Israel Pocket Library

ZIONISM

KETER BOOKS

This book is compiled from material originally published in the *Encyclopaedia Judaica*

P.O.Box 7145, Jerusalem, Israel

Cat. No. 25075

ISBN 0 7065 1326 6

Printed in Israel

CONTENTS

CONTRIBUTORS

Getzel Kressel; Writer and bibliographer, Ḥolon, Israel.
Prof. Jacob Katz; Professor of Jewish Social History and former Rector, the Hebrew University of Jerusalem.
Prof. Samuel Ettinger; Associate Professor of Jewish History, the Hebrew University of Jerusalem.
Rabbi Arthur Hertzberg; Associate Adjunct Professor of History, Columbia University, New York.
Moshe Medzini; Journalist and writer, Jerusalem.
Aharon Zwergbaum; Legal Adviser, World Zionist Organization, Jerusalem.
Dr. Chaim Yahil; Former Director General of the Ministry for Foreign Affairs; Former Chairman of the Israel Broadcasting Authority; Jerusalem.
Dr. Samuel B. Hurwich; Jerusalem.
Dr. Lucien Lazare; Educator, Jerusalem.
Dr. Jozeph Michman (Melkman); Ministry of Education and Culture, Jerusalem.
Dr. Giorgio Romano; Journalist, Tel Aviv.
Rosa Perla Raicher, Tel Aviv.
Dr. Hayyim J. Cohen; Senior Lecturer in Contemporary Jewry, the Hebrew University of Jerusalem.
Dr. Aryeh Tartakower; Former Lecturer in the Sociology of the Jews, the Hebrew University of Jerusalem; Chairman, Cultural Division, the World Jewish Congress, Jerusalem.
Dr. Theodor Lavi; Historian, Yad Vashem, Jerusalem.
Dr. Israel Klausner; Historian and former Deputy Director of the Central Zionist Archives, Jerusalem.
Yakir Eventov; Haifa.

Dr. Cvi Rotem; Journalist, Tel Aviv.
Dr. Yona Malachy (the late); Research Fellow, the Institute for Contemporary Jewry, the Hebrew University of Jerusalem.

1 THE WORD AND ITS MEANING

The root of the term "Zionism" is the word "Zion," which very early in Jewish history became a synonym for Jerusalem. It had a special meaning as far back as after the destruction of the First Temple in expressing the yearning of the Jewish people for its homeland. Thus "Zion" is found in the Psalms, "By the rivers of Babylon,/There we sat down, yea, we wept,/When we remembered Zion" (Ps. 137:1); in the prayer, "And let our eyes behold Thy return in mercy to Zion"; in the poem, "Zion! Wilt thou not ask if peace be with thy captives/That seek thy peace —that are the remnant of thy flocks" (Judah Halevi[1]); and frequently elsewhere in religious and secular literature.

The modern term Zionism first appeared at the end of the 19th century, denoting the movement whose goal was the return of the Jewish people to Ereẓ Israel. It was coined by Nathan Birnbaum in his journal *Selbstemanzipation* (April 1, 1890). Birnbaum himself explained the term (in a letter of Nov. 6, 1891) as the "establishment of an organization of the national-political Zionist party in juxtaposition to the practically oriented party that existed until now." The term was thus intended to express a political orientation toward Ereẓ Israel in place of the prevailing philanthropic approach. The extent to which the new word filled a need in the young movement can be gauged from the plethora of subtitles of *Selbstemanzipation* from its first appearance until the May. 18, 1893 issue, when the definition "Organ der Zionisten" ("Organ of the Zionists") was adopted. However, despite the precise meaning which Birnbaum intended to convey by it, the terms "Zionism" and "Ḥibbat

[1]Outstanding Jewish poet of the Middle Ages; lived in Spain

Zion" (see below) were still used interchangeably, and it was only gradually that the meaning of political Zionism, as distinguished from its "practical," almost wholly philanthropic aspect, gained acceptance. This happened finally and unequivocally with the appearance of Herzl[2].

Herzl, who knew nothing of the semantic developments of the word Zionism, first used it to denote philanthropic-supported small-scale settlement. It was only when preparations for the First Zionist Congress had commenced and when, at the last moment, two of the speakers at the Congress—R. Hirsch Hildesheimer and Willy Bambus, leading members of the Esra Society—withdrew their participation, due to Herzl's explicit political orientation, that Herzl began to stress the importance of the "Zionist" Congress, to be distinguished from the Ḥibbat Zion movement. The Basle program adopted at the First Zionist Congress explicitly endorsed Herzl's political conception of Zionism. From then on Zionist history was viewed as being divided into two epochs: Ḥibbat Zion up to the First Congress and from then on "Zionism," i.e., political Zionism. This did not, however, put an end to the prolonged struggle between the two concepts inside the Zionist movement, between the "political" and the "practical" Zionists, each of whom regarded their approach to the realization of the Zionist aim as the genuine meaning of the term "Zionism." It was at the Eighth Zionist Congress (1907) that Chaim Weizmann coined a new term, "synthetic" Zionism, which stipulated that the two approaches supplement each other and are in reality two sides of the same coin: political activity is meaningless unless it is based upon practical settlement in Ereẓ Israel, and settlement alone could not develop into desirable proportions without the support of political efforts.

 [2]See below

2 FORERUNNERS

On the threshold of modern times, as far as ethnic and historical consciousness is concerned, the Jews were better prepared for a national movement than any other ethnic group in Europe. Before this consciousness could become an ingredient of modern nationalism, it first had to undergo certain transformations. By the same token, however, all peoples had to undergo important changes in their attitudes before they could be caught up by a national movement; they had to elevate the attributes of their ethnic group to ultimate values. Jewish society achieved its nationalist transformation with the appearance of a modern idea, later called Zionism, which purged, so to speak, Jewish messianic belief of its miraculous eschatological elements and retained only its political, social, and some of its spiritual objectives. Even in this phase of development, however, Zionism leaned heavily on the old messianism and derived from it much of its ideological and even more of its emotional appeal. Yet all this was accomplished only at the end of the 19th and the beginning of the 20th century. Thus, in spite of the fact that the Jews preceded other nations in possessing the potentialities of nationalism, the development of the Jewish national movement in its Zionist form lagged behind that of most of the European nations.

The shattering of the traditional existence of European Jewry, as separate religious-ethnic entities somehow connected with the surrounding estate-structured, prenationalistic society, was followed by a transitional period that partly preceded and partly coincided with that of the forerunners of Zionism. This period was basically rationalistic, aiming principally at the integration of the Jews in the new, rapidly changing European society, but it simultaneously evolved certain features (particularly pronounced in the Haskalah period), which were later absorbed into the stream of Zionist ideology. One of them was the revitalization and modernization of the Hebrew language, which eventually culminated in the historic achievement of Eliezer Ben-Yehuda[3]; another, the striving for economic "productivization." An additional trait of this period was the emergence of the politically minded Jewish leader who appraised the world around him realistically, in the light of a defined political activity.

One cannot, however, properly speak of "forerunners" of Zionism such as Rabbi Judah Alkalai, Rabbi Ẓevi Hirsch Kalischer, Chaim Lorje, Rabbi Elijah Guttmacher, Moses Hess, and others, before the end of the 1850s or the beginning of the 1860s. Only then could they succeed in uniting the widely scattered adherents of their idea through mutual contact. The factor common to all, their faith that the future existence of the Jewish nation is conditioned by its return to the historical homeland, became a basis of social unity. The difference between the earlier period and the 1860s is not difficult to explain. The 1860s saw the completion of emancipation in most West European countries, and where it was not yet wholly accomplished, it was thought to be just round the corner. As long as the struggle for political equality of the Jews was going on, the idea of Jewish nationalism could not be tolerated, for the argument that the Jews are a separate national entity was one of the main weapons of the gentile enemies of emancipation. From the 1860s on, when the emancipation seemed all but completed, the idea of Jewish nationalism could be propagated as the next phase. Kalischer even suggested that Jewish nationalism was the natural continuation of the emancipation itself.

The old messianic idea, however, did not disappear completely under the impact of rationalism; it remained

[3]Pioneer of the modern revival of the Hebrew language; died in Jerusalem, 1922

alive in the Jewish masses. As late as 1840, there was a widespread rumor in the Balkans and in Eastern Europe that the messianic year, which was destined to bring about the great turning point in Jewish history, had arrived. Many held this belief genuinely and were waiting in a state of mental agitation. For one of these believers, Rabbi Judah Alkalai (1798–1878), his messianic expectation became a point of departure for the transition from the traditional, miraculous messianism to a realistic one. This change of conception was caused by the coincidence of the messianic expectation with the rescue of the Jewish community in Damascus, which had been charged with ritual murder, by the two leading figures of French and English Jewry, Adolphe Crémieux and Sir Moses Montefiore. As the miraculous events of the redemption failed to appear, Alkalai inferred that the rescue of this one community was a model for the messianic procedure. The future stages of redemption were to be achieved through similar activities of outstanding Jews. Alkalai was an undistinguished preacher of a little Sephardi community in Semlin, near Belgrade. Until the year of his newly found conviction, he was hardly known outside his limited circle, nor did he wish to be known. However, after he became convinced that the era of the Messiah had arrived and that the redemption would have to be achieved by human action, he felt compelled to convey this message to his fellow Jews. In the remaining 37 years of his life, not only did Alkalai publish numerous pamphlets and articles to spread his ideas, but he traveled on two occasions to Western Europe and later settled in Ereẓ Israel in order to convince Jews and non-Jews of the truth of his mission. He tried to induce people to join an organized resettlement of Jewry, or some part thereof, in their homeland and to equip themselves with the attributes of a modern nation. Although Alkalai began as a preacher imbued with the traditional, and especially kabbalistic, sources, he gradually acquired the elements of a modern national conception. He propagated the idea of Jewish national unity through an overall organization of world Jewry, with modernized

Hebrew as its common language. Religion would also play its part in the new national life, but as the controversy between Orthodoxy and Reform grew, Alkalai sought a remedy to this in the idea of national unity.

Ẓevi Hirsch Kalischer (1795–1874) developed his ideas on similar lines. A German rabbinic scholar of Polish origin, he refused to accept any position in communal life. The great experience of his youth was the emancipation of the Jews in France and in the German countries at the time of Napoleon. He explained these events in terms derived from Jewish tradition. The emancipation, and even more the ascendance of Jewish individuals (e.g., the Rothschilds) to unheard-of economic and political influence, appeared to him to be the fulfillment of the old prophecy of liberation which, according to Jewish tradition, was to terminate the exile. It is true that the prophecy was not yet realized, for it entailed the ingathering of the Jews to their homeland. Therefore, as early as 1836, Kalischer appealed to Meyer Aṇschel Rothschild to buy from Muhammad Ali the whole of Ereẓ Israel, or at least Jerusalem or the Temple area, so as to initiate the miraculous redemption "from below," and later he addressed the same request to Moses Montefiore. By interpreting the events of emancipation in terms of messianism, Kalischer simultaneously transformed these very terms. From the first stage of deliverance, which was brought about by human activity, he inferred the nature of the next stages, which were also to be achieved by human agency. Thus his interpretation of the emancipation led to the demand for the ingathering of at least some part of Jewry in Ereẓ Israel.

In order to place these theories in the correct perspective, one must bear in mind the underlying motives of their promoters. These theories of redemption were derived from a reinterpretation of the messianic tradition in the light of recent historic experiences. In view of later developments, it is important to note that modern anti-Semitism was not among these experiences. The activities of Alkalai and Kalischer took place during the flourishing period of

Middle European liberalism, e.g., between 1840 and 1875, when optimism about the possible integration of Jews into the life of European nations was almost universal. Certain obstacles to achieving full civil rights, as well as some signs of reservation in social rapprochement, were interpreted as residues of waning prejudices. Alkalai and Kalischer were among the optimists. Until the 1870s they never advanced the argument that Jews needed a country to secure their physical existence, which was later to become one of the main planks of Zionism.

The same can be stated about the motives of the socialist Moses Hess. Hess was not an Orthodox Jew but a social revolutionary and philosopher with a Hegelian tinge. His conversion to Jewish nationalism in the 1860s can be understood as the result of the unmaterialized social revolution. Hess based his Zionist ideas on the concept of a national spirit which permeated the life of the Jewish people. Since the dispersion, the "spirit" was embodied in the Jewish religious institutions, but as these institutions were rapidly disintegrating, the gradual disappearance of the Jewish spirit was the most probable—and the most lamentable—prospect. In order to rescue this spirit, the only solution was the reconstruction of national life in the ancient homeland. Hess's argument is phrased in terms of social philosophy, while the emotional climate was provided by resentment against the non-Jewish society which had frustrated the Jews' expectation of being treated as equals. In any event, any diagnosis excluding emancipation as a possible solution to the "Jewish problem" is absent from the theory of Hess, as it is absent from those of Alkalai and Kalischer. More obvious than in the theories of Alkalai and Kalischer is Hess's dependence on the general trend of nationalism in Europe. The use of such terms as "nationality," "national renaissance," and "creative genius of the nation" indicate the source of influence, i.e., romanticism, which provided all the national movements with their respective ideological tools. Hess's *Rome and Jerusalem*, as its title indicates, was written under the impact of events which had led to the unification of Italy in 1859. Hess expressly refers to this fact, calling the Jewish cause "The last national problem," after Italy had solved its own. However, impulses from non-Jewish sources can also be traced in the cases of Alkalai and Kalischer, as both use one characteristic argument in their appeal: Jews, who are the descendants of a holy and ancient nation, should not lag behind the newly created nations of the Balkans.

The real difference between Alkalai and Kalischer on the one hand and Hess on the other, is the spiritual background from which their respective drives stemmed. While the first two were originally steeped in the sources of Jewish tradition, including the Bible, Talmud, and Kabbalah, the last had only a faint idea of these sources from his childhood. He was influenced in his knowledge of Jewish history and its evaluation by the contemporary historian Heinrich Graetz. However, the fabric of Hess's outlook was woven out of strands which were of modern European, primarily Hegelian, origin. He was far from being a religious Jew, in any traditional sense, and, judging by his earlier activities and writings, he must be counted as one of those Jews who were absorbed by European movements and systems of thought.

Hess was the first figure in Zionist history who did not grow out of Jewish tradition. His Jewishness returned to him after a period of estrangement. Thus, Hess and his two contemporaries, Alkalai and Kalischer, prefigure the two main types of Zionism: one had to overcome the miraculous elements of traditional messianism; and the other, after having forsaken the tradition altogether, had to recover its cultural and political implications.

Attributing the emergence of the Zionist idea to the revitalization and modernization of the messianic utopia does not mean that the mere suggestion of regathering the Jews in their homeland was sufficient for initiating the movement. The historical connection between the Jews and their ancient homeland was indeed a conspicuous feature in Jewish, as well as Christian, tradition. The idea of the restoration of the Jews gained currency, especially in England, where the awakened interest in the Old Testament in the wake of the Puritan revolution strongly stimulated interest in the history of the Jewish nation (see Christian Zionism, below). Imaginative Jewish writers and social projectors also readvanced the idea of establishing a Jewish commonwealth, either in Palestine or elsewhere, with a view to solving the "Jewish problem." A case in point was the efforts of Mordecai M. Noah, one-time consul of the United States in Tunis, who in 1825 issued an appeal to European Jewry to establish a Jewish state named "Ararat" on the Grand Island of the Niagara River. Noah later fostered the idea of the restoration of Palestine.

At first the general Jewish public either took almost no cognizance of these ideas and their promoters or reacted to them with mockery and derision. Alkalai, who had begun his activities 20 years earlier, succeeded in finding any substantial and lasting support only in the 1860s. From this time on, a connection can be perceived in the activities of the various early Zionists. The three great figures described here not only knew of each other, but also supported each other. They succeeded in founding a more-or-less interconnected society among themselves, together with other, less conspicuous personalities who were influenced by them or who had reached the same conclusions independently. Moreover, from the 1860s onward there is an uninterrupted development, and one may speak of historical causation as the ideas and activities of these early Zionists led the way to the full-fledged Ḥibbat Zion movement, founded in the 1880s under the impact of the Russian pogroms and the rise of modern anti-Semitism in Germany.

By and large, it cannot be said that the forerunners had succeeded in realizing something of their aim, i.e., the ingathering of Jews in their homeland. Until the 1870s, when anti-Jewish troubles began in Rumania, there had been no Jewish exodus from any country in Europe. Instead of producing an idea in order to satisfy a need, the early Zionists were searching for a need which would correspond to their ideas. Kalischer seized any rumor of Jews wishing to emigrate as a God-sent opportunity to prove that people who were ready to go to Ereẓ Israel could be found. Thus he tried to refute the argument that his theory had no hold on reality, but he never tried to prove the social necessity or inevitability of his idea. The first real objectives of Zionism were realized only in the 1880s, when persecutions and defamation in Rumania and bloody pogroms and civil disqualifications in Russia set many European Jews into motion.

3 ḤIBBAT ZION

Ḥibbat Zion (Heb. "Love of Zion") was the ideology and movement whose aim was the national renascence of the Jews and their return to Ereẓ Israel. The movement in the 19th century flourished mainly in the large Jewish communities of Eastern Europe (Russia-Poland, Rumania). The Ḥibbat Zion societies merged with the Zionist Organization upon its establishment by Theodor Herzl, although some of them continued their formal existence until World War I.

Roots of Ḥibbat Zion. The Ḥibbat Zion movement derived most of its ideas from the basic values of Jewish tradition: the sense of exile, the longing for redemption, and the religious and spiritual attachment to Ereẓ Israel. Most of the Jews of Eastern Europe, however, were distant from organized political and social activity, and their religious leaders—with a few exceptions—were even opposed to it on the grounds that the coming of the Messiah should not be urged by human endeavor *(deḥikat ha-keẓ)* and that it constituted human interference in the ways of providence. The problems of the Jewish national renascence and the settlement of Ereẓ Israel were mainly discussed by individuals who were motivated to action by messianic visions or by the influence of the national awakening of European peoples. Ẓevi Kalischer and Judah Alkalai (see above) had propagated the idea of settling Ereẓ Israel as early as the 1840s and 1850s, and the former had initiated a consultation of several rabbis and representatives of the communities of Germany in 1860 in order to found a company for this purpose. Shortly after this conference Chaim Lorje of Frankfort on the Oder founded the Jewish Company for the Settlement of the Holy Land. Neither propaganda nor these activities had any substantial effect on the public, however, just as scant attention was paid to Moses Hess's *Rome and Jerusalem* and David Gordon's articles in *Ha-Maggid,* which supported the settlement of Ereẓ Israel. When the Ḥibbat Zion movement was founded, however, its religious sector was influenced by the ideas and the example of these first rabbis.

The public debate on the question of Jewish nationalism began at the end of the 1860s with the renewed strength of the movement for religious reform in Germany and Hungary. This movement called for the national and cultural assimilation of the Jews and for a break with the national tradition by removing references to Zion and Jerusalem from the prayer book and basing the Jewish religion on its "eternal truths" alone. Peretz Smolenskin[4] was among those bitterly opposed to these trends, denouncing them in the monthly *Ha-Shaḥar* which he began publishing in 1868. He placed the Jews firmly among the peoples aspiring to national liberation. Eliezer Ben-Yehuda's important articles *"She'elah Nikhbadah"*. ("An Important Question") and *"Od Musar lo Lakaḥnu"* ("We Have Not Learned Our Lesson") in *Ha-Shaḥar* (1879), relating the national renascence in Ereẓ Israel to the revival of the Hebrew language as a spoken tongue, were an essential contribution to the crystallization of Ḥibbat Zion as an ideological trend.

BACKGROUND TO THE EMERGENCE OF THE MOVEMENT. The Ḥibbat Zion movement arose at a time when developments in Eastern European states were pressing large numbers of Jews to emigrate or engage in intensified social and political activity. At the same time leading advocates of the Enlightenment (Haskalah) became disillusioned with their faith in the possibility of Jewish assimilation among the nations and were disappointed in their hopes to attain equal rights for Jews. A decisive force in this direction was the series of pogroms in Russia after

 [4]Leading Hebrew author; lived in Odessa and Vienna; died 1885

the assassination of Czar Alexander II (1881). The fact that the sincere aspiration of the *maskilim* and the Jewish youth to grow closer to the Russian people had been met with a wave of hatred and that the government had been quick to declare the pogroms as the "reaction of the people" to "Jewish exploitation" and had begun to impose severe restrictions on the sources of income, government posts, and admission to institutes of learning available to the Jews caused a severe ideological crisis among the *maskilim.* Many of those who had grown distant from their people began to return to it (visiting the synagogue, participating in fasts, etc.). Others who had previously pinned their hopes on the struggle to change the social system began to realize that this would not automatically answer the "Jewish question." Among those who advocated a national renascence the realization became apparent that a spiritual and linguistic revival was not sufficient, and that they must set their sights on a real homeland, in which the Jews would not be regarded as aliens. The example of Germany, where a widespread anti-Semitic movement arose at the end of the 1870s, served as a warning and proof that neither Enlightenment nor emancipation was sufficient to guarantee the status of Jews in their countries of residence. Jewish writers and *maskilim* embarked on a penetrating discussion of anti-Semitism and its causes. The times, however, were unsuited to ideological discussions alone. The panic-stricken flight of thousands across the borders and the suffering of the refugees in the places where they were concentrated emphasized the need for a speedy and urgent "national solution."

THE BEGINNINGS OF THE MOVEMENT. The majority of the active Jewish public felt that the only solution was to leave Russia; only a small minority, mainly the wealthy and their relatives, opposed emigration. Many societies, especially among the youth, were formed for this purpose, and there were many arguments between those who supported Ereẓ Israel as a "place of refuge" and those who favored the United States. Foremost among the Ḥovevei Zion—those in favor of going to "the land of our fathers," "to which we have historical rights"—was Moses Leib Lilienblum, who was soon joined by Smolenskin, Leo Levanda, and others. The journals *Ha-Shaḥar, Ha-Maggid, Ha-Meliẓ,* and *Razsvet* (in Russian) became the disseminators of the ideas of Ḥibbat Zion. Most of the Ḥovevei Zion societies, especially those of the young *maskilim,* advocated radical national programs. The students' society Aḥavat Zion, founded in 1881 in St. Petersburg, declared that "every son of Israel who admits that there is no salvation for Israel unless they establish a government of their own in the Land of Israel can be considered a member of the society." The charter of the Bilu society stated: "The goal of the society is the politico-economic and national-spiritual revival of the Jewish people in Syria and Ereẓ Israel." Some of the societies regarded their aim as imminent *aliyah* to Ereẓ Israel, while others emphasized preparation and the propagation of the concept of the settlement of Ereẓ Israel among the people. All of them, however, agreed upon the means toward settlement as the acquisition of land (either granted by the Turkish government or purchased) and the creation of a class of Jewish farmers and artisans in the country.

Rumanian Jewry was aroused by the idea of settling Ereẓ Israel. The Rumanian government's devious disavowal of its explicit obligation—according to the decisions of the Congress of Berlin, 1878—to grant equal rights to all its citizens and the dispossession of growing numbers of Jews from their sources of income had made the true value of those legal guarantees clear to many Rumanian Jews and brought them face to face with emigration as the sole solution. At the end of 1881 there were over 30 societies for the settlement of Ereẓ Israel in Rumania, and on Jan. 11–12, 1882, a conference of Ḥovevei Zion took place in Focsani and elected a central committee, with its headquarters in Galati. (See also below, Zionist Organization in Rumania.)

PINSKER'S "AUTOEMANCIPATION." The new movement

was provided with a systematic ideological basis by Leon Pinsker in his *Autoemancipation,* which appeared in 1882 (see below). Although initially he did not contemplate Ereẓ Israel as the most suitable territory for the Jewish state, he eventually joined the Ḥibbat Zion movement. He came into contact with societies in different localities, and after consultation with Lilienblum, Hermann Schapira, Max Mandelstamm, and others (in September 1883) a memorandum was sent out calling for the establishment of a central executive committee to be elected by a congress of delegates from all the Societies for the Settlement of Ereẓ Israel. Shortly afterward the Zerubavel society (with Pinsker as chairman and Lilienblum as secretary) was founded in Odessa and immediately became the central society of the movement; it was followed by the Warsaw society, which was headed by Saul Pinḥas Rabbinowitz and Isidor Jasinowsky.

Settlement Activities. Many of the Ḥovevei Zion pinned their hopes on the support of the Alliance Israélite Universelle and on other Jewish organizations. However, when these organizations searched for a haven for the refugees from Russia who were concentrated in Brody, they did not direct their migration to Ereẓ Israel at all: some were sent to the United States and some were returned to Russia. At the conference of delegates from various Jewish groups that met in Berlin in April 1882 to discuss the question of emigration, only Israel Hildesheimer[5] came out in favor of settling the refugees in Ereẓ Israel, and his proposal was not met with sympathy. Representatives of the societies nonetheless went ahead, and in the spring of 1882 a considerable number of settlers began to reach Ereẓ Israel, prompting the Turkish authorities immediately to publish orders to forbid further entry. The Ḥovevei Zion turned for aid to their British sympathizer Laurence Oliphant[6], and asked him to intervene with the Turkish government, but he had no influence in Constantinople.

[5]German rabbinical scholar; head of the Orthodox Berlin rabbinical seminary.
[6]British Christian Zionist who settled in Haifa. Died 1888

Among those who succeeded in reaching Ereẓ Israel in July 1882 were 14 members of the Bilu society who had gone, without any property, to work as agricultural laborers.

Despite the Turkish ban on immigration, the foundations of Jewish agricultural settlement in Ereẓ Israel were laid in that year. In July 1882 Zalman Levontin and his companions established Rishon le-Zion, and shortly afterward members of the Moinesti society from Rumania settled in Rosh Pinnah (which had previously been settled and then abandoned by Jews from Safed). At the same time, the settlement in Petaḥ Tikvah, which had been founded by Jerusalem Jews in 1878 but had later been abandoned, was revived. At the end of 1882, a group of Rumanian Jews settled in Zammārīn (later Zikhron Ya'akov). However, the meager resources of the new settlers, their lack of preparation, and the difficulty of local conditions worked against them, and soon after the establishment of the new settlements they were in need of help. It soon became apparent that the various societies in Russia and Rumania were in no position to provide the required assistance, and Baron Edmond de Rothschild was persuaded by Samuel Mohilever and Joseph Feinberg (of Rishon le-Zion) to assist a group of Jewish farmers from Russia to settle in Ereẓ Israel (they later founded Ekron) and to take the settlement of Rishon le-Zion under his protection. In the course of time most of the settlements became sponsored by the Baron de Rothschild; the exception was Gederah, which was founded by the Bilu'im in 1884. The regime of strict supervision of the settlers through the agency of Rothschild's officials was a constant source of friction and rebelliousness. Meanwhile, settlements continued to be founded until the end of the 1880s.

The Organization. Although it was clear to all the active members of Ḥibbat Zion that the movement had to be unified and organized, opinions differed on the form of organization. Younger and more radical elements demanded emphasis on the ultimate national aspirations and open opposition to the philanthropic organizations, while more bourgeois elements advocated moderation and supportive activities. The 100th birthday of Moses Montefiore provided the movement with a suitable occasion for convening all its active members, and the first conference of Ḥibbat Zion took place on Nov. 6, 1884, at Kattowitz (a town in southern Poland). Thirty-five delegates participated in the conference; most of them were from Russian societies, and the rest were from Rumania, Germany, England, and France. An account of the movement's achievements proved rather unimpressive. The great tide of Jewish emigration had been stemmed, and even the large Jewish organizations had abandoned hope of guiding and directing it; the Turkish government had closed the gates of Ereẓ Israel, and those few who had succeeded in reaching the country were considered infiltrators. It is therefore not surprising that the main value of the conference was its demonstration of the unity of Ḥibbat Zion and of the Jewish people as a whole. Pinsker hoped to attract Jewish personalities and organizations from the West into the movement. It was decided to call the organization Mazkeret Moshe be-Ereẓ ha-Kodesh and to establish a central committee with headquarters in Berlin, since conditions in Russia made legal activities on behalf of the movement impossible there; until the establishment of this committee, it was decided to set up a temporary committee in Odessa and a subcommittee in Warsaw. The resolutions accepted at the conference concerned mainly practical matters—organizational methods and ways of supporting the settlements. There was no mention, either in the debates or in the resolutions, of the major questions of national revival or the great national goal.

These concessions, however, were in vain. In Germany, not a single Jewish personality of any stature was found to head the proposed committee, and the resolution to establish a Berlin center was cancelled. Neither did other societies of Ḥibbat Zion that were founded in German and English towns succeed in achieving importance. Even the society in Kattowitz, which in 1883 had published the

German-language movement organ, *Der Kolonist,* lost its importance. Only the student organization Kadimah in Vienna, which published *Selbstemanzipation* from 1885 on, survived. The movement in Rumania stagnated until the beginning of the 1890s, and the Russian societies were involved with minor affairs. The organization consolidated itself, however; there were almost 100 societies with a membership of approximately 14,000, which collected about 30,000 rubles a year from donations and another 20,000 rubles from various enterprises. Propaganda among the masses was emphasized; preachers (e.g., Ẓevi Hirsch Masliansky and Judah Leib Yevzerow) and entertainers (e.g., Eliakum Zunser) did much to spread the ideas of Ḥibbat Zion. Nonetheless, there was friction between the different societies, and opposition to the existing leadership emerged.

In June 1887 the second conference, this time of Ḥovevei Zion in Russia, met in Druskieniki and resolved to call the movement Ḥovevei Zion. Mohilever attempted to impose an Orthodox authority over the movement, but was foiled by younger representatives, such as Menaḥem Ussishkin from Moscow, Ze'ev Berman from St. Petersburg, and Meir Dizengoff from Kishinev. Pinsker was finally reelected to lead the movement, with six advisers, three of whom were famous rabbis: Mohilever, Naphtali Ẓevi Yehudah Berlin, and Mordecai Eliasberg. It was also decided to renew efforts to gain permission from the Russian government to organize the movement. In 1890 Alexander Zederbaum, editor of *Ha-Meliẓ,* succeeded in obtaining government sanction for the Society for the Support of Jewish Farmers and Artisans in Syria and Palestine, which became known as the Odessa Committee. The founding conference, which took place legally—for the first time—that year in Odessa, was attended by numerous delegates from all over Russia. Increased contributions enabled the establishment of the settlements of Reḥovot and Ḥaderah (1890–91), the consolidation of Mishmar ha-Yarden, and provided support for the veteran settlements.

An executive committee was set up in Jaffa under Vladimir Tiomkin to supervise the distribution of support and the acquisition of land. The Ezra society in Berlin and other societies in Frankfort, Paris, and London intensified their activities. The second "Russian Exodus," which took place after the expulsion of Jews from Moscow in 1891, led to increased *aliyah* and to speculation in land, and the Turkish authorities renewed their ban on immigration and settlement.

THE SPIRITUAL CENTER. The "practical" activities of Ḥibbat Zion gave rise to harsh criticism, especially on the part of Aḥad Ha-Am[7]. This criticism was partially inspired by Aḥad Ha-Am's view that Ereẓ Israel could not provide a solution for the masses of emigrants, but should rather serve as a "spiritual center" to unite all parts of the disintegrating nation. It was in this spirit that the Benei Moshe[8] society was founded. The crisis in settlement activities after the short-lived increase in *aliyah* at the beginning of the 1890s sowed fresh disillusionment in the ranks of Ḥibbat Zion and strengthened the influence of Aḥad Ha-Am, who had several supporters among the members of the Odessa Committee. Emphasis on the need for spiritual preparation brought about an intensification of the ideological and cultural activities of Ḥibbat Zion, especially after the founding of the Aḥi'asaf publishing house. Despite the importance of Aḥad Ha-Am's criticism, however, his approach could not serve as a basis for the activities of the movement. It is not surprising, therefore, that upon the appearance of Herzl and political Zionism, the vast majority of the Ḥovevei Zion societies joined the new Zionist Organization.

[7]Zionist thinker and philosopher; died in Tel-Aviv, 1927

[8]Exclusive order within Ḥibbat Zion founded by Aḥad ha-Am and concentrating on cultural activities

4 IDEOLOGICAL EVOLUTION

THE SHOCK OF THE 1880S; POLITICAL ZIONISM. Modern Zionism began with need and in disillusion. The new thinking was a reaction to dramatic and tragic events in Russia. Czar Alexander II was assassinated early in 1881 by revolutionaries, among whom there was one young Jewess in a minor role. Immediately thereafter a wave of pogroms spread all over the country. The physical results of the murder and pillage were dire, but the moral impact of these outrages was even more devastating. It was commonly believed that the perpetrators of these attacks were encouraged and even organized by governmental circles; it was certainly beyond doubt that the authorities did little to defend the Jews against the pillagers and murderers. What was perhaps even more upsetting, at least to elements of the advanced Jewish intelligentsia, was that many liberal and revolutionary circles did not defend the Jews but preferred to see in these outbreaks the first stirrings of social change, in which the Jews were being attacked for their supposed exploitation of the Russian peasants and laborers. The whole system of anti-Jewish restrictions had locked the Jews of Russia into a few miserable middleman occupations, in which they could not help but be "unproductive"; the Jews were as much victims as those whom they were supposedly victimizing. Yet all this was ignored by so advanced a group as the leaders of the populist (Narodnik) movement, even though there were some Jews among them, as they hailed the pogroms as the first necessary revolutionary convulsion.

The conclusion drawn on all sides from this shock was that there was no future for Jews in Russia in the existing regime. A segment of the Jewish intelligentsia turned to revolution and lost all hope in the possibilities of reform in the land. Great masses followed in the path of the substantial trickle of emigration that had begun in the 1870s, and, despairing of any economic future in Russia, they moved westward, chiefly to the United States. In the years between 1881 and 1914 some 2,600,000 Jews from Russia and its immediate neighbors emigrated to the "new land." Some contemporary figures, chiefly Leon Pinsker and Moshe Leib Lilienblum, drew other conclusions. They did not believe that hatred of Jews was limited to Russia alone or that the problem was ultimately to be solved by emigration to friendlier countries or even by the achievement of emancipation in legal theory. The young Lilienblum was in Odessa in 1881 as an "enlightener," a *maskil,* completing his own secular education, in the certainty that the road to freedom for Jews required their westernization, which would then make them acceptable to "benevolent Russia." He was then also mildly socialist in his political outlook. But cowering before the pogrom mob, it became clear to him, as he was soon to write, that the revolution might take place and yet not bring freedom to the Jews; that they might still be excluded and hated even in a new order; and that the future of Jews lay in the restoration of Jewish nationhood. The more important, and more famous, immediate reaction to the pogroms and to the failure of hope which attended them, was that of an even more committed "enlightener," Leon Pinsker. He left Russia for Central Europe in those months to search for allies for his new views, which he published in German in a pamphlet called *Autoemancipation.* The simple assertion of this essay was that anti-Semitism, which he called Judophobia, was a permanent psychopathological phenomenon, not only a social one, so long as the Jews were a "ghost nation"—everywhere a minority and nowhere a normal national majority, everywhere "guests" and nowhere "hosts." Anti-Semitism was "xenophobia," the hatred of the stranger, but it differed from all the usual varieties of such tensions, if not in kind then in degree, as it was the longest lasting and most pervasive form of this malaise. In the light of pogroms Pinsker finally rejected the notion that any amount of change by Jews to make themselves over into the image of their gentile neighbors could finally gain them acceptance in the majority society. He thus agreed with the anti-Semites that by their ill-will they had proved their case, that the Jews were irretrievably and forever alien, and that the dream of assimilation was not possible, not because the Jews could not assimilate but because the majority would not let them. It followed rationally from these premises that the way to solve the Jewish problem was to remove the Jews from the places of their dwelling, from the situation of abnormality surrounded by hatred, to a territory of their own where they would become a normal nation. Such a place was not necessarily the land of the ancestors in Ereẓ Israel, though Pinsker was aware that there were historic and emotional ties to the land, but rather the most readily available land that was suitable for settlement, preferably on the American continent, where Jews could develop their own autonomy. For all of his disbelief in the promise of the era of the emancipation that Jews would be personally accepted as equals in Europe, Pinsker's outlook was still emancipatory, still rooted in the desire to engineer the acceptance of the Jews as equals in the modern world. What was new was that Pinsker saw this world as consisting of nations which disliked foreigners, so Jews had to cease being foreign by becoming a proper nation. He was in the first stage of awareness that such national equality was not granted as a gift from on high, because the peoples were not generous, but rather as a result of the national effort of those who desired their national dignity.

Those to whom Pinsker turned in Western Europe showed sympathy for him but thought that he had been totally unnerved by the sight of the pogroms in his country. In Russia itself the few who organized the Ḥibbat Zion movement in 1882 were motivated also by other impulses than the national theorizing of Pinsker. Their concerns were, like those of Alkalai and Kalischer of the previous generation, a blend of the older, religious longing for the messianic restoration of Zion and the new language of modern nationalism, allied to the notion that gradual settlement in Ereẓ Israel was at least a step in the direction of the ultimate consummation. Pinsker reluctantly found in these groups the only possible adherents and he consented to become their leader. Aḥad Ha-Am, his younger contemporary who was to become the major ideologist of this strand of Zionism, insisted after Pinsker's death, and in contrast with Theodor Herzl, that Pinsker's major concerns had been "the revival of the spirit," i.e., the renaissance of the Hebraic culture in a modern key, and that he had never wavered from his commitment to Zion as the only possible land for the endeavor of a Jewish renaissance—and, for that matter, that Pinsker had never dreamt of more than an elite, representative Jewish community in the Land. All this was fairly adequate as a statement of Aḥad Ha-Am's own premises, but Theodor Herzl was thoroughly right in his assertion that, had he known of the existence of Pinsker's *Autoemancipation,* he would not have written *Der Judenstaat*. Herzl's views were indeed almost exactly those of his Russian predecessor.

It is now no longer believed that Herzl wrote *Der Judenstaat* in immediate reaction to the beginnings of the Dreyfus Affair, which he witnessed and on which he reported as the correspondent in Paris of the leading daily paper of Vienna. Herzl's shift from a fashionable journalist who believed in the assimilation of Jews into the majority culture had begun earlier, in reaction to renewed anti-Semitic agitation of the German-speaking world in the 1880's culminating in Karl Lueger's appointment as mayor of Vienna on an anti-Semitic platform. Kaiser Franz Joseph had vetoed his election three times, but that such a party could prevail in cosmopolitan Vienna was a major shock. The beginnings of anti-Jewish agitation in the very home of the emancipation, Paris, where the French Revolution had first given equality to some European Jews in 1791, could only confirm that the trouble was real, and pervasive. Herzl was, if anything, even less involved in Jewish cultural concerns than Pinsker, who had been a leader of the "enlighteners" before his conversion to Jewish nationalism and had even so labored among his people in that period. What gave particular bite to Herzl's views was that he made no distinction, explicit or implicit, between "Eastern" and "Western" Jews. This (and not some intellectual belief in the indivisibility of the Jewish spirit) was the meaning, in the context of his thinking and writing in 1896, of his oft-quoted sentence, "We are a people—one people." What he saw was one Jewish situation all over the world, that of a national group which was an anomaly. His first thought had been that of total assimilation and at first he even fantasized about the possibility of leading all Jews to the great cathedral of St. Stephan in Vienna, where their baptism would make an end of anti-Semitism. He turned away from this "solution" (in which he had been preceded by such figures as David Friedlaender[9] and Napoleon a century earlier, at the dawn of the era of emancipation) because he knew that it would not work, that anti-Semites hated Jews even after they were totally assimilated. Herzl therefore proceeded to argue in *Der Judenstaat,* exactly like Pinsker, that the essence of the Jewish problem was not individual but national and that the Jews could gain acceptance in the world only if they ceased being a national anomaly. He too spoke of the creation of a commission which would survey the possible territories on which the Jewish State would be founded and he left open the question as to whether it would be better to opt for Palestine with its historic associations or for some vacant land in Argentina. Intellectually, what was original in Herzl's analysis was his dialectic use of the conception of anti-Semitism as a "reasonable" form of hatred of the unlike. Herzl argued, on the basis of his bold assertion that

[9]German Reform leader; died in 1834

he alone understood this phenomenon correctly, that even anti-Semites could and would be enlisted in laboring for a Jewish State, for it would help them solve problems that they had with Jews, who were "unnecessary" in the host societies and whose very existence disturbed social peace. Since he accepted without question that men were reasonable and not demonic (Herzl went so far as to say that the emancipation was basically irreversible), he could only presume that history would inevitably move forward and produce the only possible solution to the tension between the Jews and the majority society, a Jewish State.

The very nobility of his person, the appearance of a man who suggested the ancient prophet and seemed the equal of great statesmen of his own day, lent resonance to Herzl's words, and he was particularly moving to masses of Jews in Eastern Europe precisely because he was a "Westerner" come back to his people. His tactics were perhaps even more important as an original contribution to the formation of the Zionist movement. Into the teeth of the anti-Semites who had made the word "Jew" into an insult, and of the assimilationists who used such circumlocution as "Hebrew" and "Israelite," he spoke boldly of the *Judenstaat,* which means not "The Jewish State" but, literally, "The Jew State." He saw the Jewish question as an international political question to be attacked in the forum of international politics. He therefore organized the Zionist movement at the First Zionist Congress in 1897 in such fashion that the gathering had about it the aura of a Jewish parliament in session, and he made of his presidency of the movement something reminiscent of the role of a head of state or a prime minister. All of the new instruments that were created—the Zionist Congress as a political forum, the buying of the shekel as an act of allegiance to the national movement, a bank (the Jewish Colonial Trust) to be financed by the buying of shares, and an official press in several languages to inform the adherents of the political activities of the central body and its principal leader—these did indeed constitute the adumbration of Herzl's bold

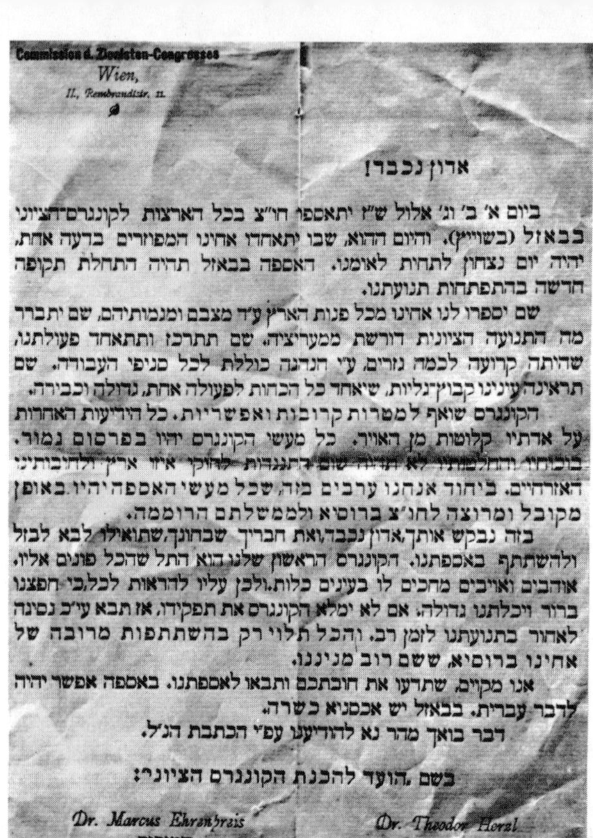

Commission d. Zionisten-Congresses
Wien,
II., Rembrandtstr. 11.

אדון נכבד!

ביום א׳ ב׳ וג׳ אלול ש״ז יתאספו חו״צ בכל הארצות לקונגרס־הציוני בבאזל (בשוייץ). והיום ההוא, שבו יתאחדו אחינו המפוזרים בדעה אחת, יהיה יום נצחון לתחית לאומנו. האספה בבאזל תהיה התחלת תקופה חדשה בהתפתחות תנועתנו.

שם יספרו לנו אחינו מכל פנות הארץ ע״ד מצבם ומגמותיהם, שם יתברר מה התנועה הציונית דורשת ממעריציה. שם תתרכז ותתאחד פעולתנו, שהיתה קרועה לכמה גזרים, ע״י הנהגה כוללת לכל סניפי העבודה. שם תראינה עינינו קבוץ־גליות, שיאחד כל הכחות לפעולה אחת, גדולה וכבירה.

הקונגרס שואף למטרות קרובות ואפשריות. כל הידיעות האחרות על אדתיו קלוטות מן האויר. כל מעשי הקונגרס יהיו בפרסום גמור. בזכויותיו והחלטותיו לא תהיה שום התנגדות לחוקי איזו ארץ ולחובותינו האזרחיים. ביחוד אנחנו ערבים בזה, שכל מעשי האספה יהיו באופן מקובל ומרוצה לחו״צ ברוסיא ולממשלתם הרוממה.

בזה נבקש אותך, אדון נכבד, ואת חבריך שבחוגך, שתואילו לבא לבזל ולהשתתף באספתנו. הקונגרס הראשון שלנו הוא התל שהכל פונים אליו. אוהבים ואויבים מחכים לו בעינים כלות, ולכן עליו להראות לכל, כי חפצנו ברור ויכלתנו גדולה. אם לא ימלא הקונגרס את תפקידו, אז תבא ע״כ נסיגה לאחור בתנועתנו לזמן רב. והכל תלוי רק בהשתתפות מרובה של אחינו ברוסיא, ששם רוב מנינגו.

אנו מקוים, שתדעו את חובתכם ותבאו לאספתנו. באספה אפשר יהיה לדבר עברית. בבאזל יש אכסניא כשרה.

דבר בואך מהר נא להודיעו עפ״י הכתבת הנ״ל.

בשם „הועד להכנת הקונגרס הציוני״:

Dr. Marcus Ehrenpreis
המזכיר

Dr. Theodor Herzl
ראש־הועד

Invitation to the First Zionist Congress at Basle, 1897. It is signed by Herzl as head of the preparatory committee and Marcus Ehrenpreis as secretary. Jerusalem, Central Zionist Archives.

assertion in his diary at the First Zionist Congress in 1897, "here I have created the Jewish State."

 In the few years that were given him at the head of

Zionism, he held consistently, until near the very end of his days, to the line that only the attainment of a charter, of a political document granting Jews near-sovereign rights in the territory that they were to settle, was the first objective of Zionism. He therefore fought against turning the Zionist movement into an instrument of piecemeal settlement, and the aid that was given the early settlements in his lifetime, little though it was, was a concession that he made to his opponents in the movement, the "practical" Zionists.

Herzl bitterly opposed the turning of Zionism toward cultural endeavors either by linking it with the secular Hebrew revival or by coupling Zionism with the national religious orthodoxy of the Mizrachi faction which was arising near the end of his days. For that matter, even though he was himself a certain kind of aristocratic social reformer (he dreamt of a seven-hour day in the Jewish State and even wanted its flag to contain seven stars to mark this social advance) Herzl opposed the setting up of the socialist faction within Zionism. For him the movement that he had created existed for one purpose: the translation of "a people without a land" to some "land without a people." He did indeed turn his first and major ongoing efforts toward negotiating with the sultan of Turkey for a charter for Jews in Palestine or in its immediate vicinity, but those who opposed him in 1903, when he wanted to accept the proposal of the British government for a Jewish settlement in East Africa (the Uganda Scheme), were not entirely wrong in remembering that Herzl's commitment to Zion was unlike theirs, and that on theoretical grounds he had always remained a Zionist created by the "plight of the Jews" *(Judennot)*, and not by cultural commitment.

Nonetheless, the bulk of Herzl's followers, even though all assented to his political vision of a national movement treated as an equal among the powers of the world, came to his Zionism with less clearcut, more complicated motivations. It was not only that individual parties and factions arose each of which wanted the future Jewish State to take a certain shape and to be constructed consciously in such a direction. More fundamentally, the needs that Zionism served among the mass of its East European believers were not always identical with those which had moved Pinsker and Herzl.

CULTURAL AND "SYNTHETIC" ZIONISM. The basic distinction in contemporary polemics was made around the turn of the century by Aḥad Ha-Am: he refused to believe that it was humanly possible, even under the most favorable conditions, in the light of the Jewish birthrate, for the majority or even any substantial fraction of the Jews of the world to emigrate to their national homeland and thus significantly reduce the population in the Jewish Diaspora. He thus saw the "Jewish plight" as intrinsically insoluble by purely Zionist means, and the Jews could only do what they had already done in the Exile in bad times: either emigrate to more favorable countries, such as America, or temporize with the conditions in Russia. Aḥad Ha-Am himself did a bit of both, eventually emigrating to London, where he practically stopped writing but served in an important way as spiritual guide to the young Chaim Weizmann and a coterie of others. The fundamental problem of the modern age, and the one to which Zionism could indeed address itself, was the crisis not of the Jews but of Judaism, i.e., the rapid and radical disintegration of Jewish faith and identity that was going on everywhere. A secularist and positivist himself, Aḥad Ha-Am did not believe that the process of loss of religious faith was reversible. The function that revealed religion had performed in talmudic and medieval Judaism, that of guaranteeing the survival of the Jews as a separate entity because of their belief in the divinely ordained importance of the Jewish religion and people, it was no longer performing and could not be expected to perform. The crucial task facing Jews in the modern era was to devise new structures to contain the separate individuality of the Jews and to keep them loyal to their own tradition. This analysis of the situation implied, in its very first assertions, a view of Jewish history which Aḥad Ha-Am produced as undoubted and which has since become the common coin of secular Zionist and Israel historiography: that the Jews in all ages were essentially a nation, and that all other factors profoundly important to the life of this people, even religion, were mainly instrumental values.

A thousand years earlier Saadiah Gaon[10](d. 942 C.E.) gave expression to the *raison d'être* of the Jew in the pre-modern era when he pronounced that "the Jewish people is a people only for the sake of its Torah," i.e., that Jews exist as the instrument of Judaism. To accept this definition in the modern age of disbelief would mean that contemporary Jews have broken radically with their past, that continuity no longer existed in Jewish history, and that whatever solution could be found for the present situation would address itself to masses of individuals who still bore the name "Jew," in varieties of suffering or quiet desperation and on various levels of pride or self-hatred, to help them make the best of their situation. Such an understanding of Jewish modernity could lead to an assimilationist conclusion, as it had throughout the 19th century. It could also support the basic thesis of Herzl that the Jews existed as a community in his day only because they shared a negative situation, anti-Semitism, and that this was the one problem which they could, in the here and now, solve together. Those who chose to deal with that problem only by national and political means would then be free to evolve whatever culture might suit them. This view of modern Jewish culture was maintained by Hebrew writers and ideologists, such as M. J. Berdyczewski, J. Ḥ. Brenner, and Jacob Klatzkin. They could accept neither Aḥad Ha-Am's notion of ongoing continuity in Jewish history nor, more fundamentally, his description of the "national spirit" as an authoritative guide and standard to which he attributed a majesty comparable to that which the religious had once ascribed to the God of revelation. Brenner[11] regarded the national past and most of the Jewish heritage as weak,

[10]Leader of the Jewish community in Babylonia: philosopher, rabbinic authority, translator of the Bible into Arabic

[11]Hebrew author, journalist, essayist, novelist. Killed by Arabs in Jaffa, 1921

desiccated, cringing, and unworthy. There was thus created at the beginning of the 20th century, in part under the influence of Friedrich Nietzsche, a school of thought which wanted to create a Jewish state not only because there had already been a radical break with the Jewish past but in order to realize such a change. These writers wanted to establish a bold and earthy people, whose hands would not be tied by the rules of the rabbis or even by the self-doubts of the prophets. (This trend toward a total break was never attractive to more than a small minority among the Zionists, but it eventually evolved into a heresy to be represented by those few Israel writers and intellectuals who opposed the very notion and term of Jewish peoplehood and Zionism—and were called "Canaanites.")

Of all the schools of thought that were arising within the Zionist movement in its very first few years, Socialist Zionism was, at least in practice, the most important. In the work of its founding father, Nachman Syrkin, and a few years later, of the younger, Marxist, Ber Borochov, a socialist explanation of the "plight of the Jews" was constructed. In this view, the Jews were everywhere rejected aliens because their economic pursuits were "unproductive" or peripheral. For their masses were locked in the Pale of Settlement without any outlet into the modern development of the general society and its economy. They were middlemen, small craftsmen or *luftmenschen* who were not integrally bound to the roots and basic aspects of production and especially not to farming, modern industry, and other forms of primary economic activity. Socialist Zionists did not, of course, blame the Jews for this unhealthy economic situation, for they knew that it was not only a result of many centuries of persecution and discrimination but also of the "judophobia" of the gentile peasants and workers who regarded the Jews as alien "exploiters" and unwanted competitors; the anti-Semitism which attacked Jews because of their marginal economic role was the source of the very phenomenon that it attacked. This vicious circle produced the "inverted pyramid" of the Jewish economy in the Diaspora, the phenomenon that Jews were fewest in production and became more numerous the further away one went from farms and factories. That was the cause of an inevitable process of mass flight from Russia, Rumania, and other countries, which would, in the view of Borochov, eventually propel Jews toward the land within which a proper kind of national economy, a "normal" pyramid, would be created. However, the non-Marxist Labor Zionists, particularly those in Ereẓ Israel, such as A. D. Gordon, who was influenced by Tolstoy, affirmed neither such a historical inevitability of a mass emigration to Ereẓ Israel nor its socialist future, nor did they theorize about the need to create a Jewish national community as a necessary precondition for "healthy class struggle," which could not take place in the Diaspora where both Jewish workers and their employers were trapped by unhealthy circumstances. For Gordon and his pioneering disciples Zionism was an act of will, an affirmation about the dignity of physical labor and the rootedness of man in his own soil, of the desperate necessity to create a new Jewish man in the Land of Israel to replace the disfigured human being who had been shaped by his misery and alienation from nature in the Diaspora. The men of the Second Aliyah, the young pioneers who went to Ereẓ Israel in the first decade of the 20th century, adhered in their majority to some version of the Socialist Zionist faith and especially to the notion that the "new man" whom they were creating and exemplifying through themselves was the essential positive feature of Jewish history in the modern era. This group was eventually to become the dominant element among the founders of the State of Israel. It had no doubt from the beginning of its career that it was the creative center of the Jewish world and that, most immediately, the Zionist movement was important insofar as it made their image of the Jewish settlement in Ereẓ Israel possible (See below: Socialist Zionism).

The major thrust of Zionism in the era immediately after Herzl was neither toward his purely political activity for the achievement of the "charter," nor toward small-scale settlement combined with cultural evolution; it was toward "synthetic Zionism." This term was coined by Chaim Weizmann, who had been a young opponent of Herzl in his lifetime and who succeeded to the acknowledged leadership of the movement by 1917, when the Balfour Declaration was obtained from the British government as the result of prolonged negotiations during which he had been a central figure. Weizmann was, however, not alone in this shifting of the Zionist outlook and policy. Even Herzl's immediate heir in the presidency of the movement, David Wolffsohn, and most of those with whom he surrounded himself, especially Nahum Sokolow, were committed or at least inclined to the cultural, Hebraic renaissance and to the gradual upbuilding of Jewish settlement efforts in Palestine as the ongoing immediate tasks of the movement, while continuing diplomatic efforts and hoping that the time would come when major political arrangements would be possible. Moreover, the very struggle for these achievements, the labor of securing, step after step, "one cow, one dunam" in the Land of Israel, or the laying of the foundations for an educational system in Hebrew culminating in the creation of the Hebrew University in Jerusalem, were the routine ongoing life of Zionism, while those who engaged in these daily endeavors continued to dream of the eventual Jewish commonwealth, to be achieved at some political turning point in history. The handful who were taking the lead in the early years of the century by going to Palestine were moved by visionary considerations, and they regarded themselves, and were regarded within the Zionist hinterland, as a kind of secular priesthood preparing the way for those who would follow. Even in the United States, where the Zionist movement consisted almost entirely of recent immigrants of the same origins as the pioneers in Palestine (so that these American Zionists were then not themselves candidates for joining the pioneer vanguard) the labor for Zion became a quasi-religious experience. Even those "Western" Jews in America who had become Zionists, because they said they wanted to extend philanthropic help to Jewish refugees who chose to go to Palestine, belonged to a generation in American life which was dominated, among both Jews and gentiles, by the "social gospel," the teaching that the meaning of religion is not in metaphysical faith or theology but in the work of social reform in this world. "Synthetic" Zionism thus provided those who adhered to it, everywhere, with such daily commandments as the collecting of money to help the Jewish National Fund purchase dunams for new settlers; with tales of courage and suffering by the pioneers in Palestine; with spiritual uplift at the sight of a cultural renaissance; and with the ultimate hope, sustained even in the decade between 1904 and 1914, that some great political event would come to pass.

The cultural and "synthetic" Zionists emphasized more than the purely "political" Zionists the activity called in Zionist debates *Gegenwartsarbeit,* i.e., "work in the present," in the Diaspora. They included in it not only the task to "conquer" the Jewish community councils, proclaimed by Herzl himself, but also the need for modernized Hebrew education, in new-type *ḥadarim* (called *"ḥeder metukkan"*) and in secular-type schools; the establishment of Jewish athletic and sports clubs for the young (Bar Kokhba, later Maccabi, etc.); and, most important of all, the active participation, on separate Jewish tickets, in parliamentary and local elections, particularly in the Austrian Empire, in order to emphasize the existence of specific Jewish national interests in multinational states, crystallize the Jewish public around them, and thus erect a barrier against political assimilationism.

Zionism was transformed into a mass movement and into a major political force by World War I. At the outbreak of hostilities the seat of the Zionist Executive was in the capital of one of the major warring powers—Berlin; and even though an office was soon established in neutral Copenhagen, there was no possibility of effective central direction in a situation in which major Jewish communities were on both sides of the line. The situation was all the more complicated by two facts: that Palestine was under the control of Turkey, which joined the Central Powers in 1915; and that the largest Jewish community in the world, and the one most disaffected from its own oppressive government, was in Czarist Russia, which was allied to the Western powers. The situation created complex interplays of political forces which resulted in such events as the partial expulsion and total harassment by the Turks in 1917 of the Jewish population of Palestine; the protection of Jews in Palestine by German influence in Turkey in order not to lose support of Jewish opinion in the world as a whole and especially in then neutral America; and, above all, the long deliberations which resulted in the publication by the British government on November 2, 1917, of the Balfour Declaration, in which it declared itself to be in favor of the establishment in Palestine of a Jewish national home, provided that the civil and religious rights of the non-Jews were not impaired. This act resulted from the desire of the British to appeal to U.S. Jewish opinion, whose support for the Allies was questionable until the U.S. entered the war at a very late stage in the British deliberations on Zionist aspirations, and to keep Russia in the war despite its revolutionary upheavals in 1917. Beyond these immediate purposes there was, however, a new atmosphere compounded out of markedly increased Jewish fervor for Zionism. This was a corollary to the rising nationalism among all peoples in Europe, including the Austro-Hungarian Empire, which the Allies were exploiting by promising such subject nations as the Czechs and the Poles their national freedom after the war. The self-determination of subject peoples was made into a central war aim by President Wilson when he announced his Fourteen Points.

LEGION AND SELF-DEFENSE. It was clear early in the war that this convulsion involving all the major European powers would inevitably lead to new political arrangements and thus give room for Jewish aspirations. Some of the Zionists, especially Joseph Trumpeldor, the Russian Zionist leader Vladimir Jabotinsky, and later also such young labor pioneers from Ereẓ Israel as David Ben-Gurion and Izhak Ben-Zvi believed that one way of making sure that Jews would be taken seriously at the peace table was to organize Jewish military units to fight on the side of the Allies. As a practical matter this was the way to enlist Russian Jews in the West, particularly in England, for while they would not return to their native land to fight for Russia, even if that had been possible, many were eager to enlist as Jews in the Allied cause. The British government was at first not overly enthusiastic or cooperative, but these efforts did result in the establishment of the Jewish Legion—the Zion Mule Corps, which fought at Gallipoli in 1915 and in the Jewish battalions which took the field in 1917. As military formations they were of some importance, but their main significance was in the creation of the modern Jewish military tradition as a conscious national act. In the preparation of the claim for normal Jewish nationhood at the end of the war, something more than a symbolic army had fought beside the ultimate victors. Even earlier, with the very beginnings of Zionist settlement, Jewish armed guards (the Ha-Shomer) had increasingly protected settlements against thieves and armed robbers. Both of these military traditions coalesced after World War I, when difficulties soon developed in Palestine between Jews and Arabs, into the creation of a semisecret Jewish self-defense organization, the Haganah. There was never sufficiently prolonged quiet in Palestine between the two world wars for Jews ever to be able to imagine that they would be safe without their own self-defense. By the late 1930s there was continuing open warfare between the Jewish and Arab communities, in which the British played an ambiguous role, at best, and in which the Jews could largely depend for their safety only on themselves. By this time "illegal" immigration in the teeth of British restrictions had become a life-and-death matter for those Jews who could escape Europe. The Zionist movement as a whole, in all its factions, and not only the Revisionists, who had left the Zionist Organization because of its lack of militancy, was in a military struggle with both the Arabs and the British. There had thus evolved a new element which had been implicit in the Zionist ideological vision of a normal nation: an increasingly independent military force, which, however small by international standards, was almost from its beginning a substantial power in the immediate region. The existence of armed strength added further "sovereign" dimensions of Jewish self-liberation to the vision of Zionism.

POST-WAR CONSENSUS AND DIFFERENTIATION. As World War I ended, the major arena of Zionist activity was, however, not in Ereẓ Israel but in Paris, where the victors were meeting in 1919 to define the terms of peace. A variety of Jewish groups were officially in the lobbies of this conference. The most assimilated elements from France, England, and the United States would, for the most part, have preferred that the Jewish position at the Peace Conference be simply the demand for full individual liberty in all the states that were then being created in Central and Eastern Europe. The "Western" Jews were projecting the image of what they hoped was and would remain their own status, that of Frenchmen, Englishmen, or Americans who differed from others only in their private adherence to a differing religious faith. The Zionists, headed by Weizmann and Sokolow, came to Versailles to make sure that the intent of the Balfour Declaration (as they hopefully understood it to mean: an act pointing to the creation in measurable time of Jewish political independence in Palestine) would be incorporated in the peace arrangements. The delegates from Eastern Europe were mostly interested in insisting that such new states as Poland and Lithuania, and all the rest, be made to pledge the most solemn guarantees for the rights of national minorities within their borders. For Jews this meant self-definition as a national minority, parallel, for example, to the Ukrainians in Poland, with the right to conduct educational institutions with public money in their own national language, be it Yiddish or Hebrew; the right to self-governing community councils with status before the law; and, most sensitively, the right to appeal to the international community, which was seen to be represented by the League of Nations, over the head of the national government, if minority rights were violated.

There was internal struggle among these various parties in Paris. Out of their interaction there, and largely through the leadership of Louis Marshall[12], a kind of consensus was achieved which became the actual premise for all Jewish political life in the next decades, the interwar years. It was agreed that all would stand together for the minority rights of Jews in those countries in which the local Jewish population desired such a formulation of its identity. In practice this meant that the Jews of Eastern and Central Europe were publicly defined in new international arrangements as a separate people; for the Zionists this definition meant the possibility of struggling effectively within these Jewish national institutions to orient educational endeavors toward the new Hebraic culture and to prepare the hearts of the people to realize that only in complete national concentration in Ereẓ Israel could there be a Jewish future. Throughout the 1920s and 1930s various other factions were in combat with the Zionists within these new structures of the Jewish community. There was ongoing friction with assimilationist opinion, but this trend never achieved importance in the inner life of the East European Jewish communities outside the Soviet Union. The more serious battles were with the religiously orthodox, who were by then organized to a great degree around Agudat Israel; this party found Zionism to be too secular. As a counterforce to these views the Orthodox wing of the Zionist movement itself, the Mizrachi, achieved particular importance during these years; it represented the possibility of a synthesis between the new national ideal of self-realization in Ereẓ Israel, through cooperation even with nonbelievers who were laboring in the Zionist cause, and preserving and even refreshing traditional Judaism. The

[12]U.S. communal leader; a member of the Committee of Jewish Delegations at the Versailles Peace Conference

enemies of Zionism on the left were even more serious, because both the Jewish Socialist Bund and the Jewish elements within the mostly illegal Communist Party, in Poland and in several other adjacent countries, had substantial followings. The Zionists countered these visions of a new, revolutionary era by insisting, especially through their own socialist wing, that the new socialist society would have to be formed by the remaking of individual national societies and that, at least in the case of the Jews, rampant anti-Semitism, which had culminated in the mass slaughter of the Ukrainian pogroms in the post-revolutionary period and became a bitter reality in independent Poland, required that, whatever be the nature of the internal life of a Jewish independent society, the solution to the Jewish problem had to take a Zionist form. Several varieties of Zionist Socialism had been defined in the 1920s, ranging from moderate social democracy to the ultimately Marxist pro-Communism of Ha-Shomer ha-Ẓa'ir.

Almost every one of these versions of Zionism, except for the most radical Communist option, had existed as a school of thought and even as an organization, in some form, before World War I. However, these parties came to serious maturity in their encounter with the postwar realities: the internal struggles of East European Jewry and, of growing and soon of predominant importance, the battle for the definition of the life and character of the *yishuv,* the Zionist settlement in Palestine, as it increased tenfold, from roughly 60,000 in 1919 to 600,000, in the 1940s. In the interwar period a fully developed form of Jewish communal autonomy and self-government existed there, legally, in the Keneset Yisrael with its executive body, the Va'ad Le'ummi, which was confirmed by the British Mandate government and, extra-legally, in the internal discipline and cohesiveness of the Jews in the country. An even more important political process involved these very forces, both in the *yishuv* and among the Jewish masses of Eastern Europe, in their interaction in the World Zionist Organization. The League of Nations' Mandate for Palestine stipulated that an appropriate " Jewish agency" cooperate by right with the British authorities in the upbuilding of the Jewish national home, and the Zionist Organization, though obliged to seek the cooperation of non-Zionist Jews as well, was recognized as such an "agency." The most poignant problem during most of those years was the question of Jewish immigration, which was always strictly limited by the British in reaction to Arab opposition and violent outbursts. The World Zionist Organization exercised effective control over the distribution of "certificates," that is, entry permits for new immigrants, up to the number permitted in any one year by the British. How these permits were divided in the Diaspora became a cause for impassioned struggle, both among the various Zionist factions which accepted the discipline of the world body and especially with the Revisionists, who regarded themselves as discriminated against. (This militant group eventually broke away, mainly for political reasons, and declared its Zionist independence in 1935.) The basic solution was an agreement to operate by the "party key," which meant that "certificates" were distributed on the basis of the respective strengths of the various parties in the world Zionist movement and especially in the nascent *yishuv*. The result was that the political composition of the Jewish community in Palestine remained remarkably stable despite the growth of its proportions. This party influence on immigration was part of a picture in which many of those who came, especially after 1933 in flight from Hitler—even though they were admitted as individuals and not as the holders of certificates—had also to find their way within a community which was dominated by parties. Kibbutzim, banks, educational facilities from university down to elementary school, jobs in the administration and many other things besides were controlled or influenced by parties, which tended to be complete Jewish societies living side by side, each one involving most of the elements of human life, almost from the cradle to the grave. There were parties even before 1914, but in the 1920s the internal life of the Jewish community in Ereẓ Israel had crystallized into the political parties, which largely exist to the present day. The forces which were contending over the nature of the new society were divided into three broad groups. The most powerful were the several kinds of Socialist Zionists, with their roots in the Second Aliyah, in the kibbutz movement, and in the labor unions, which had together formed the overarching organization of all the Jewish workers in Israel (later including Arabs also), known as the Histadrut. These forces strove for a socialist, economically egalitarian, secularist Jewish society. The central sector of the developing Jewish community consisted of middle-class elements. In part, and especially in the case of the first refugees to come from Germany after 1933, these forces consisted of people who arrived with some property. Not all those who came from Eastern Europe wanted to be pioneers in kibbutzim. Some had been accustomed to a middle-class, urban way of life and they wanted to live that way in the new environment. This middle-class group contained many General Zionists allied to the anti-socialist Revisionists. On doctrinaire grounds they insisted with vehemence that the very future of the Jewish settlement depended on the releasing of the energies of free enterprise. There was one wing of General Zionists who refused to identify, both in Ereẓ Israel and outside it, with any specific middle-class program in the country and who followed the lead of Chaim Weizmann, in particular, in accepting economic and cultural support for the labor sector as well as for private enterprise. But another wing of the General Zionists clung to a more partisan view, so that a continuing battle was fought between Socialist Zionism and the middle-class groups. The tension was often sufficiently great for bitter accusations to be hurled. Such leaders as David Ben-Gurion, in his role as secretary-general of the Histadrut, spoke for the Socialists in accusing the Revisionists of being "Fascists"; the partisans of Jabotinsky replied by charging that the Socialist Zionists were using their power not for the good of all but to increase their own political and organizational dominance.

Parallel with this quarrel there was continuing tension over the issue of religion. There had been Orthodox Jews of the old *yishuv* in some numbers in Ereẓ Israel before the new Zionist immigration began, but the earliest arrivals after 1900 were in their overwhelming majority socialist and secularist, and many of them were anti-religious in a doctrinaire way. The religious Zionist movement, Mizrachi, had indeed been founded in the early years of the century and it had existed as a trend even before, but its direct presence and influence on the life of the new Jewish community in Ereẓ Israel began to be felt only after World War I. By then a labor wing of the religious party, the Ha-Po'el ha-Mizrachi, had arisen, and it proceeded to create its own kibbutz movement. Many of the middle-class immigrants who were arriving in the 1920s and 1930s were personally Orthodox, and they could not imagine a Jewish presence in the land which did not exemplify the values and practices of the religious tradition. Religious Jewry was led by the Ashkenazi chief rabbi, Abraham Isaac Kook, until his death in 1935, who, though he was himself beyond party, was regarded as the spiritual voice and teacher of all religious Jews who accepted a Zionist vision. For Kook the new settlement in the Land of Israel was the "beginning of the redemption." Both his temperament and outlook were broad enough to embrace even the most partisan secularist as an instrument of the divine purpose. Those who followed him could accept such a notion in theory. In practice they were dedicated to the building of an institutional power base for religious Jews, so that they could compete as equals with the other groups and provide equal opportunity in the new country for those who shared the Orthodox religious faith. This body of opinion was deeply concerned that the total temper of the Jewish community should not be secularized. They did not want to become a religious ghetto in a non-religious Jewish society, and they believed that it was their duty to bring religion even to those who opposed it. Orthodox Jews in Palestine joined the battle, immediately after the beginning of the

British Mandate government, for the ever wider influence of traditional Jewish practice on the life and the law of the *yishuv*. The struggle between the socialist and the middle-class elements in Israel's society has been muted in the generation of statehood, for a mixed economy now prevails. The conflict over religion and its relationship to public life has, if anything, become sharper within the sovereign parliamentary life of the Jewish state.

BETWEEN POGROMS AND HOLOCAUST. Ideological stamps were thus deeply impressed on the Jewish community in Palestine. Great numbers of those who came in the 1920s and even in the 1930s chose their paths because they believed in some version of the Zionist vision and found in it their path toward national and personal realization. Nonetheless, the dominant element in creating many more candidates for immigration to Palestine than were ever permitted to arrive was not Zionist ideology, at least not in its cultural, "synthetic" form, but the growing horror of anti-Semitism, at a time when other doors to safety were closing or were entirely closed to Jews. The sense of disaster was already deeply embedded in the consciousness of European Jews by the events which followed right after the end of World War I. The far greater horrors of the Nazi Holocaust have by now half obscured the murder of about one hundred thousand Jews, including women and children, in the Russian-Polish borderland, where Ukrainian and counter-revolutionary Russian army units systematically engaged in killing Jews in the years 1919–21. These pogroms had a profound effect on the Jewish delegation in Paris, which agreed to plead unanimously for national minority rights because the hatred of Jews as Jews was so rabid in Eastern Europe. Moreover, major figures among Western Jewry increasingly became less doctrinaire. Men such as Louis Marshall could not accept the Zionist notion that all Jews everywhere belonged to a national entity other than that of the majority of the people in the political state into which they were born, and they could not therefore agree that Jews ought to be working for their ingathering in

Zion. Nonetheless, such figures responded to the dire need of East European Jews both by trying to alleviate the immediate situation and by accepting that, on purely humanitarian grounds, those who wished to go to Palestine should be helped to do so. Even after the pogroms ended and a certain amount of surface stability was created in Eastern Europe, the largest community outside the United States, that of Poland, was increasingly harassed by a regime of economic exclusion and of *numerus clausus* at the universities and in the professions. Year by year the life of these Jews was becoming more unbearable, and there were occasional pogroms in Poland in the 1930s to underline their misery. The situation was only relatively better in some of the other countries in the area. The "non-Zionists" who were persuaded by Chaim Weizmann in 1929 to join with the Zionists on the basis of parity in creating the "enlarged" Jewish Agency were moved by a sense of the direst Jewish needs and a growing undercurrent of fear of worse things to come. This, rather than Zionist ideology of any variety, was the dominant note in the development of Zionism itself even before Hitler appeared on the scene, and certainly after 1933.

The sense of need and foreboding had come to formal expression in Zionist thought immediately after World War I. Louis Brandeis, by then a justice on the Supreme Court of the United States, who had served as the leader of American Zionism during the war years, believed that, with the achievement of the Balfour Declaration, the political struggle of Zionism was over and that, henceforth, the Jewish settlement in Palestine should be fostered through the orderly processes of investment, on the highest principles of business accountability. This soon led to a shattering struggle with Weizmann, who continued to believe in the need for a movement of Zionist national consciousness. He wanted the Zionist movement to work toward a *yishuv* which would be a left-wing liberal, in part moderately socialist, Hebrew-speaking society and he saw its embodiment mainly in the collective and cooperative enterprise of the labor pioneers who needed non-profitable funds, such as the Keren Hayesod, to create their network of settlements and institutions. In short, Weizmann intended to realize the "synthetic" Zionism which he had defined in the days of his youthful opposition to Herzl. Both Brandeis and Weizmann, despite their difference, wanted to create the Jewish community in Palestine step by step, according to plan, with the presumption that there was time aplenty to do it. Right after World War I Max Nordau, the still-living colleague of Herzl, and later also Vladimir Jabotinsky, arose against such views. Nordau and Jabotinsky did not believe that the Jews of Eastern Europe would find safety in any years of seeming quiet that might follow after the Russian-Polish upheavals and they were equally convinced that the British government, the holder of the Mandate, would find reasons of its own for making the large-scale immigration of Jews into Palestine an ever more difficult enterprise. Nordau proposed, melodramatically, that without any meticulous planning or preparation, or even arrangement for solid housing, Jews, mainly from the pogrom-afflicted areas, should be led in their hundreds of thousands simply to appear in Palestine. He agreed that many might suffer extreme hardship, but that it was better for that to happen than to wait for the slower horrors in Europe and the hardening of the anti-Zionist policy of the British. At least, this mass movement would immediately achieve majority status for Jews in Palestine and would assure possibilities for the future. This then wild idea of "catastrophic" Zionism was rejected but it remained dormant, and even in the quieter years of the 1920s it was the countertheme to the then dominant notion of "building step by step," according to plan. By the 1930s Jabotinsky and the Revisionists called for the implementation of the "Nordau plan" and for an orderly mass "evacuation" of East European Jewry. Though this call evoked bitter internal controversies among Zionists, Jewish need, and the growing foreboding of worse horrors to come, were ever more the driving force attracting support to Zionism as a solution all over the Jewish world, and beyond its confines.

RELATION TO THE ARABS. Until the immediate aftermath of the Balfour Declaration the Zionist movement had given little serious thought to the question of the Arabs

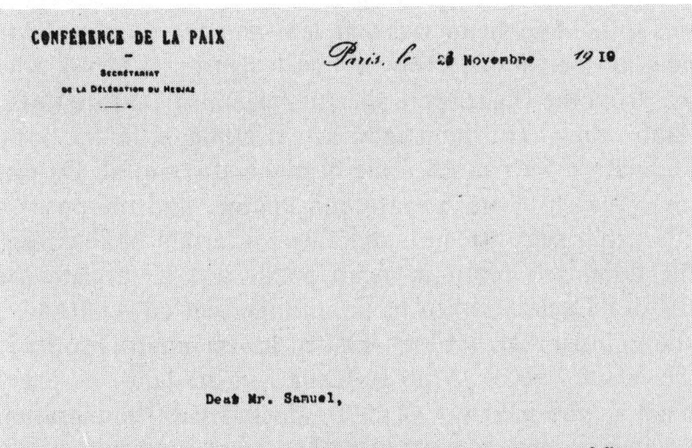

CONFÉRENCE DE LA PAIX

SECRÉTARIAT DE LA DÉLÉGATION DU HEDJAZ

Paris, le 23 Novembre 1919

Dear Mr. Samuel,

I am in the receipt of your letter of Nov. and very much regret to know of the opposition of the Damascus Press to Zionism.

I personally deprecate any difference between the Arabs and the Jews who ought to unite their efforts in word and deed for promoting the developement and happiness of our country.

Mr. Sokoloff with whom I had a long conversation will, I hope, convey to you my views about this matter and assure you of my unabated efforts, and the means I am taking for safeguarding our common interests and strengthning the old bonds of friendship and co-operation between Arabs and Jews.

Believe me

Yours sincerely

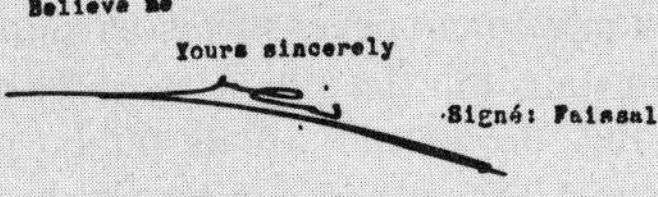

Signé: Faisal

Letter from Emir Feisal, head of the Arab delegation at the Paris Peace Conference,to Herbert Samuel, Nov. 23, 1919, expressing his positive attitude toward Zionism. Jerusalem, Central Zionist Archives.

resident in Palestine. Moses Hess in 1861, a generation before Herzl, had imagined that a highly Westernized element such as the Jews would be welcomed by the Arabs because of the leadership that Jews would provide in creating in the entire region an advanced economy and an advancing society. Chaim Weizmann took a comparable tack in 1919 in his encounters with the Arab leader of the time, the Emir Feisal, with whom he signed an agreement in this spirit. The theme was that Jews and Arabs proposed to be good neighbors. However, such figures as Feisal, who was from the Hejaz, were alien to the immediate Palestinian Arab scene. The politically active elements in the local population were much more hostile and resentful. Despite large Jewish efforts toward conciliation, and the positive effect that such attempts did have on certain Arab circles, the dominant motif in Arab policy was to declare the Balfour Declaration to be an infringement on Arab rights and to insist that, at best, a limited Jewish minority could in the future live on Arab sufferance in the land. At every point in the interwar years at which Jewish immigration became of some consequence, there were Arab riots which invariably caused the British to issue further restrictions against the Jews. This became particularly marked in the decade after 1929, when there were major riots by Arabs. Zionism had thus, perforce, to define itself in much more complicated terms than those of a "people without a land on the way to a land without a people." The very example of its own energies and national purpose was helping to evoke some comparable national emotion among the Arabs in Palestine. In theory, throughout this period the bulk of the Zionist movement never surrendered the ultimate vision of a Jewish state, but the only wing of the movement which made of this the essence of its public position was the Revisionists. All the others concentrated on two immediate objectives: immigration, while trying not to displace Arabs in the process and to compensate generously the few displaced ones, feasible by constantly increasing the "absorptive capacity" of the land through new endeavors; and the devising of formulas for ongoing life together with the Arabs in which no absolute minority ceiling would be placed on the Jews. Among one group on the extreme left, the Marxist Ha-Shomer ha-Ẓa'ir, a bi-national state of absolute parity between Jews and Arabs was defined as its version of the political purpose of Zionism as a whole. A handful of Jewish pacifists of high station, led by such figures as Judah L. Magnes[13] and Martin Buber[14], formed the Berit Shalom program in the 1930s; they were willing to go even further than Ha-Shomer ha-Ẓa'ir in placating Arab fears for the sake of peace, but even they, like all the other Jewish groups or leaders (including Ben-Gurion), could find no Arab representatives of rank and power with whom to come to terms. Jewish misery was growing constantly in Europe and the need for mass immigration was ever greater. No Zionist group (and, for that matter, after the appearance of Hitler, no responsible non-Zionist body) could accept the halting of the growth of the *yishuv* even if it meant open hostility with the Arabs, and that is what it indeed meant by the mid-1930s and for the rest of the decade. Jews required freedom of immigration; Arabs demanded its absolute end. The British floundered in the middle, issuing "white papers" and setting draconian quotas on future Jewish arrivals. The situation could not last for all the positions were irreconcilable.

Throughout the years of the British Mandate of Palestine the government in London appointed a whole series of commissions, whenever conflict between Jews and Arabs broke out into open violence, in the vain quest of finding some acceptable compromise. Such efforts became more frequent in the 1930s, when the basic Jewish demand was, as it had to be, mass immigration which could not ever be restricted by Arab veto.

The logic of events, compounded out of the first years of

[13]U.S. Reform rabbi who became first chancellor of the Hebrew University, Jerusalem

[14]Religious philosopher who taught in Germany and, from 1938, at the Hebrew University

Hitler and the increasing clashes in Palestine between Jews and Arabs, evoked the single most serious study of the Palestine question which was ever undertaken, that by the Royal Commission of 1936, chaired by Lord Peel. In its many hearings, some of them in no less impressive a place than the House of Lords in London, and others in Palestine itself, the major spokesmen of all varieties of Arab and Jewish opinion were heard. There was little essential difference among the views of the Zionist representatives, for even such old antagonists as Weizmann and Jabotinsky spoke in the same terms. Both emphasized the spiritual and cultural elements in Zionism, the vision of the movement of a "new Jew" who would be born in freedom to achieve his own proper dignity. However, the main theme, in the testimony of both, was the misery of Jewish life at that moment. Before the Peel Commission and later, at the Zionist Congress of 1937, when Weizmann proposed that the movement accept, in principle, the Commission's proposal to partition Palestine, he looked especially closely at the life of the Jews in Poland. He said openly that this community was doomed. A third of it, the old people, would no doubt die in Poland; for another third he had no hope; but it was the responsibility of all who could help to make it possible for the last third, the young people, to come to Palestine and start a new and decent life.

In this atmosphere the Peel Commission proposed the division of Palestine into three geographical entities: an Arab state, a Jewish one, and a large enclave, including Jerusalem, to be governed by the British. The proposed map was very nearly impossible, though, for it presumed the kind of goodwill between Jews and Arabs which, had it existed, would have made partition unnecessary. What the proposal did achieve, from the perspective of the Zionist movement, was the first formal suggestion by the ruling power that a Jewish state in at least part of Palestine was a realistic necessity; secondly, the proposal was based on the premise that Jews had a right, because of their need, to large new immigration into the land and that they could achieve this only if they were in political control of their own national destiny. The Zionist movement, after heated debate, which reflected the objections that the proposed state was unviable and that to accept it meant to give up the claim on the whole of the land, reluctantly accepted the partition proposal as a basis for discussion. The negotiations soon died, however, because the Arabs rejected the idea and the British, in the era of appeasement of Hitler, had no stomach for forcing any radical solution. On the eve of World War II, Zionism had, however, defined itself as charged with the responsibility of creating or exercising, whether legally or illegally, as much independence as was necessary to do everything that was possible for the saving of Jews. This had become the dominant motif, and it had a directness and moral urgency which ever wider circles of Jewish and world opinion could not help but accept. The contrast between Jewish farmers in Palestine and their native-born sons, farming their fields and shooting back if necessary at Arab raiders, and the Jews being spat upon in Warsaw or sent to concentration camps, or worse, in Germany was, even before 1939, clear and unmistakable.

AFTER THE HOLOCAUST: "CATASTROPHIC" ZIONISM REVIVED. On the very eve of World War II the British government issued a White Paper in which, in effect, Jewish immigration was limited to a final 75,000. This meant that the Jews of Europe were being left to their destiny; the clear intent was to condemn the Jews in Palestine to be a permanent minority. The whole of the Jewish world was well nigh unanimous in its opposition, in declaring this act to be not only wrong but utterly devoid of moral or legal validity. Soon the war broke out and the Zionist movement, indeed the entire Jewish community everywhere, was inevitably on the side of the Allies. The Jews in Palestine soon tried to organize a volunteer force to fight with the British in the critical Middle Eastern arena, but, on the grounds of "parity," because no such volunteers were forthcoming from the Arabs, the offers were initially rebuffed. The Jewish Brigade eventually came into being.

It played a military role especially in the campaign in Italy, but its most important achievement was that here, directly, much of the immediate foundation of the future army of Israel was laid. "Illegal" immigration had been going on straight through the war, for the Zionist movement as a whole had accepted the slogan of David Ben-Gurion: "To fight Hitler as if there were no White Paper and to fight the White Paper as if there were no Hitler." Some of the brutalities that the Nazis had perpetrated were to be seen in Italy, as the Jewish Brigade advanced within the Allied army; and as the war was ending, the men of the Brigade began the work of finding friendly out-of-the-way ports and cooperative officials elsewhere to make it possible to transport to Palestine those Jews who had survived. The armies on the eastern and the western fronts, and especially the Jews among them, were concurrently discovering the unspeakable crimes of Buchenwald and Auschwitz. Perhaps a million Jewish refugees were alive in camps in Europe in May 1945. All those who saw them were overwhelmed by one conviction—that they must be given the kind of new life where they could never again be the object of the horrors that had been done to them. The survivors themselves were most vocal everywhere that they had to be allowed to go to Ereẓ Israel, to take their place in an independent Jewish state.

During the war years the Zionist movement itself had almost completely stripped away all tentativeness or vagueness from its ultimate aims and it had abandoned, at least for the moment, any public concern with the nature of the new Jewish society. That did not mean that within Palestine itself, and within the world Zionist movement, the various parties did not continue to jockey for control of whatever they could regarding resources and position, but from the mid-1930s forward these issues became ever more internal to the immediate scene in the *yishuv*. As a world movement Zionism spoke of "a home for the homeless," and the more bitter and obvious the homelessness was, the greater was the support for all the actions that this slogan required. By 1942 a Zionist conference, the most representative possible under the circumstances, met in New York at the Biltmore Hotel. It announced in the "Biltmore Program" that the "establishment of Palestine as a Jewish Commonwealth" was the war aim of the Jewish people. This program was tacitly adopted by non-Zionists as well. The many years when such words were not spoken even by most Zionists, for fear of complicating the immediate situation among Jews, Arabs and the British, had thus been ended. Within the next year or so, after a bitter battle within the ranks of American Zionism between those who were willing to wait for the end of the war and trust President Roosevelt, and those who believed that American public opinion needed to be enlisted on the widest possible basis, Abba Hillel Silver emerged the victor over Stephen S. Wise and, in 1943, Zionism in America entered a militant phase which continued until the State of Israel was achieved. Here, too, it was the growing knowledge and then the absolute certainty of what Hitler had been doing to Jews that made the Zionist demand for freedom, dignity, and independence a great force in American public life.

At the end of the war the Jews were indeed, as the anti-Zionist British foreign minister Ernest Bevin said, "pushing to the head of the queue." No doors, not even those of the United States, were wide open to the refugees of the greatest single disaster that had ever befallen a people, and it was therefore inevitable that Palestine would have to provide the major part of the immediate solution. The British, weakened greatly by the war, were even less affected and less resolute than they had been in the 1930s; the Arabs were at least as intransigent; the Jews, both in Palestine and elsewhere, were at the highest point of outrage and self-assertion in their entire history. Many intricate maneuvers in Europe, Palestine, and the diplomatic centers of the world resulted finally in the great debate before the United Nations in November 1947 on the future of Palestine. The Jewish Agency, even though it was not a government, was admitted to the debate as the representa-

New York Jews in a mass protest against British and American policy on Palestine, July 1947.

tive of the Jewish people; it stood solidly for the legal and moral right of those to whom promises had been made in the Balfour Declaration and who had suffered so greatly in the recent past to a state of their own in the land which had belonged to their ancestors and in which they had already created much in the 20th century. The end result was a decision reminiscent of the proposals of the Peel Commission a decade before—partition of the land in an unworkable map. This time, however, nothing prevented the formal declaration by the Jews of their own state on the appointed day, May 14, 1948—neither the ambiguous attitude of the United States in the decisive stage nor the war against this new state which was begun by the Arabs both in Palestine and on its borders even before the formal declaration.

ZIONISM AND THE STATE OF ISRAEL. After the costly battles ended and the state was secure, and even as the war was still going on, refugees by the tens of thousands were brought into Israel. There was little surface difficulty in the immediate years after the achievement of statehood in defining the purpose of Zionism. The state was young, weak, and threatened; the refugees were many and in direst need. The purpose of Zionism, and of the Jewish world which it was by then leading, was to help root the state in secure ground, defend and explain it before world opinion, and either raise funds directly or provide inspiration for such endeavors. Almost immediately, however, the question of Zionist purpose and definition began to be a critical issue, first in isolated instances and then in prolonged debate which raged through the 1950s and into the 1960s. As early as 1949 there was a public break between David Ben-Gurion, the first prime minister of Israel, and Abba Hillel Silver[15], then the major Zionist figure in the Diaspora. The essence of the quarrel was the unwillingness of the government of the new state to accept any presumption of tutelage from the Zionist movement.

[15]U.S. Reform rabbi who played leading role in Jewish Agency and in U.S. Zionism

Now that a state existed, Zionism could clearly no longer engage in the kind of international politics to which it had been accustomed. The fund-raising had increasingly been engaging Jews of all shades of opinion, and many of the richest and most generous were not Zionists, at least in the formal sense. The bodies which raised funds for Israel were not everywhere, and especially not in the United States, really under Zionist leadership. There were a number of attempts made by post-state Zionism in the Diaspora to define the ongoing purpose of the movement as the cultivation of Jewish national consciousness, the fostering of Hebraic education and the creation of a Jewish life which had as its emotional and spiritual center the life in Israel. Against this there stood, implacably, the figure of David Ben-Gurion, and the majority opinion in Israel which he led. He held that fund-raising and other forms of aid extended by Jews to Israel were an endeavor which was, and quite properly, common to the entire Jewish people. This entitled those involved to be considered "friends of Israel." A Zionist, in the proper sense of the term, could be only one who was preparing himself and his family, no matter how comfortable the society in which he was living, to come in measurable time as an immigrant to the new Jewish state. This outlook finally prevailed in international Zionist councils in the 1960s, and the seal was set on it with a proclamation in 1968 of the Jerusalem Program by the Zionist Congress. In this document the acceptance of *aliyah*, of personal migration as the ultimate ideal, became a sine qua non of belonging to any recognized Zionist group.

It had taken two decades, however, for Zionists in the Western countries to be willing to reach such a conclusion. In the early years after the establishment of the State of Israel American Zionists in particular had argued that "America is different," that there is a distinction between a Diaspora where Jews were persecuted and the Diaspora of the free countries, where anti-Semitism was not a major factor and was not likely to increase, because of the rooted democratic tradition of a country such as America, which had no medieval past of hatred of Jews. The unwillingness to accept *aliyah* even as an ideal was ended in part by ongoing pressure from Israel opinion and in part by changing loyalties within American society as a whole, which was becoming less nationalist in the 1960s. The most important cause was, however, internal. During most of this era the president of the World Zionist Organization was Nahum Goldmann, and he became aware, soon after the heady days of the creation of the State of Israel, that intermarriage and spiritual and cultural evaporation were becoming a major threat to the survival of Jewish life in the free world. He argued that the task of the time was to prevent in the very age of Zionist achievement the rapid assimilation of world Jewry. Ever wider circles in the Jewish communities in the Western countries began looking to Israel, to various educational and work programs in the country, especially for young people from all communities of the Jewish world, to provide the occasion and the source for Jewish commitment. In such an atmosphere of growing concern for the Jewish continuity of hundreds of thousands of Jewish families all over the world, the notion that those who chose to live in Israel would certainly remain Jewish in a creative way conquered many previous reservations about *aliyah* as the ultimate personal ideal of a Zionist.

In the 1970s the world Zionist movement retains substantial functions in the upbuilding of Israel's society, both in the bringing of new immigrants, especially from lands where Jews are being persecuted, and in all other areas in which public funds from the Diaspora are properly spent. It continues to conduct and even to expand its endeavors in the strengthening of ties between Jews all over the world and those in Israel. Its governing body, still called the Jewish Agency, formally expanded again, in 1971, under the leadership of its chairman Louis Pincus, after the pattern of an earlier, practically abortive expansion in 1929, to include on the basis of parity representatives of the major Jewish pro-Israel fund-raising organizations everywhere in the world. In these new arrangements the World Zionist Organization and its Executive divested themselves, in favor of the new body, of direct responsibility for the financing and directing of *aliyah* from places of need and of the tasks which flow from this responsibility. Regardless of the formal changes, and even the increase in activities, the question of Zionist definition remains, however.

A major turning point was the Six-Day War in 1967. The days that led up to that event were filled with fear that a small state surrounded by enemies might become the object of a new holocaust. The swift and total victory evoked joy that Jews were now masters of their own destiny and recognized as such throughout the world. The Jewish Diaspora in all countries did not know how deeply it identified both with the fears and the triumphs of Israel until it was in the midst of the actual events. There then came an outpouring of money, political support of the most public kind, and volunteers, the equal of which had not been seen except briefly during the months of Israel's War of Independence. The years between 1948 and 1967, of continued integration of Jews into U.S. society, and into several West European countries, had not affected the strong emotions of self-identification and of identification with Israel which had clearly existed two decades before. Nowhere, during those days, did Jews hesitate to exert pressure on the governments of their countries of residence to support Israel. In France, where de Gaulle had reversed his previous policy and stood against Israel when war came, Jewish demonstrations in Paris evoked from him a remark about the Jews as an "elite people, sure of itself, and domineering." After the initial outrage over the negative rhetoric in which de Gaulle's opinion was couched, the Jews of the world were by 1967 willing to accept the proposition that Jews were indeed a community with opinions, ties, and characteristics which were distinct, and that the major contemporary affirmation of this Jewish distinctiveness was the whole set of relationships which involved all Jews in Israel. Zionism had thus finally succeeded in having the Jewish world accept the idea—and, what is more, feel deeply—that in the 20th century the Jews were a people and not only an international religious community, and that this people found its central expression in the renascent life in Israel.

Tensions in the U.S. and the U.S.S.R. In the last years of the 1960s two other events deeply affected the contemporary understanding of Zionism. In the United States this was the era of major social tension and Jews were not far from the center of all the problems. Race relations deteriorated by the latter years of the decade to physical confrontation and even armed clashes between blacks and whites. In all of the largest cities of the United States Jews had, for historical reasons (they were usually the last occupants of the neighborhoods into which blacks then moved), a substantial stake in the economy of the black ghetto, as storekeepers and landlords. They were often the most visible white men in the life of blacks in the north. In another dimension, younger, politically radical Jewish elements had been among the founders of the most activist movements of black protest, but, as black consciousness became ever more exclusivist, Jews and all other whites were systematically excluded from these movements. Certain administrations, such as that of the public school teachers in New York City, were dominated by Jews, and blacks began to fight hard to occupy their places. On a variety of levels the dream of peaceful integration was thus replaced by confrontation in the name of group identity and group interests. Within such an atmosphere many Jews were pushed toward identification with the specific interests of the Jewish community and its own peculiar destiny. The alternative for some of the young who had cut their teeth politically in the black movement, was to come to Israel.

There was no such direct correlation between the rising tempers over the war in Vietnam and Jewish consciousness. Young Jews were very prominent among the makers of the political protests which rocked the American campus in the late 1960s; but only a very few of those who chose not to fight in the war in Vietnam came to Israel. What was more fundamental was the growing disillusionment in all circles, not only Jewish ones, with the "American dream." For a person to emigrate from America to some less problematic, more satisfying place was now thinkable, and indeed some were even doing so. At such a moment the problem of "dual loyalty" which had troubled the past generation of Jews in America, their need to prove that it was not anti-American to care about Israel, or even to want to go and live there, was no longer of consequence. Fear for their future as Jews was not major, but some element of reaction to anti-Semitism was widespread. *Aliyah* from America, which neared 10,000 for the first time in the year 1970, was mostly, however, propelled not by the "push" of disappointment in American life, but by the "pull" of the attraction of Israel to Jews who wanted to live its kind of life, as the realization of their own Jewish identity.

In the late 1960s the Jews of the Soviet Union, who had remained inert on the surface under Stalinist persecution, began to assert their Jewishness and their identification with Israel in the most overt ways. The underlying factors here were the classic ones of bitter resentment that Russian Jews felt at the anti-Semitism which still existed in Soviet society and its administration after half a century of Bolshevik rule, coupled with a surprising amount of deep Jewish feelings, and especially of proud identification with Israel, which still persisted despite the absence for at least a generation of any Jewish schools or communal organizations—for even the Communist schools and press in Yiddish had been destroyed under Stalin. In the Soviet Union, too, the Six-Day War had been a turning point. The government was on the Arab side and remained the chief protector and supplier of Egypt and of the most anti-Israel of the other Arab states. Official propaganda was violently anti-Israel, anti-Zionist with strong anti-Semitic overtones. The Jews of the U.S.S.R., through their most vocal elements, had, however, lost their fear of repression and proceeded to demand the right to leave and to go to Israel. A trickle of such immigration had been permitted by the Soviet authorities earlier and, spasmodically, it was renewed in 1968, even during the years of the most bitter vituperation of Israel by Soviet diplomacy and propaganda. The numbers of those who were permitted to leave reached relatively considerable proportions and the requests that were submitted by Jews were in the tens of thousands. Hebrew was being studied in semi-underground conditions and in many ways connection was maintained, amidst difficulty and some-danger, with the Jews beyond the "iron curtain." The right of Soviet Jews to emigrate had become by the end of the decade an international issue of considerable magnitude. The activity on their behalf was widespread throughout the Jewish world, and it acted to recall many Jews who were themselves otherwise alienated, to a sense of their own Jewish identity. In the Soviet Union itself this reassertion of Jewishness was clearly the harbinger of a new era of rebellious national consciousness after the two generations when cultural and linguistic de-Judaization was forced upon the Jews while the doors of gentile society to complete equality and assimilation were not opened to them. For Zionism the Jews coming out of the U.S.S.R. represented an element that had been aggrieved and had so strongly asserted itself as to be a classic fundamental assertion of Zionist theory: the assertion that in any social system the Jew would ultimately find himself in a situation different from that of the majority and discriminated against and that he would have to make his life in terms of that reality.

IDEOLOGICAL PROBLEMS IN ISRAEL. In Israel itself, the first generation of statehood produced essentially two sets of internal cultural problems. Both were not new; both were deeply embedded in tensions inherent in Zionism almost from the beginning. Religious and secular forces fought each other over the role that Jewish religion was to play in the life of the total community. For the religious such questions as whom one married, or whether public transport and all public services were to function on the Sabbath, were not matters of private conscience. They went to the very roots of the issue of why a Jewish state had to be created in Zion in the first place. It was to be something more than a refugee camp, or a large-scale attempt to create a "Jewish Albania." The purpose of this effort was to make it possible for a characteristic Jewish life in line with tradition to be lived in contemporary settings of one's own. Amid the secular forces the imposition by the state of the Orthodox religious rules on personal status, so that, for example, one was not free to marry out of the faith if one chose, or the legal definition of "who is a Jew" only by the norms of rabbinic law (so that children of gentile mothers born and raised in Israel as Jews were not so registered by secular law until 1970), raised great anger. On the view of the secular thinkers a modern state and society required an absolute separation between religion and public order. Another continuing battle was that between those who preferred to regard themselves as Israelis, with little concern or identification either with the Jewish past in the Exile or with the present-day Jewish majority in the Diaspora, and those who kept insisting that Jews in the new state were still primarily Jews and not Israelis. The events of 1967 and the rise of Jewish passion in Soviet Jewry effectively made an end to this latter debate. It became clear to almost everyone that Israel and the Jews of the world stood together in crisis; that even the Jews of the U.S., the richest of Diasporas, did not feel themselves as living on a different plane from the Jews in Israel; and that everywhere the rescue of the Soviet Jews was regarded as a prime purpose. The seal was thus set on a development which had begun with the very foundation of the state in one of its earliest constitutional acts, "the Law of Return," under which any Jew anywhere has the right to claim Israel citizenship upon arrival in the country and his right to immigrate into Israel is inalienable. The government of Israel had made it its duty to intervene diplomatically on behalf of Jewish communities in trouble, from the very beginning of its existence. Israel had never allowed any doubts to persist that the defense of Jewish interests all over the world was an integral element of its foreign policy. It had certainly presumed that world Jewry would stand with Israel and that its policies on all matters of major concern would parallel those of the state. In June 1967 these presumptions of worldwide Jewish support for Israel were fully realized. Soon thereafter there was another demonstration of the principle that defense of Jews all over the world was central to Israel's policy. It took the leading role in the battle which soon broke into the open for the rights of Soviet Jews.

Perhaps the most difficult, in the long run, of the problems of Jewish self-definition in Israel was its relationship to the Arabs. On the one hand there was lasting tension; on the other there was increased contact after 1967 and an ever greater straining to recognize and encounter Arabs as equal human beings. Here, too, the new generation was heir to a moral concern as old as the very beginnings of Zionism. At the beginning of the 20th century Aḥad Ha-Am had expressed the fear that the new Jewish settlement in Ereẓ Israel might be so constructed as to harm the Arabs and he had pleaded for sensitivity to this possibility. In actual day-to-day life throughout the years of Zionist immigration there were not only riots and battles but also friendships and accommodations between the two communities. Eventually every Zionist theory had had to face the question of the Arabs. The newest note after the Six-Day War was sounded by those intellectuals and politicians in Israel who saw the main road to peace in active consent and even cooperation by Israel in the establishment of Palestinian Arab independence in a part of the previous area of Palestine (including Transjordan).

Looking toward the last third of the 20th century Zionism as an organized movement was weaker than it had been a generation before, but the result of its labors, the State of Israel, was strongly established. As an organization the world Zionist movement inevitably no longer occupied the central place in the Jewish world, for it had been replaced by the government of Israel, but Zionist sentiment now pervaded the whole of Jewish organized endeavor. The possibilities of substantial new immigration were again in view and the Zionist movement continued to assert that the encouragement of such processes was its most characteristic task. But the basic question that Zionism had posed when it first appeared, even before Theodor Herzl, still remained open—and embattled: What would be the nature of the new Jews and of the new Jewish society? To what degree would it be conventionally modern and Western and to what degree would it be connected with the classic Jewish past—or, for that matter, to what degree would the Jews in Israel "de-Westernize" in order, hopefully, to come to terms with the Middle Eastern world within which they were living? If, at the very least, there would be major Jewish communities in the Diaspora for a long time to come, and perhaps permanently, what was to be the continuing relationship between the Jewish national community in Israel and that Diaspora? How, for that matter, was the continuity of Jewish loyalty in the far-off communities to be fostered and preserved? What, in short, was the new Jew, the Zionist and Israel successor to his ghetto ancestors, to be? In 1972 there were as yet no answers—but it was equally clear that these questions would continue to be wrestled with and lived through for many years to come.

5 ZIONIST SOCIALISM

A new type of Jewish socialism, Zionist Socialism, challenged the hegemony of the Bund in the years immediately preceding the first Russian revolution. The ideologists of this new movement were from various backgrounds: there were former "bourgeois" Zionists, such as Nachman Syrkin, who were unable to withstand the great influence of Russian radicalism and moved to the left but without abandoning their Zionist principles; and former Russian socialists, such as Ber Borochov, whose encounters with Russian anti-Semitism, including the proletarian variety, helped to push them into the Zionist camp. The Zionist Socialists agreed with the Bund in recognizing the predominant role of the Jewish proletariat in modern Jewish history, and in recognizing the dual nature of this role—both social and national. However, they were also in fundamental agreement with the Zionist analysis of the Jewish predicament, namely that anti-Semitism was endemic to the Diaspora and that the reversal of class relationships through revolution, however desirable, did not constitute a solution. Their problem was to create an ideology which, rejecting both the Bund's russo-centrism and the all-class character of bourgeois Zionism, would combine the revolutionary determinism of the former with the doctrine of territorialism articulated by the latter.

The early Po'alei Zion circles found it easier to attack the Bund than to formulate a clear alternative. Their attack was based on the theory that the Jewish working class did not constitute a proletariat, a theory somewhat reminiscent of the views of those who opposed the agitation tactics of the early 1890s. The Jewish working class, it was argued, was incapable of transforming itself into a proletariat because of the very nature of the Diaspora, which precluded the possibility of a normal Jewish existence. It was, and would remain, incapable of a meaningful class struggle, and therefore the entire Bundist program was based on a class with no future. Thus the failure of Jewish workers to enter the great factories was not a temporary phenomenon but a symptom of the Jewish people's abnormal situation, which no social revolution could alter. The Jewish strike movement, while perhaps of psychological value, was a palliative rather than a cure. The peculiar nature of the Jewish proletariat, cited by the circle participants in their polemics with Kremer[16] and Gozhansky[17] and by the Bundists as proof that the Jewish artisans would be particularly amenable to the class struggle, was presented as proof of the bankruptcy of the Bund's position. Thus the emotional argument against the Bund, the rising tide of anti-Semitism symbolized by the Kishinev pogrom (1903), was given "scientific" backing by studies proving the absurdity of Jewish strikes and the absence of Jewish workers from the great factories.

As socialists, however, the Bund's critics were also obliged to base their hopes on the Jewish proletariat (or at least on the "laboring masses"). Therefore they evolved the concept that the Jewish question could be solved only through the territorial concentration of the Jewish working class, where a meaningful class struggle would be feasible and would lead to a Jewish socialist society. This territorial concentration, however, would not come about as the result of the will of the Jewish people—Herzl's famous slogan, "If you will it, it is no dream" was unacceptable to the Marxist and semi-Marxist intelligentsia—but as the inevitable result of the Jewish proletariat's search for a base from which to conduct the class struggle. Thus both the Bund's error and Zionism's ultimate victory were proven in "scientific" terms, as was the pioneering role of the Jewish proletariat in

[16]Central figure in the Jewish labor movement in Russia in the 1890s, described as "father of the Bund" (1865–1935)

[17]Leading member of the Bund (1867–1943)

the Zionist movement. Marxist determinism was introduced to lend certainty to the Zionist ideal, a fact of great psychological significance to those who had previously suspected Zionism of being Utopian. Herzl's slogan was turned on its head; since it was proved that "it is no dream," therefore "we shall will it."

While Zionist Socialists (see below) agreed that the abnormal situation of the Jewish working class, itself symptomatic of the incurable disease of the Diaspora, ruled out a Diaspora solution to the Jewish question, there was no agreement on a number of extremely difficult problems inherent in the basic ideology. There was, for example, the problem of the "two levels." Should the Zionist Socialists participate in the political and economic struggle in Russia, or should they concentrate solely on efforts to obtain a territory? The latter alternative was not particularly attractive, since it was not clear exactly how a political party, with its base in Russia, might work to hasten the territorial solution. On the other hand, if the Jewish question could not be solved in Russia, and if the Jewish proletariat was incapable of waging the class struggle, what was the point of organizing a party in the Diaspora at all? It was logical that, despite the "negation of the exile" implied in the theses of the Zionist Socialists, their involvement in the Diaspora should nonetheless increase as their popularity among Jewish workers and intellectuals grew. From a practical point of view it was clear that the territorial solution, especially after the episode of the Uganda scheme, was far off, and that the Jewish masses would remain in Russia for the foreseeable future. Along with this was the fact that the rising revolutionary storm in Russia, which reached its peak in 1905–06, could not be ignored by the Jewish socialists, whether Zionists or not. Thus Zionist Socialists, revealing an apparent contradiction between their theory and their practice, often became as involved in the Russian struggle like their antagonists, the Bundists. This was particularly true during great upheavals in Russia, when the temptation to participate and therefore to prove one's revolutionary worth was too great to withstand. The problem of the "two levels" remained crucial for all Zionist Socialists, just as the peculiar composition of the Jewish proletariat and the participation of workers in pogroms remained a problem for the Bund. This problem helped split the socialist Zionist camp in 1917 and during the civil war, the greatest Russian upheaval of them all.

Another basic problem was the question in which territory the Jews were to be concentrated. For many Zionist Socialists, who believed along with Herzl in the imminent collapse of Diaspora Jewry (a belief naturally strengthened by the Kishinev pogrom), any territory would do, and therefore they supported the Uganda scheme, an issue which divided the Zionist movement from 1903 on. Moreover, it was difficult for socialists to accept the Palestinian orientation of bourgeois Zionism, since it seemed to be based on mysticism and was unsupported by any scientific, socialist analysis. The eternal bond between the Jewish people and Ereẓ Israel appeared to be a fitting slogan for the Mizrachi movement but not for Marxists. It is therefore paradoxical that the most consistent Marxist of all, Ber Borochov, nonetheless insisted on Palestine, though he too justified his choice on utilitarianism rather than on appeals to Jewish tradition. The problem of "why Palestine," like the problem of Hebrew versus Yiddish, remained a difficult one for Zionist Socialists, especially for Marxists torn between their loyalty to the national movement and their adherence to scientific socialism.

Other issues also separated the various socialist Zionist groups, which included strict Marxists, semi-Marxists, and Populists. To cite one example, some rejected the "catastrophe" approach to the Jewish Diaspora and insisted that the territorial solution, though necessary, could be achieved only after a long process of development in the Diaspora. During the first Russian Revolution three distinct parties formed out of the ideological confusion: the Marxist, Palestinian Po'alei Zion, the Zionist Socialist Workers' Party (known as S.S.), which despite its name was territorialist, and the Jewish Socialist Workers' Party, also known as the "Sejmist" party, which called for the nurturing of Jewish national life in the Diaspora (under the aegis of a Jewish parliament, or Sejm) until the time was ripe for a territorial solution. Together, these parties spelled a serious challenge to the hegemony of the Bund. Unlike the Bund, all suffered from the tension between the ultimate goal, a territorial solution, and the inescapable need to participate in the struggle for socialism, Jewish national rights in the Diaspora, and the improvement of the economic lot of the Jewish masses. The three parties, all claiming to represent the Yiddish-speaking, economically and culturally deprived Jewish laboring masses, found that their activities overlapped. It is significant that the objective situation led all of them to champion national cultural autonomy for Russian Jewry, a stand also taken by the Bund. In fact, though kept alive by polemics between party leaders, ideological distinctions tended to be blurred in the daily struggle. Thus Bundists, socialist Zionists, and socialist territorialists all cooperated in the establishment of Yiddish schools, seen as the mainspring in the creation of Jewish national autonomy. While the gulf between the Bundist and Zionist Socialist analysis of the Jewish question remained as wide as ever, so long as the Jewish masses remained concentrated in the Pale and elsewhere in Eastern Europe, the practical platforms of the various Jewish socialist parties were bound to grow more and more similar.

In Eastern Europe, beyond Russia's borders, it was Galicia that offered the most fertile ground for the growth of Jewish socialism. Both the Bund and the Zionist Socialists made inroads in this Austrian province, which combined economic conditions even worse than those in the Pale with a much more moderate political system. Vienna, a magnet for Galician Jewish intellectuals, became an important Po'alei Zion center, though the absence of a substantial Jewish proletariat made Bundist incursions impossible. The waves of immigration brought to the U.S. numerous East

European Jewish socialists, including illustrious Bundists and Zionist Socialists, who formed groups of their own. Such organizations, aside from their local activities, were of great importance for their sister organizations in Eastern Europe and Palestine, since they were in a position to offer both political and financial support. Thus just as the significance of American Zionism within the world Zionist movement increased, so did that of the American Po'alei Zion within world labor Zionism, all the more so since most of the prominent Po'alei Zion leaders were at one time or another active in America.

The Bolshevik Revolution (1917) and the establishment of the Communist International inaugurated a period of schisms within the Jewish socialist movement, as within virtually all socialist parties. It became necessary to choose between affiliation to the victorious Communist movement and continued adherence to democratic socialism. For the Jewish parties this choice was particularly difficult; the Russian Communist Party, while clearly opposed to anti-Semitism, inherited an assimilationist attitude toward the Jewish question and was hostile to both Zionism and Bundism. Hence to join the Communist movement meant, essentially, to abandon a specifically Jewish program (though not the use of Yiddish to reach the Jewish workers). In the Soviet Union, of course, there was no freedom to choose. The Bund, which was anti-Bolshevik during the revolution, was not tolerated by the new regime. After the failure of efforts to maintain organizational autonomy as the so-called "Kombund" ("Communist Bund"), the Bund was forced out of existence by 1921. The various Zionist socialist movements, though they lasted longer than the Bund, were finally crushed in the Soviet Union during the later 1920s.

The world Po'alei Zion movement, which had come to overshadow the socialist territorialist parties after the failure of the Uganda project and which naturally benefited from the Balfour Declaration, split in 1920 over the issues

 of whether or not to adhere to the Communist International

and of their relations with the Zionist movement. The left faction, drawing its strength chiefly from Russia and Poland, actually accepted Zinoviev's celebrated 21 points for admission to the Comintern, while the right, based mainly on delegations from the United States and Palestine, refused to go that far (though it too took a positive attitude toward the Bolshevik revolution). However, the Left Po'alei Zion did not join the Comintern, not because it decided against this step but because the world Communist movement could not accept its program for Palestine. It thus existed, mainly in Poland, as a Zionist party too far left to have anything to do with the official Zionist movement and as a revolutionary Marxist party unacceptable to the Comintern. This unenviable position, complicated still further by the party's ambivalent attitude toward Hebrew and toward *aliyah* (emigration to Palestine), reduced its appeal and its ability to compete both with the Bund and with the more moderate Zionist socialist movements. No other organization illustrated more clearly the inherent contradictions of a Diaspora-based Marxist Zionist party. On the other hand the Right Po'alei Zion, identifying with Aḥdut ha-Avodah in Palestine, with the pioneering movement, and generally with progressive Zionism, became ever stronger within the world Zionist movement. In Poland, for example, by the 1930s the moderate socialist Zionist faction had become the strongest force within the Zionist movement. Generally speaking Right Po'alei Zion became less socialist and more nationalist, following the lead of party developments in Palestine, where Syrkin's non-Marxist ideology was more influential than Borochov's strictures. If to Left Po'alei Zion Palestine appeared less important than world revolution and Yiddish more important than Hebrew, Right Po'alei Zion broadened its national base. It thereby followed the course taken by so many other socialist parties which, once they had gained a certain degree of power (in this case in Palestine), spoke less and less of the proletariat and the class struggle.

Jewish socialism in the interwar period was highlighted by

pioneering youth movements. To a certain extent these movements followed in the footsteps of the Ẓe'irei Zion ("Youth of Zion") circles, whose history began in Russia in the early 20th century. A fervent supporter of settlement in Palestine, nationalistic, at the outset non-socialist, and even nonpolitical, the Ẓe'irei Zion rejected the Marxist determinism and intense involvement in the Diaspora of the various Jewish socialist parties. Their voluntarism and emphasis on personal salvation through *aliyah,* which established an alternative for Jewish youth to the existing parties, whether Bundist or Zionist, was also the hallmark of the pioneering youth movements established during and after World War I. Thus Ha-Shomer ha-Ẓa'ir, founded in Galicia during the war by middle-class youths seeking their way between the Polish world which rejected them and Jewish bourgeois existence they found so distasteful, turned not to Marxism and not to party organization but to self-fulfillment through pioneering, through an act of will which would make them productive proletarians building a just society in Palestine. Both Ẓe'irei Zion and Ha-Shomer ha-Ẓa'ir shared a natural sympathy for socialism, and neither was able to withstand the pressure to organize into political groups. In 1920 the left faction of Ẓe'irei Zion created the Zionist Socialist Party (Z.S.), which later merged with Right Po'alei Zion, while the right faction merged with the Palestinian nonsocialist party, Ha-Po'el ha-Ẓa'ir, to form the Hitaḥadut. Both these parties offered a moderate labor Zionist alternative to the radical Left Po'alei Zion. As for Ha-Shomer ha-Ẓa'ir, it developed from a self-styled vanguard of romantic idealists into a Marxist movement based on the organizational structure of the Ha-Kibbutz ha-Arẓi, founded in Palestine in 1927. The attraction of Marxism for the Zionist Socialists of the early 20th century had been that it could make Zionism appear determined rather than a mere dream. For the voluntaristic members of Ha-Shomer ha-Ẓa'ir, on the other hand, it functioned as a cement which held the movement together in Palestine, guarding against internal collapse and amalgamation with other elements. The history of both Ẓe'irei Zion and Ha-Shomer ha-Ẓa'ir demonstrates that organizational and ideological consolidation could not be avoided by groups whose initial mission was personal redemption through proletarianization. The acceptance by the Ẓe'irei Zion, for example, of the principle of Jewish national autonomy in Russia, and their active struggle for Jewish rights in the Diaspora, is reminiscent of the history of Po'alei Zion. But the political offshoots of Ẓe'irei Zion, active in an era when *aliyah* was a clear possibility, were firmly centered on Palestine and less subject to the dilemma of the "two levels." The problem of "which territory," of course, had completely disappeared.

This also held for the various pioneering youth movements, Ha-Shomer ha-Ẓa'ir, He-Ḥalutz ha-Ẓa'ir, etc., whose major problem in the Diaspora concerned the likelihood of *aliyah* and the impact of *aliyah* on the local organization. What tied the youth movements of the 1920s and 1930s, whether Marxist or not, to the Jewish socialist tradition, was their preoccupation with the necessity to create a just Jewish society based on productive labor. If Liebermann[18] and later the Bundists and Zionist Socialists discovered the Jewish proletariat, members of the pioneering movements proposed to turn themselves into proletarians in Palestine, an extreme solution which reflected the crisis of East European Jewry in the period between the two world wars.

The Jewish socialist tradition was eliminated in Eastern Europe by the Holocaust, and in America by the unparalleled opportunities offered by American society. Its chief impact has been in Israel, where ideas formed in Eastern Europe were molded to fit the task of building the *yishuv*.

[18]Aaron Samuel Liebermann (1845–1880), pioneer of Jewish socialism; lived in E. Europe and for a short period in London

6 NON-ZIONISM AND ANTI-ZIONISM

Zionism, though initially a minority movement, became so central in Jewish thought that eventually the other Jewish ideological trends had to define themselves largely in terms of their attitude to the Zionist idea or to certain essential elements of it, as, e.g., the revival of Hebrew language and culture, the "fixation" on Ereẓ Israel as the only territory for ingathering the Jewish mass migration, the national unity of Orthodox and secular Jews, etc.

Autonomists and Yiddishists. Before World War I the bulk of the Jews of the world were living in two multinational empires, Russia and Austria-Hungary. In both of these regimes minority peoples were conducting struggles for their respective national autonomies. The situation of the Jews was different from that of all other minorities, for they were nowhere a majority in any particular piece of territory that was historically associated with their national identity. Nonetheless, Jews in these regions continued to speak a language of their own, Yiddish, and they were bound together by ties of history and culture and by a network of communal institutions. Zionism was not the only possible national movement among Jews. A variety of other ideologies and movements arose, which refused to accept the idea that Jews were in any sense alien to the places of their dwelling in Europe, or to believe that anti-Semitism could be ended only by mass emigration. These movements argued that Jews were one of the historic tribes of Eastern Europe, with as much right in the region as the Poles or the Ukrainians. The discrimination against Jews could, and should, be ended by a more vigorous battle for a just social order and by the achievement of national equality for all the national communities in the region. "To do battle at one's positions" was the slogan directed against the Zionists by such schools of thought. Most such non-Zionist nationalists regarded the Hebrew revival as a piece of romanticism and as disguised clericalism. In their view the spoken language of the people, Yiddish, was its natural contemporary speech. A healthy national life could be built only by strengthening that language and its literature and raising it in public esteem from the level of a dialect to that of a respected language.

The most important theoretician of Diaspora nationalism was the historian S. Dubnow. He himself did not deny the importance of Hebrew, or of Russian, for he wrote all his life in both these languages as well as, of course, in Yiddish; nor did Dubnow deny that there was significance in the developing Jewish community in Palestine. In his historiography Jewish life had always found its leadership in some new emerging center of energies as an older community was declining. In his own day he saw Eastern Europe as the lead community, then erecting tributary centers in Palestine and the United States. He envisaged that Jews everywhere would labor to achieve nationally cultural autonomous institutions, including especially an educational system of their own in their own language. His spiritual disciples organized a party which labored for a system of "Sejms," Jewish "parliaments" or "diets," which should direct the affairs of the various Jewish communities and of the Jewish people as a whole. This principle of "autonomism" was adopted also by the Russian Zionists at their conference in Helsingfors (1906), when czarist Russia seemed to be on the threshold of genuine parliamentary democracy. They, however, regarded it not as an end in itself, but as an element of Zionist *Gegenwartsarbeit:* an instrument for Jewish social and educational activity with the clearly defined aim of an ultimate migration and settlement in Ereẓ Israel. Dubnow faced squarely the question that the national situation of the Jews in the Diaspora, in the minority everywhere, was an anomaly, but he did not arrive at the conclusion that this situation should be rectified by the creation of a Jewish commonwealth in Ereẓ Israel. At the core of his outlook was the vision of a future for all humanity in which all of the historic nations would rise to a higher stage of existence in which they would be freed of their dependence on any particular land and would exist as communities on the basis of historic and cultural ties. The paradigm for such communities was what the Jews had become in the Diaspora after the beginning of the Exile; they had persisted in this new and higher form; and so Dubnow saw his vision of Diaspora Jewish national autonomism, or a formulation of the modalities of human association, to be the newest and most profound teaching by Jews for mankind.

There were other, more mundane versions of Diaspora nationalism. Several schools of thought, chiefly under the influence of Chaim Zhitlowsky[19], were in favor of the centrality of Yiddish in the national Jewish experience and labored toward the recognition of that language, and of those who lived out their lives in it, as one of the several cultural linguistic communities of Eastern Europe, and of the Western world as a whole. This ideology was crystallized formally at a conference of Yiddishists in 1908 in Czernowitz. Right after World War I this ideology was expressed by the foundation in Vilna, with branches in other parts of the Jewish world, of the Yidisher Visenshaftlekher Institut (YIVO-Institute for Jewish Research), which survived World War II and now continues its scholarly and educational endeavors in New York.

The most important single movement to arise in Eastern Europe in the 1890s, in the very months when Herzl was appearing on the Jewish scene, was the Jewish Socialist Bund. This organization was created not primarily in reaction to Zionist stirrings but through tensions within the Russian revolutionary movement. Most of the young

[19]Philosopher and essayist, born in Russia: in New York from 1908. Died in 1943

Jewish revolutionaries of the day were joining and taking prominent part in the various underground factions, but some began to feel that the Jewish workers could not be approached and made active in the Jewish revolutionary cause except through Yiddish. The announced purpose of the founders of the Bund was thus not a Jewish national one, for initially they proposed only the temporary use of Yiddish as a means to the end of bringing the Jewish workers into the mainstream of the Russian revolution. Yet the gibe by no less a figure than Plekhanov, the father of Russian Marxism, that Bundists are "Zionists who are afraid of seasickness," soon acquired a measure of truth. A Yiddish-speaking party representing the revolutionary will of Jewish workers could not help but become aware that these workers had problems not only with their employers but also with gentile workers. Under the pressure of Zionists, and especially of Socialist Zionists, the Bund moved in the direction of accepting the separate culture of Jews as a lasting value worth preserving through "personal cultural autonomy," i.e., the right of every individual to enjoy national, educational, and linguistic life in the framework of a legal minority organization. It clashed on this issue with its fellow social democrats, Jewish and non-Jewish, Menshevik and Bolshevik.

RELIGIOUS AND SECULAR ANTI-NATIONALISM. There were also anti-nationalist reactions to Zionism, and these were much more clearly occasioned by the fact that an organized Zionist movement had arisen. The First Zionist Congress had been intended for Munich and it did not take place there because most of the rabbinate of Germany made a public declaration against the movement, for it would, in their view, call into question the absolute loyalty and integration of Jews as a purely religious community in the European nations. Some 20 years later, in the debates within the British war cabinet which preceded the announcements of the Balfour Declaration, the only Jewish member of the cabinet, Edwin Montagu, argued along the same line, that the recognition of the Jews as a nationality with its homeland in Palestine would call into question his political identity as a British subject who was a Jew only by religion. In 1929 when a group of distinguished non-Zionists joined a reorganized and "enlarged" Jewish Agency for Palestine, on a plane of parity with the representatives of the World Zionist Organization, the non-Zionists maintained that their interest in the Jewish settlement in Palestine was philanthropic and not political and they indeed remained opposed to any talks of an eventual Jewish state. In the 1940s in the United States anti-Zionist sentiment was represented at its most extreme by the American Council for Judaism, which maintained not only that its members were Jews by religion alone but that their religion made it incumbent upon them to take only a universalist position, which meant in practice a pro-Arab and anti-Jewish nationalist view of their responsibilities. "Dual loyalty" worried wide circles of Jews, especially in the Western countries, in varying degrees into the 1950s. By then it had become generally accepted, as Nahum Goldmann maintained, that all men have many "loyalties" which lived in some tension with each other. The purpose of at least the most extreme of these anti-Zionists was the rapid assimilation of Jews into the total population, and they opposed Zionism because they saw it as a stumbling block to this end.

Zionism was attacked from another side by schools of thought which found it too secular, too modern, and thus too destructive, in their view, of the traditional Jewish values. The religious forces which joined Ḥibbat Zion in the 1880s and which later formed the religious Zionist organization, the Mizrachi, during the first few years of the modern Zionist movement, were a small minority among the Orthodox. The overwhelming majority, especially in ḥasidic circles, saw in such human efforts for the restoration of Jewish nationhood an affront to the command to wait patiently for the Messiah. More seriously, they understood that the definition of Jewry as a modern nation, which meant in immediate Zionist practice that religious believers were to accept equality within Jewry with nonbelievers, portended the eventual end of the supremacy of the Orthodox faith within Jewry. On this point older believers in Eastern Europe found allies in some circles of Westernized Jewry, especially in Germany. Together these groups formed in 1912 the Agudat Israel, which maintained a consistent involvement in the Jewish community in Ereẓ Israel but was opposed to Zionism as too secular. Its main emphasis was on the defense of the Orthodox Jewish faith everywhere in the world.

TERRITORIALISM AND AGRICULTURAL SETTLEMENT. The movement that was closest to Zionism, Territorialism, arose out of a split within the Zionist movement itself. In 1903 Herzl brought before the Zionist Congress the proposal of the British that the Jews be given land in East Africa for the development of their own autonomous community. The occasion for this proposal was the dire need of Russian Jewry, in the light of renewed pogroms, and the despair of quickly achieving from the Turks rights for settling Palestine. Thus it seemed that Herzl himself had "moved away from Zion" toward immediate, practical mass settlement to alleviate Jewish need. The proposal to examine the feasibility of the British offer won a bare majority at the last Zionist Congress presided over by Herzl, but it was overwhelmingly defeated after his death. Israel Zangwill, the writer who had been one of Herzl's first followers in England, left the Zionist Organization and founded the Jewish Territorial Organization (I.T.O.) in 1905. This and similar territorialist bodies continued into the 1930s and 1940s to search for a territory in some part of the world sufficiently empty and available to give the Jews room for the creation of their own national polity. These efforts never succeeded, but something very like what they intended was indeed realized by a non-ideological body, the Jewish Colonization Association (ICA) which was founded in 1891 by Baron de Hirsch, one of the Jewish magnates to whom Herzl had turned and who had refused to join the Zionist endeavor. Agricultural colonies were created by this trust in several places in the United States and, especially, in

Argentina. Though on the local level a kind of autonomous "all-Jewish" life did develop in some places on the American continent for one generation, they never coalesced into full-fledged "territorial" communities. Nowhere did these settlements survive the attraction for their young of higher education in the dominant language and the economic and professional opportunities of the cities.

SOVIET JEWISH CULTURE. In the first two decades after 1917, a kind of Jewish Communist nationalism arose and flourished in the Soviet Union and it was attractive to many Jews outside the borders of the U.S.S.R. But it was short-lived and took a tragic end. In reaction to the Jewish Socialist Bund and to the Zionists the young Stalin had declared in 1913 that there was no such thing as a united Jewish nation, for it lacked a land of its own. Only separate ethnic Jewish groups did exist and were doomed to disappear by assimilation. Nonetheless, during his early years in power he continued the policy of Lenin, to permit the Jews to organize a system of cultural life in Yiddish, provided the Jewish nationality, like all the others in the Soviet Union, made Communism the central political purpose of its cultural activity. Schools on all levels and even college courses in Yiddish were created in the 1920s. Hundreds of books were published and a press and theaters were encouraged. Additionally, with the help of such Western Jews as the Chicago millionaire, Lessing Rosenwald, who was opposed to Zionism, there was some settlement of Jews on the land in southern Russia and the Crimea. An even more grandiose attempt was made to create an autonomous Jewish region on a stretch of land in Siberia, Birobidzhan. In the later 1930s and particularly after 1948 all of this, including Jewish cultural life in Birobidzhan, was brutally ended. But into the 1930s the reality of Jewish autonomy and the vision of state-sponsored Yiddish creativity in the Soviet Union, allied with its official outlawing of anti-Semitism, seemed to some Jews in the West, not only of the extreme political Left, an option to be preferred to Zionism. There is no longer any such ideology because repression in the Soviet Union has ended every genuine expression of Jewish life in that country. What does exist there now (1972) is conducted as an act of semi-clandestine resistance to an unfriendly repressive regime.

7 ZIONIST POLICY

Throughout the 19th century, and with increasing potency during the 20th century, nationalism emerged as probably the most powerful political force in Europe, the Americas, and later in Asia and Africa as well. It led to the dismemberment of established empires and to the unification of nations (Italy and Germany); it released creative forces hitherto often suppressed by foreign rule; but it also had other consequences: the identification of state and nation left little room for free and equal development of "minorities." Unlike the Greeks or Rumanians, who lived on their own land, the Jews could not attain national self-determination by merely throwing off a foreign yoke. That these developments could not but affect Jewish thought was only natural.

Nineteenth-century Jewry carried very little political weight. Its strivings and efforts could only be of a religious, spiritual, or philanthropic nature. There was no lack of literary expression: countless pamphlets, memoranda, petitions, and sermons were bequeathed by men of renown and by anonymous writers in that century, as well as in earlier times. The general upheaval kindled new hopes. Not only Jewish names, such as Montefiore the magnate, Hess the socialist, and Disraeli the statesman, are connected with that period, but also many gentile names, such as Lord Palmerston, Lord Shaftesbury, Ernest Laharanne, J. H. Dunant (father of the International Red Cross), and George Eliot. Gentile support for the idea of the Return to Zion reflected the realization that emancipation of the Jews was not enough, and that in addition to recognition of their civil rights, Jews were also entitled to the recognition of their rights as a nation. The sympathy of the few, however, was far outweighed by the hostility of the many. The old anti-Semitism had been reinforced by "scientific" racial teachings. The last two decades of the century saw the outburst of violent persecutions and pogroms in Eastern Europe, particularly in Russia. These were followed by a mass flight westward, especially to the U.S. The little that Ḥibbat Zion could do in the circumstances was totally inadequate. While hundreds of thousands surged through the gates of the New World, only hundreds succeeded in infiltrating through the more than half-closed doors of the ancient homeland. That these few would in time lay the cornerstone of the Jewish state could only be foreseen by dreamers and visionaries.

THE HERZL PERIOD. If Ḥovevei Zion had sought to reach their goal by quiet and modest labor, Herzl's aim was to achieve a dramatic *coup,* to secure vast funds in order to obtain a guaranteed political basis ("Charter") for a large-scale settlement of Jews. Securing the cooperation of the Baron de Hirsch or Baron de Rothschild and the consent of the sultan and the German kaiser looked like a shortcut to the goal. He believed that with "millions" it would be possible to obtain a charter or, with a charter, to obtain the millions. Hirsch and Rothschild had already been involved in assistance to Jews in the East in cooperation with the Alliance Israélite Universelle, which had established, inter alia, the first Jewish agricultural school near Jaffa in 1870. Rothschild extended a helping hand to the early settlements in Ereẓ Israel, and Hirsch had set up the Jewish Colonization Association (ICA) with an endowment hitherto unheard of in Jewish affairs. Herzl was received by Hirsch in June 1895 and the result was nil. It was after that interview that Herzl wrote *Der Judenstaat*.

The publication of this clarion call had several consequences. The Jewish national idea, hitherto discussed in small and uninfluential groups, became the subject of heated debate in wider circles. The excited support that came from various quarters—as well as criticism and derision—confirmed Herzl's instinctive feeling that the idea was viable. The territorial aspect also became clearer in his mind: it was to be the ancient homeland and not Argentina or some other place. The keys to Palestine were to be found in Berlin and Constantinople. A man of action, Herzl took his first political steps. He began by seeking a way to approach William II, and the initial results were not discouraging. Anxious to make rapid progress, however, he went to Constantinople (June 1896) in an attempt to see Abdul Hamid II. This proved to be impossible, but Herzl spoke to a number of high officials and a minor order was conferred upon him in the sultan's name.

After further visits to London and Paris in search of political and financial backing, Herzl saw no alternative to organizing a mass movement. Support of a growing number of Zionist groups, especially of students and youth, and encouragement from some Jewish notables enabled him to brush aside the opposition of the assimilated and of rabbinical circles (even Ḥibbat Zion remained cool, fearing Baron Rothschild's displeasure). The First Zionist Congress met in Basle, Switzerland, in August 1897 and, amid scenes of great enthusiasm, adopted the following formulation of its aim: "Zionism seeks to establish a home for the Jewish people in Palestine secured under public law." The Congress also created the instrument for the implementation of its plan: the World Zionist Organization. Herzl wrote in his diary the prophetic words: "In Basle I founded the Jewish State." And he added a forecast as to the date when the state will become a reality: " . . . maybe in another five years, at the utmost fifty years." It was 50 years later—almost to the day—that the highest international body, the United Nations, gave its stamp of approval.

One of Herzl's immediate aims—turning the Jewish problems into a "world political problem"—had been achieved in part by the discussions that took place at the Congress itself, in the press, and in the public. Herzl could not have known, for instance, that the German embassy in Berne sent to Berlin a not unsympathetic account of the

Fasse ich den Basler Congress in ein Wort zusammen – das ich mich hüten werde öffentlich auszusprechen – so ist es dieses: in Basel habe ich den Judenstaat gegründet.

Wenn ich das heute laut sagte, würde mir ein universelles Gelächter antworten. Vielleicht in fünf Jahren, jedenfalls in fünfzig wird es Jeder einsehen.

Extract from Herzl's diary for Sept. 3, 1897, after the First Zionist Congress: "In Basle I founded the Jewish State .... Maybe in five years, certainly in fifty, everyone will realize it." Jerusalem, Central Zionist Archives.

proceedings, or that this account reached the kaiser's desk and evoked William's remarking that he is all for the Jews moving to Palestine, "the sooner the better." On the other hand, the German consul in Jerusalem made light of the Congress and characterized Zionist aims as utopian. There was to be a change in the kaiser's approach, however. Urged by the grand duke of Baden, one of the more liberal and influential princes in Germany, he reconsidered his previous attitude. On the eve of his visit to Constantinople and Jerusalem in 1898, the kaiser wrote to the grand duke that "the basic idea has interested me, indeed, moved me," and he had come to the conclusion that they were dealing with a "problem of far-reaching significance." Great importance was attached to Jews turning to Germany with gratitude, and he was ready to receive Herzl during his visit to Turkey.

Anxious to have the kaiser put in a good word for Zionism in his talks with Abdul Hamid, Herzl obtained a preliminary audience with William in Constantinople (Oct. 18, 1898) and it seemed that the kaiser had received in a positive spirit both his views and his plea. Von Buelow, the German foreign minister, showed little enthusiasm. It was decided that a Zionist delegation would be officially received by the monarch later, during his visit to Jerusalem. The second audience took place as planned (Nov. 2, 1898), but the spirit was almost totally different. It seemed that the kaiser mentioned the matter in his talks with the sultan, and the latter did not react. The final outcome of Herzl's tremendous effort had been deeply disappointing even though, on the credit side, the whole chapter added somewhat to Zionism's political weight in the eyes of the world, Jewish and non-Jewish.

In search of new approaches, Herzl sought contacts with England and even with Russia; nor was Constantinople written off as yet. Indeed, a new mediator—the orientalist Armin Vambery—succeeded in obtaining the decisive audience with Abdul Hamid himself (May 17, 1901); but it proved fruitless. Coupled with the disheartening difficulties on the way to establishing the financial instruments of the movement, which were intended to help in obtaining the charter (the Jewish Colonial Trust), it brought Herzl to the realization that the old road led nowhere and the search would have to turn to other areas, closer to Ereẓ Israel or further away.

England was the first to be approached, and the territory in question was around El Arish, on the southern border of Ereẓ Israel. London was interested, as it sought to secure the eastern approaches to the Suez Canal. A commission of experts went out to explore the area, which, not unexpectedly, proved to be poor in agricultural land and water resources and could at best absorb a limited number of settlers. Herzl himself visited Cairo (in the spring of 1903) to negotiate with the British representative there, Lord Cromer, and with the Egyptian authorities, but he could not secure the main precondition for any attempt in El Arish—supplies of water from the Nile.

Theodor Herzl (at center) during a visit to Rehovot, 1898. Courtesy Central Zionist Archives, Jerusalem.

This episode did not sever the first links with London. The second, and more serious suggestion, to come from there related to Uganda. The name Uganda stood then for a number of tribal areas in East Africa where British penetration—first missionary, then commercial and military—went on through the 1870s and 1880s and originally did not prosper. In 1892 the British government decided to abandon the territory, but reversed itself under pressure of missionary and trade interests. Sleeping sickness killed about 250,000 people among the local tribes between 1901 and 1909. Herzl did not know those details when British Colonial Secretary Joseph Chamberlain first spoke to him about the place. Before the matter came up officially, he made another attempt to tackle the Palestine issue by trying to obtain Russian support. In August 1903, several months after the Kishinev pogrom, he traveled to St. Petersburg and interviewed the notorious minister of interior Plehve (who was assassinated within less than a year) and the minister of finance Count Witte. Once again, the Russian government would not or could not help. On his return journey, he received official news of the new British proposal.

Uganda was not Zion. Herzl knew that and said so at the Sixth Zionist Congress, which met immediately after his visit to Russia. As long as Ereẓ Israel was not obtainable, however, the persecuted people needed a temporary asylum. Opposition from the old, "pre-Herzlian" Zionists was to be expected, but it was sharper and more widespread than foreseen. In fact, it revealed an accumulation of old dissatisfactions in considerable sections of the movement, especially among the young. The affairs of Zionism were conducted in a way that was far from democratic. Had it produced results, the rank and file would have acquiesced; but all those comings and goings in spheres of "high diplomacy" led away from the main goal, which was Zion. The basic difference between the approach of the leadership and that of the critics became increasingly apparent. The "political Zionists" believed that immigration and settlement could only follow the grant of a "Charter," which would secure the rights of the Jewish people to the land; anything else would be "infiltration" doomed to fail. The "practical Zionists" believed that Jewish rights to Ereẓ Israel were self-evident; immigration and settlement there could not be called "infiltration" and had to proceed under all circumstances. Both sides, however, were conscious of the political significance of the British proposal: at last a mighty world power had recognized the national aspirations of the Jews and was willing to extend a helping hand.

The Uganda Scheme became the Uganda crisis. The Sixth Zionist Congress did not reject the idea outright; with 295 delegates voting for, 178 against, and 132 abstentions, the movement formally accepted the leadership's proposal that a commission be elected to act in an advisory capacity when the Executive sent a mission to the area proposed by England. But the storm that broke loose came as a shock, and it was realized that it would be virtually impossible to proceed with the plan. There were also reports of strong opposition on the part of the British settlers in East Africa and criticism in England itself. Thus, the first debate on Zionism took place in the House of Commons in June 1904, with the participation of the prime minister, A. J. Balfour, and one of the opposition leaders, David Lloyd George.

In the closing stages of the Zionist Congress, Herzl sought to conciliate the opposition and stressed his continued devotion to what he called "the only country where our people can find rest." But he felt that the breach could hardly be healed. After eight years of superhuman effort and tremendous personal sacrifices, he saw the end approaching. In a final spurt of energy he turned to Rome, where he was received at the beginning of 1904 by King Victor Emmanuel III and by Pope Pius X. The king displayed a warm interest, but there was not much that Italy could do. The pope was ice cold: "If you come to Palestine and settle your people there, we shall prepare churches and priests to convert them." Within a few months after these interviews, Herzl died.

THE TRANSITION PERIOD. That the political activities of the movement could, after the leader's death, no longer be conducted in the same centralized, personal way had been clear to all concerned. After the "natural" successor, Max Nordau, refused to take over, the task fell to another close friend, David Wolffsohn. But he was hardly a political leader, and if the inevitable change came but gradually, it was because the desire to remain faithful to "Herzlian Zionism" dominated the heirs to the leadership and because the main problem inherited by them, Uganda, called for immediate decisions. By then, neither side, the Zionists nor the British, were interested in proceeding with the project. A group of experts went to East Africa in December 1904 and reported in April 1905: the proposed area was not suitable for mass settlement. Meanwhile, practical work in Ereẓ Israel gained priority even before any official change took place in the policy of the movement. One of the first visits paid by Wolffsohn was to Edmond de Rothschild, who promised to aid in practical undertakings in the country. Wolffsohn also visited Vambery, who was not optimistic. In his view, the best way for Zionists was to settle Palestine through quiet work within the existing laws. It was in this direction that the Zionist movement gradually veered after Herzl's death, though it never gave up the political element of its philosophy. The turning point came at the Seventh Zionist Congress (1905) which witnessed the first split in the movement when supporters of Uganda refused to concede defeat. They saw themselves as "territorialists," and with the gates of Ereẓ Israel virtually closed, the "Ugandists" refused to reject a proposal made by a great power at a time when the need to find a refuge for the victims of persecution was at its highest.

The departure of the Ugandists, who established the Jewish Territorial Organization under the leadership of Israel Zangwill, was bound to weaken the movement. But it strengthened the "practical" wing in Zionism (led by M. M. Ussishkin), which, for the first time, obtained representation on the Zionist Executive. The latter was now composed of three "political" Zionists, three "practical," and Wolffsohn as the balancing force. The controversy did not end at that, and difficulties arose when the territorialists sought to negotiate with governments. Tensions relaxed somewhat when the two organizations found themselves cooperating at a conference called by the Zionists (Brussels, January 1906) in order to discuss assistance to Russian Jews. This also produced meager results.

Wolffsohn and his advisers looked for new political initiatives, though this time—in accordance with an explicit ruling of the Seventh Zionist Congress—not beyond Ereẓ Israel and "adjacent areas." El Arish and Sinai drew renewed attention; Syria and Mesopotamia were considered. Sinai was then causing difficulties between Constantinople and London, which wanted the Turkish-Egyptian border to be fixed as far away from the Suez Canal as possible. A suggestion that the establishment of a Jewish settlement in Sinai may serve as a "compromise" found no support. France displayed no interest at all; when Nordau sought its help on behalf of persecuted Jews in Russia, he was told that France cannot add to the many difficulties of an allied government.

There were other attempts, among them discussions with the foreign minister of the Netherlands about raising the problem of Jewish migration during the second Peace Conference at The Hague. Another proposal spoke of calling a special international conference to deal with the subject. The Dutch thought that it would be appropriate for the initiative to come from England; London felt that a Dutch initiative would be better. A German official promised to take it up with his foreign minister, but no more was heard of it. In the meantime, a fleeting hope arose that it might be possible to renew some of the contacts with Turkey. The sultan's financial troubles were greater than ever, and his officials were looking for help. Twice during the year 1907 Wolffsohn visited Constantinople, and there were moments when he felt that "substantial" progress had been achieved. He no longer spoke of a "Charter" and concentrated on immigration and land acquisition. But the Turks needed vast sums of money, which were, as before, far above the financial ability of the Zionists. The results were therefore the same as during Herzl's desperate journeys. On the credit side, a start had been made for the opening of a bank in Constantinople (The Anglo-Levantine Banking Co.) in which the controlling interest was to be in the hands of the Jewish Colonial Trust (enabling it to appoint the bank's deputy director, who would represent Zionist interests, both financial and political).

THE YOUNG TURKS. When Wolffsohn next visited Constantinople, it was after the situation there had undergone a dramatic change. The revolution of the Young Turks (July 1908) brought to the fore new rulers and widespread hopes. It also restored a relatively liberal constitution; abolished the rule of corrupt palace cliques, of spying, and censorship; and established a parliament. Abdul Hamid survived for another eight months and—after a briefly successful counter *coup*—was replaced by Muhammed V. The years that followed were turbulent and saw almost constant warfare, beginning with the Italian campaign in Tripolitania (1911–12) and through two Balkan wars (1912–13) to World War I and beyond. It was hardly a time for gaining sympathy for Zionism. Whatever progressive ideas the Young Turks may have had initially, chauvinistic tendencies soon prevailed among them. They rejected suggestions for a less centralized regime and for a degree of freedom for the minorities. As far as Palestine was concerned, they proved as inflexible as the rulers they displaced. Nevertheless, conditions of political work in Constantinople itself underwent a slight change.

The Zionist leadership sought to avail itself of the few opportunities that were now to be found on the Bosphorus, mostly for the purpose of explaining the aims and purposes of Jewish settlement in Ereẓ Israel. With the opening of the Anglo-Levantine Banking Co., the post of deputy director was entrusted to Victor Jacobson, a Russian Zionist with some experience in the Near East. Since the main task had been the proliferation of authoritative information, he was joined by another Russian Zionist, the journalist Vladimir Jabotinsky. A small Turkish publication in French was turned into a well-edited daily, *Le Jeune Turc*. Apart from propaganda, however, there was little that could be done in the political sphere. A visit by Nordau, who had friendly ties with some of the Turkish leaders, produced no change. He was told that the Jews would be allowed to take part in the development of Turkey but would not be allowed to concentrate in any particular area, such as Palestine. Wolffsohn revisited Constantinople (June 1909) to review the situation. This was to be his last visit there. In 1911 he retired from the Executive and was replaced by Otto Warburg, a "practical" Zionist, as chairman. This time Wolffsohn paid special attention to the attitude of Turkish Jews, of whom only a few showed interest in Zionism; others were indifferent or unfriendly. The community saw much in-fighting: between Sephardi and Ashkenazi leaders, between those influenced by the French-oriented Alliance

Israélite Universelle and the adherents of the German-Jewish Hilfsverein der Deutschen Juden. Prominent among the opponents were Chief Rabbi Haim Nahoum (later chief rabbi of Egypt) and a Jewish member of parliament from Baghdad.

THE ARAB PROBLEM. The Arabs themselves had become a significant political factor. As one of the subject peoples, they had little direct say in the past. In Palestine difficulties arose, from time to time, between Jewish settlers and the local population in connection with land purchases, commercial competition, labor disputes, or robberies. Labor troubles multiplied after the Second Aliyah brought young pioneers who sought to "conquer" labor opportunities in all Jewish settlements. But there, as elsewhere in the empire, Arabs were dominated and roughly treated by Turkish officials. The Arab national movement was in its infancy. One of the few who thought of it was Aḥad Ha-Am, who wrote as far back as 1891, in a famous article "Truth from Ereẓ Israel":

> "We abroad are accustomed to believe that Ereẓ Israel is almost totally desolate at present . . . but in reality it is not so . . . Arabs, especially those in towns, see and understand our activities and aims in the country but keep quiet and pretend as if they did not know, and that because they don't see any danger to their future in our activities at present, and they try to exploit us, too, and profit from the new guests while laughing at us in their hearts. But if the time comes and our people make such progress as to displace the people of the country . . . they will not lightly surrender the place."

The situation began to change after the revolution of the Young Turks. There were some 60 Arabs and a couple of Jews in the parliament, which counted less than 300 members. The Arabs influenced policy (mostly through personal contacts), introduced interpellations, and, in 1911, initiated two full-fledged debates on the dangers involved in Jewish immigration and land acquisition. In one of these debates, the only speaker to refute their accusations was a Bulgarian socialist member. Government spokesmen more than once made hostile statements stressing Zionist separatist aims. Zionist representatives sought to counteract the assaults by denying separatist intentions. Jacobson also sought to establish contact with Arab members of parliament. The latter feared that government leaders belonging to the Committee of Union and Progress might be unduly influenced by Jews who were among the earliest supporters of the Committee. The Turkish authorities, on their part, chose to make promises to all and fulfilled very few of them.

Not many realized at the time that the struggles in which Turkey had been involved, in the Balkans and elsewhere, were but the opening skirmishes in an approaching world war. Though talk of "partition" of the Ottoman Empire was heard long before and early Zionism itself had been influenced by it, the Zionist movement had to base its day-to-day work on repeated assurances that it did not seek to harm the unity of that empire. When Turkey found itself at war with Italy in Tripoli, Nordau supported a proposal that a unit of Jewish volunteers be organized to fight side by side with the Ottoman forces. Another Zionist suggestion later spoke of organizing a medical unit to help the Turks in the Balkans. When the veteran Zionist leader Jacobus Kann of The Hague published a book about a visit to Ereẓ Israel in which he openly stated that the ultimate aim of Zionism is the establishment of a Jewish state there, Jabotinsky, then in charge of Zionist press activities in Constantinople, vigorously protested to Wolffsohn and demanded the suppression of Kann's book.

This attitude did not seem too convincing to the Young Turks, while it made Zionism further suspect in the eyes of Arab nationalists. On the other hand, Zionist tactics were almost inevitably the outcome of the contradiction between the movement's immediate needs and its long-range goals. The immediate neccessity was to preserve the existing *yishuv* and to increase, however slowly, the number of new immigrants and settlements. The hopes engendered by the changes in Turkey were soon reflected in growing Jewish activity: the number of settlements established in the years

1908–14 reached almost a dozen and a half. The same period also saw the opening in Jaffa of the Palestine Office of the Zionist Organization under Arthur Ruppin, the foundation of Tel Aviv, and the formation of organized public bodies of the new *yishuv*. All these naturally strengthened Arab opposition and coincided with the formation of local Arab nationalist groups and the appearance of their first newspapers in the country. Though the stirrings among the Arabs found little reflection in the Jewish press, some Zionist leaders soon realized their importance, and as far back as 1908 Wolffsohn used an expression which was later to be repeated by others: Governments change, but the people remain.

During the last year before the outbreak of World War I the first Arab-Jewish contacts that could be seen as politically significant, were introduced. When the Young Turks started taking stringent measures for the "Ottomanization" of their empire, some of the active Arab nationalists were in search of allies. A few turned to the Jews, who, they hoped, could help them with the press and public opinion in Europe. A director of *Le Jeune Turc*, S. Hochberg, received an invitation to visit Beirut and Cairo in order to meet Arab nationalists. He went there, with Jacobson's consent and with the knowledge of the Young Turks, and, according to reports to his superiors, established a measure of accord. The support of *Le Jeune Turc* had been promised for Arab aspirations, without prejudice to the unity of the empire, as well as help in the European press, while the Arabs undertook to drop their opposition to Jewish immigration and to support Arab-Jewish understanding. Some of this spirit was also reportedly felt at a conference called by the same Arab activists in Paris in July 1913. This time, Jacobson joined Hochberg in the talks but these were inconclusive, though only muted opposition to Jewish immigration was voiced at the conference.

Another attempt at Arab-Jewish understanding was made in 1914. Arab politicians were again in need of propaganda assistance and, in conversations with Zionists in Constantinople, concentrated on Jewish financial aid for the expansion of Arab education, large-scale public works in Arab regions, and preventing the dispossession of Arab fellahin. The latter point was met by suggestions that agriculture be intensified, thus making room for new settlers as well as for the existing farmers. Parallel with these conversations, other talks were conducted by Nahum Sokolow, member of the Zionist Executive, who visited Beirut and Damascus in May 1914. Arab participants in these talks suggested a joint conference to be convened later in the summer and attended by members of the Zionist Executive like Sokolow himself, and not by representatives unauthorized to take decisions. Some of the Arabs called for the assimilation of the Jewish settlers among the local majority through the establishment of mixed villages and mixed schools. In the meantime, heavy clouds covered the international horizon. The joint conference which was to meet at the beginning of July was postponed for a few weeks. But on July 28 the first shots of World War I rang out in the Balkans, and on November 5 Turkey became involved in the war on the side of Germany and Austria.

THE STRUGGLE FOR THE FUTURE. That the vast conflict was bound tragically to affect a people whose masses lived on both sides of the frontiers in regions which turned into battlefields soon became all too obvious. The Zionist movement, national in spirit but international in structure, was also bound to find itself in a precarious position. Its headquarters were in Berlin, but the majority of its followers lived in countries at war with Germany or neutral. There were suggestions that the central office should move to Scandinavia. British and U.S. Zionists wanted it transferred to the United States and placed under the leadership of Louis D. Brandeis. Russian Zionists feared that such a step would cause affront to Germany and further antagonize Turkey; they wanted a coordinating bureau in neutral Copenhagen. Thus the old central office remained in Berlin and its representatives stayed in Constantinople, their task more vital than ever: to see to it that the young *yishuv* weathers the storm. Two members of the Executive (Sokolow and Tschlenow) were sent to London to take charge of political activities there, while another member, Shemaryahu Levin, went to the United States. Nonetheless, one of the results of the fact that the Zionist headquarters never left Central Europe was the widespread and persistent impression that the movement was under German influence.

Whether Germany itself took it for granted was far less certain. Berlin never took Zionism seriously. Its international character had always been suspect. The recent struggle of the *yishuv* (1913) against German as the language of instruction in the German-Jewish Hilfsverein schools, including the newly founded Haifa Technological Institute, caused considerable irritation. Having achieved the huge political success of involving Turkey in the war as an ally, Berlin would do nothing to place any strain on the friendship. Repeated Zionist initiatives directed at obtaining Turkish—or at least German—expression of sympathy for Jewish aims in Ereẓ Israel were repeatedly rebuffed. Even where the proposals concerned the rights of Jews in Russian Poland, which was occupied by German troops (Count Bernstorff, German ambassador in Washington, urged his government to promise them equality of rights in the future), Berlin responded negatively, ostensibly because such a step could make it more difficult to achieve a separate peace with Russia at some later date.

Nonetheless, in the military and political vacillations that were to follow, the Germans sought to preserve the precarious status quo in and around Palestine, but even that proved difficult. Soon after the outbreak of hostilities, one of the most ruthless members of the Turkish ruling group, Jamal Pasha, assumed command in Syria and Palestine and began a series of expulsions, some of them explained as military measures, others as the result of the fact that many of the Jews in the country were foreign (mostly Russian) citizens. The grave danger to the very existence of the *yishuv* (which numbered about 85,000) alarmed not only the

Zionists but Jewry as a whole. The largest Jewish community (Russia) could do little; its political influence was nil and it had been overwhelmed by its own huge refugee problem, created by the mass expulsion of Jews from the war zones by the Russian army conmmand. There remained only one large section of the Jewish people not directly involved in the war. U.S. Jewry immediately offered a helping hand both to the Jewish victims of the fighting in Eastern Europe and to the *yishuv*. Furthermore, U.S. Jewry had political weight, and the United States was at the time represented in Constantinople by Henry Morgenthau, who was willing to help. Coming on top of the Turkish atrocities, of which the Armenians were the main victims, reports of harassment in Ereẓ Israel created an atmosphere that was harmful not only to Turkey but to its allies as well. One of the main aims of the Central Powers had been to keep the U.S. neutral. The unpopularity of czarist Russia in wide circles of the United States public played into their hands. There were also great economic interests involved in the struggle for U.S. sympathies. This helped to make the rulers of Turkey realize that turning Jewish Palestine into another Armenia by large-scale massacres may be too costly, and, although Jamal Pasha often acted on his own, the worst fears that were felt in the first months of the war only partly materialized. Before the end of 1915 the German ambassador in Constantinople, Count Metternich, sent a confidential circular letter to his consulates in Turkey explaining their government's "friendly attitude" toward Jewry's aspirations concerning the raising of the spiritual and economic standards of the Jews living in the Ottoman Empire and furthering Jewish immigration and settlement there (Palestine was not mentioned); all this, of course, provided no harm was done to Turkish or German interests.

In the meantime, a Zionist political campaign was slowly gaining ground in Britain. It centered around a younger leader who had become prominent as one of the critics of Herzl's policies—Chaim Weizmann. One of his closest advisers was a much better known critic of Herzl—Aḥad Ha-Am. The political climate in England was unlike that of Germany. For a long time Britain guarded the integrity of the Ottoman Empire until the latter's misgovernment, the steady penetration of German interests into Turkey, and the expansion of Britain's own interests in the Near East made that policy no longer tenable. The future partition of the vast Ottoman domains raised great problems and offered great opportunities, including some for the non-Turkish elements in the empire and for the Jews in Palestine. Weizmann was one of those who soon grasped the suddenly unfolding prospects. The history of his efforts is the history of the Balfour Declaration. It was a dramatic struggle in which the chief participants were outstanding leaders of the British government, foremost among them Balfour and Lloyd George, leaders of the Jewish community, split in their attitude to the very idea of a Jewish center in Palestine, and numerous other personalities. An early advocate of the idea was a member of the government, Herbert Samuel. The search for an acceptable policy formulation proved to be a most complicated task, mainly because other Entente partners, above all France, were also involved.

When the first tentative approaches were made, the Zionists knew nothing of the secret negotiations between Britain and France, which resulted in the Sykes-Picot Agreement of February 1916, that had already settled the future of Palestine. With the exception of a small enclave including Haifa, in which Britain had a long standing interest, the country was to be placed under an international administration. Later, Russia was also promised large areas of Turkish territory. These undertakings tied Britain's hands when the discussions on Zionist proposals began making headway. But they also spurred interest. The creators of British policy in the Near East had always viewed France as an undesirable neighbor in the vicinity of Suez. An opportunity to reopen the question, especially as far as Palestine was concerned, increased that interest. The potential propaganda value in America and even in Russia, with their millions of Jews, was not overlooked. The Jews, on their part, were becoming more active in giving expression to their wishes and expectations. The British government consulted the government of the U.S., and obtained the support of Wilson and his administration for the pro-Zionist attitude of the British government. L. Brandeis and S. Wise[20] played an important role in securing the U.S. support. As early as the first days of the war, before Turkey joined the Central Powers, proposals were made that Jewish battalions be raised to fight for the liberation of Ereẓ Israel. In August 1914 London was visited by a well-known figure in the Russian revolutionary movement, Pinḥas Rutenberg, who sought to obtain the support of Weizmann and others for this idea. In the meantime, young Jews expelled from Ereẓ Israel to Egypt began volunteering for service with the British forces, and the Zion Mule Corps was established in 1915 under British command with a former officer of the Russian army, Joseph Trumpeldor, playing a central role when the unit went to Gallipoli later in the year. This was but the beginning of the prolonged campaigning for the establishment of the Jewish Legion that was stubbornly pursued by Jabotinsky in London and took another two years to obtain its goal. Rutenberg, who went to the United States in 1915 for the same purpose, had been persuaded to postpone it because of the threat of Turkish retaliations in Palestine, and those who influenced him most were two labor leaders from Ereẓ Israel, David Ben-Gurion and Izhak Ben-Zvi, who later, however, in 1917, themselves promoted the idea of the Jewish Legion and joined its "American" battalion. Much of this activity, including Weizmann's political initiative, had not been authorized by the official supreme organs of the Zionist movement; a meeting of its General Council held in Copenhagen in 1916 resolved that the Executive may not negotiate with any country at war with Turkey.

[20]U.S. Reform rabbi and one of the leaders of U.S. Zionism

The turning point on almost all the fronts came in 1917. The beginning of March brought the Russian Revolution which overthrew the czar and led, eight months later, to the overthrow of the revolutionary government itself and the establishment of the Soviet regime. April brought the American declaration of war on the Central Powers (but not against Turkey). Soon afterward permission was granted in London for enlistment in Jewish battalions. At the beginning of the same year, the British government, now led by Lloyd George, started "unofficial discussions" with the Zionists. One of the first obstacles that had to be removed was the previous commitment under the Anglo-French Sykes-Picot Agreement. Indeed, it was Sir Mark Sykes himself who conducted the discussions with representative Jews, and with his assistance important moves were made in Paris and Rome. On behalf of the Zionists, Sokolow conducted the negotiations there. This time, even the Vatican was less unbending. Benedict XV told Sokolow: "We shall be good neighbors." A short time later, Sokolow received from the French government assurances of "sympathy for your cause, the triumph of which is bound up with that of the Allies." It may have been a reluctant concession, but it opened the way for a decision by the British cabinet. Significantly, the most persistent opposition there came from Edwin Montagu, the Jewish secretary of state for India, but it could not overcome the equally great persistence of the prime minister and of the secretary of state for foreign affairs. Montagu succeeded, however, in delaying the approval of his government's pronouncement and in watering it down. On Nov. 2, 1917, the Balfour Declaration was issued.

WORDS AND DEEDS. The impact of the Balfour Declaration on Jewish public opinion was immediate, and enthusiasm spontaneous. In many lands there were huge demonstrations and processions displaying the Union Jack side by side with the Zionist flag. But the Jews in Germany and Austria could only celebrate between four walls, and in Russia there were by then large areas under Bolshevik rule or in a state of flux where open identification with an "imperialist power" became imprudent. If one of the purposes of the declaration had been to influence developments in Russia, it came too late, even assuming that Jewish opinion could have had any significant influence amid the political storms that were raging there. On the other side of the trenches, in Germany and Turkey, the semi-official reactions were unexpectedly mild. The German Foreign Ministry was unmoved; Zionist efforts in Berlin to obtain a similar declaration were rebuffed. But in December 1917, Talaat Pasha, one of the Turkish ruling triumvirate, told a Zionist correspondent of a prominent German newspaper that Turkey was favorably disposed to Jewish settlement in Palestine, that existing restrictions would be removed, and immigration would be free within the "limits of the country's absorptive capacity," and that Jews will have the right to free economic and cultural development and to local self-government in the framework of Turkish laws. After the publication of the interview, Jewish and Zionist representatives were called to the Foreign Office in Berlin and an undersecretary told them that his government welcomed Talaat's statement.

The general military situation at the time had not yet been viewed by the Central Powers as hopeless. Even Turkey was far from giving up the struggle, in spite of the British advance in Palestine, which caused, inter alia, the removal of Jamal Pasha (September 1917), but not before he hanged a number of Arab nationalists in Damascus. Turkey was pinning its hopes on a Russian withdrawal from the war, chances of a separate peace or, at least, a relatively lenient treatment at a future peace conference. But 1918 brought the series of events that left no more illusions. Bulgaria collapsed at the end of September. A few days later came the disintegration of the Austro-Hungarian Empire. Turkey capitulated on October 20, and Germany herself, her power broken on the western front and her people rebelling, deposed the kaiser and signed an armistice on November 11.

Months before this denouement, the new Zionist leadership headed by Weizmann took the first steps toward the implementation of the Balfour Declaration. A Zionist Commission for Palestine had been formed, including representatives from Britain, America, France, and Italy, and started out for Ereẓ Israel. Two representatives from Russia were elected, but their departure had been postponed. Before leaving, Weizmann was received by King George V. There were high hopes but few illusions. It had been difficult to obtain the international promise; turning it into a reality was bound to be much more difficult. The Turks were out; the Arabs felt immeasurably stronger; the British military administration was totally indifferent and often openly hostile. The Jewish people as a whole had been greatly weakened by the war. Russian Jews were among the chief victims of the internal chaos that followed the October Revolution and of the civil war that was beginning to engulf most of Russia. Polish Jewry was in dire need of help. American Jews saw their most urgent task in rushing aid to Eastern Europe.

The arrival of the Zionist Commission in Ereẓ Israel in April 1918 opened three decades of incessant struggle. The commission's immediate task was to help in restoring the impoverished *yishuv* and preparing the conditions for future immigration. The almost totally negative attitude of the military authorities was a major obstacle, and it also impeded understanding with the Arabs. Contacts were established with Emir Feisal, about to become king of Syria. Weizmann's talks with him, first in Akaba and later in London and Paris, led to the signing of an agreement in January 1919 with Colonel T. E. Lawrence acting as intermediary. But Feisal's hopes to remain in Syria had been frustrated. The French forced him to flee Damascus in 1920, and though he was compensated by the British, who secured his election as king of Iraq, his understanding with the Arab world were bound to involve Palestine, where they were soon directed—partly made to be directed—against the Jews. For the first time attacks were organized on a large scale. In the spring of 1920, Trumpeldor and seven others fell while defending Tel Ḥai in Upper Galilee. Within a few weeks Arab rioting in Jerusalem claimed further victims. Some of the organizers were sentenced to years of hard labor. For the sake of evenhandedness, Jabotinsky and members of the Jewish self-defense received similar treatment. Moreover, official explanations published by the British authorities made the Balfour Declaration look like a scrap of paper. The political pattern then established was to last until the end of British rule in the country.

Elsewhere on the political front things looked somewhat less dismal. Zionist leaders had been given an opportunity personally to present their case at the Paris Peace Conference. They also had a say in the lengthy process of drafting the League of Nations Mandate for Palestine, even if many of their proposals had not been accepted. The Mandate itself had been entrusted to Britain at San Remo in 1920, although some British leaders wanted it to be taken on by a more than reluctant America. On June 30, 1920, Sir Herbert Samuel arrived in Palestine as its first high commissioner, with every goodwill to serve the people of Palestine as a whole, the Jewish National Home, and British interests. While he was taking the initial steps in establishing a civilian administration, Zionist leaders met in London for their first postwar conference, and the internal difficulties which dogged the movement from its early days again came to the surface. Instead of "political" and "practical" Zionists, it was "east" and "west" this time, symbolized to a great extent by two names: Weizmann and Brandeis. The former wanted a comprehensive program of action embracing political, economic, and cultural matters. His opponents viewed the political chapter as closed with the attainment of international recognition and approval of the Mandate; henceforth efforts were to be concentrated on economics, and particularly on fostering private enterprise. Those in Weizmann's camp proposed the establishment of a large foundation fund—Keren Hayesod—for the upbuilding of the National Home and for the encouragement of private initiative. The "Brandeisists" opposed it. There was a widespread feeling that unless Jewry put to good use the opportunities created by the wartime achievements, they might be irretrievably lost. But the general situation did not work in Zionism's favor, regardless of trend. The strongest appeals addressed to world Jewry evoked only a faint echo. The funds raised were miserably inadequate. Even the limited number of immigrants could not find immediate employment, and crisis chased crisis.

These difficulties opened new opportunities before the opposing side. Samuel's efforts to placate the Arabs were rebuffed. Winston Churchill's efforts as head of the Colonial Office to do the same by making Feisal king of Iraq and Abdullah emir of eastern Palestine (called Transjordan) where the "Jewish clauses" of the Mandate were not to be applied, fared no better. Less than a year after Samuel's arrival, the country was shaken by the worst outbreak of Arab rioting yet seen there. Its political repercussions led to the publication (in June 1922) of the first of the series of White Papers (statements of British policy) which undermined the foundations of what was intended to be the Jewish National Home. No concession, however, satisfied the Arab political leadership, which sought to stop all Jewish immigration and take over the government of the country through institutions with an Arab majority or by other means. This general erosion gave rise to great discontent within the Zionist movement. Weizmann was accused of not being strong enough in his dealings with the Mandatory government since he constantly insisted on Jewish-British relations based on mutual trust. Others accused him of extending too much support to the Zionist labor movement and to unsound economic policies. One of the opposition groups was led by Jabotinsky, who had been brought into the Executive in 1921 but resigned in 1923. Moreover, Brandeis laid down his post as honorary president of the Zionist Organization (June 1921), thus bringing U.S. Zionists into disarray for a number of years. For different reasons, Ussishkin was also soon to leave the chairmanship of the Zionist Executive in Jerusalem (which replaced the Zionist Commission). Even before that, there were changes in its Political Department whose first chief, Commander Bianchini (Italian Jewry's representative on the commission) had been killed by Bedouin in an attack on a train near the Syrian border. His successor, M. D. Eder (a former territorialist), returned to London in 1922, and Weizmann sent to Jerusalem a career officer with diplomatic experience, Lt. Col. F. H. Kisch, who was to remain at his post for nine difficult years.

Seeking to break the vicious circle of economic predicaments and political setbacks, Weizmann and his colleagues decided to open a new page by bringing into the national effort important non-Zionist elements in Jewry. The idea encountered strong opposition, mainly among those already opposed to Weizmann. However, after lengthy preparatory work, the first conference of the "enlarged" Jewish Agency met in Zurich in 1929 in the presence of a number of outstanding Jews of the generation, among them Albert Einstein, Leon Blum, Ḥ. N. Bialik, Sholem Asch, Louis Marshall, and others. The impression produced by this remarkable gathering had been powerful, and the hopes it reawakened were great. But the reaction in Palestine came almost immediately. After months of Arab incitement motivated by the most potent of weapons—Muslim religious hatred aimed at depriving the Jews of their traditional rights at the Western Wall—there came a wave of murderous attacks. The outbreak was followed by two inquiries. An international commission studied and reported on rights of access to the Western Wall, and a British commission reviewed the political aspects of the situation. The resultant White Paper (1930) issued by the colonial secretary, Lord Passfield (the Labor leader Sidney Webb), led to Weizmann's resignation as president of the Jewish Agency as a protest and a sign that the government can no longer expect his cooperation. A storm followed in the press and in the British Parliament. Official explanations were published by Prime Minister Ramsay MacDonald, but they could but slightly reduce the damage done. Weizmann's own position became untenable, and at the 1931 Zionist Congress Sokolow was elected president in his place. No essential change in the policy of the movement, however, followed. Indeed, Chaim Arlosoroff, who took over the Jewish Agency's Political Department in Jerusalem from Kisch (who resigned before the Congress), had been Weizmann's devoted disciple. It was also the first time that a representative of Zionist Labor had been entrusted with the political portfolio, which was to remain in Labor hands. Furthermore, with Weizmann away from his old office in London, the center of Zionist policy-making gradually moved to Jerusalem, and this shift was virtually completed after Ben-Gurion joined the Executive in 1933.

Kisch was the model civil servant; Arlosoroff was the statesman-philosopher. Realizing that no change in the situation could be expected unless there was some progress toward a modus vivendi with the Arabs, Arlosoroff was determined to concentrate much of his work in this field. Consequently, he appointed Moshe Shertok (Sharett) as secretary of the department for his knowledge of Arabic and his strong ties with the country. Arlosoroff's brief term, less than two years (he was murdered on the Tel Aviv seashore in June 1933), coincided with the first years of service of the British high commissioner, Sir Arthur Wauchope. The two established a sincere mutual understanding, and this played a part in government actions when, at the beginning of the Hitler regime, it became imperative that Palestine be opened to a large number of immigrants from Germany. Nonetheless, Arlosoroff also came to the conclusion that although there was no immediate alternative to the former political course of the movement, future alternatives had to be explored. He considered Revisionist demands for a complete change of the system of government in Palestine as unrealistic. But the road hitherto followed, without greater political assistance from Britain and vast sums from the Jewish people, would clearly not bring Zionism nearer to its goal. The world situation also militated against it. In 1932 Arlosoroff foresaw a new international conflagration "in five to ten years." It was imperative to elaborate alternative, even "revolutionary," plans, while continuing to "muddle through." The ideas discussed in those days included plans for the division of the country into "cantons" on Swiss lines. This was an old suggestion made by Jacobson, then head of the Zionist Office at the seat of the League of Nations in Geneva. More radical proposals spoke of establishing a Jewish state in a part of the country where Jews formed a large section of the population (by then the *yishuv* counted about 180,000).

In spite of their vital importance, long-range issues had to give way to urgent current problems, and even these could not be adequately handled when the budget of the Political Department in Jerusalem amounted to $20,000 a year. The latest White Paper (1931) brought in its wake additional inquiries into the problems of land and absorptive capacity—or lack of it, according to British experts. The Jewish Agency tried to reopen the question of settlement in Transjordan; a group of influential sheikhs entered into negotiations with the Jewish Agency on the subject, presumably not without Emir Abdullah's knowledge. The British were adamant: Transjordan was to remain closed to Jewish settlement. Such policies could only weaken the position of the few Arab leaders who were inclined to some sort of understanding with the Jews. Desultory attempts to open discussions with them were made during those years by prominent *yishuv* personalities (J. L. Magnes, Rutenberg, Moshe Smilansky) and, less important, by a small group called Berit Shalom, which was seeking a bi-national solution. They found, however, no one in the Arab camp able to enter into binding agreements. The mufti of Jerusalem, Hājj Amin al- Husseini, intended to turn the Palestine problem into a general Muslim problem by calling a Muslim Conference in Jerusalem. Tension and agitation were also fostered by inciting broadcasts from Fascist Italy. In Egypt the beginning of the

1930s witnessed violent disturbances and a general strike in 1933. In the year 1937 independent Egypt was admitted to the League of Nations. The year 1936 saw a general strike in Syria, too, but French consent to grant Syria independence was later repudiated by Paris. Iraq, which joined the League of Nations in 1932, experienced a military coup in 1936. The examples proved infectious. In order to force the British to stop Jewish immigration and place Palestine under an Arab government, and also in order to subdue the moderates within the Arab camp itself, al-Husseini and his followers proclaimed an Arab national strike in 1936. It did not take long for what was supposed to be passive resistance to turn into open rebellion. An Arab Higher Committee was formed to conduct the struggle.

The inquiry instituted by the British this time was the most authoritative ever. The Royal Commission headed by Lord Peel had been appointed, and before it left for its destination, unusually stringent measures were taken in Ereẓ Israel to restore a semblance of order, with the aid of almost 20,000 British troops. Formally, the Arab leaders only stopped the strike when called upon to do so by the rulers of Iraq, Saudi Arabia, Yemen and Transjordan (Egypt was not among them), but later decided to boycott the commission because the government approved new immigration permits. The commission stayed in the country from November 1936 until the end of January 1937, and toward the conclusion of its hearings Arab representatives testified before it in compliance with another call from the same rulers. The Jewish Agency appeared before the commission in full force, headed by Weizmann who was again its president (reelected in 1935). Sittings were held abroad as well, and statements were heard from Jabotinsky and Samuel, among others. Politically, the results were more dramatic than after any previous inquiry. The commission concluded that the Mandate proved to be unworkable because it was impossible to secure even the minimum of mutual understanding between the two sections of the population necessary for its implementation.

After analyzing the various proposals for finding a way out of the impasse, the commission chose partition: dividing the country into a Jewish state, an Arab state, and a mandated zone which was to include Jerusalem. The establishment of a Jewish state had thus become for the first time a proposal from a formal British body. What could not have been foreseen was that at least three other commissions would have to go into the matter and a second world war and the holocaust of European Jewry would be witnessed before the plan—largely modified—would be implemented.

The approaching war was casting ominous shadows. Britain could not face increased complications in a vital strategic region. Parliamentary reactions to the partition plan were unfavorable. Emir Abdullah stood to gain a great deal, for he could do in 1938 what he did in 1948—take over the area allocated to the proposed Arab state. Abdullah's supporters were secretly with him, but for public consumption their attitude was negative. The Husseini camp was totally uncompromising and ready to renew the fight. Soon the government was compelled to take drastic steps, including the suppression of the Arab Higher Committee and the deportation of extremist leaders; some of them, including al-Husseini, had fled the country earlier. The riots continued, however, and to a large degree became an internecine Arab struggle, claiming numerous victims, mostly among the moderates. The fact that the Jews were also split in their attitude to the partition plan made Britain's retreat from the plan much easier. In spite of Weizmann and Ben-Gurion's pleading in its favor, only a vague compromise resolution could be forced through the Zionist Congress in 1937. By 299 votes to 160 it was agreed that the Executive should "ascertain" in discussions with the British "the precise terms for the proposed establishment of a Jewish State." The non-Zionist partners in the Jewish Agency were far more negative. They did not want a Jewish state; their decisions, including a request to the government to convene a conference of Jews and Arabs, made progress even more difficult.

In 1938 another commission visited Palestine. Though it was called the Partition Commission, there had been a widespread feeling even before it reached Jerusalem that its real purpose was to bury the plan. In the autumn it presented its report, which was negative. It was welcomed not only by Arabs, but also by anti-partition Zionists. But even before that happened, Hitler made his first decisive steps toward war: the annexation of Austria in April and the beginning of the destruction of Czechoslovakia in November. The same month also brought the *Kristallnacht*[21] in Germany. By then the propaganda offensive of the Axis in the Near East had heightened. Anxiety among Jews abroad mounted and led, inter alia, to the presentation of a memorandum on the subject to President Roosevelt by 245 members of both Houses of Congress and 30 governors. In Poland a Jewish Emigration Committee was established under government pressure to seek new "territories"; a study mission went to Madagascar and returned with empty hands. Other territories were mentioned with little hope. By then, an air of inevitability began enveloping Europe and the world. No conditions could be less propitious for an attempt to achieve in 1939 what proved to be elusive before: a fair settlement.

Britain nonetheless considered that the urgent needs of the hour precluded further postponement. Taking up the suggestion that an Arab-Jewish conference be called, the British broadened the scope and invited, in addition to the parties to the conflict, representatives of Egypt, Iraq, Saudi Arabia, Transjordan, and Yemen. Inevitably, the inclusion of the Arab states almost led to a boycott of the conference by the Jews, but the situation was far too grave for that. The Jewish delegation was large and weighty; it included Zionists, non-Zionists, and Agudat Israel. With regard to the leadership of the Palestine Arab delegation, London began by declaring Amin al-Husseini persona non grata

[21]The night of Nov. 9–10, marked by extreme anti-Jewish excesses throughout Germany and Austria

and ended by accepting his representative and kinsman, Jamāl al-Husseini, over the opposition of moderate Palestine Arabs. The augury was plain: no agreed proposal could come from such a gathering. The Arabs insisted on their full program: abolishment of the Jewish National Home, an end to Jewish immigration, and Arab self-government. There was no room for give and take. The government of Neville Chamberlain saw itself facing one overriding task: to prepare for the coming war with Hitler. The Arabs could be a menace; the Jews had no choice. Thus, a new White Paper was issued in May 1939. A Palestine state was to be established and the population was to be prepared for self-government over a ten-year period. The future constitution was to include safeguards for the holy places, for the special position of the Jewish National Home, and for British interests. Full independence was made conditional on the creation of good relations between Arabs and Jews. As to immigration, 75,000 Jews were to be admitted in the next five years, after which the continuation of immigration would depend on Arab consent. The regulation of land sales, or their banning in certain areas, was left in the hands of the government.

The White Paper was rejected outright by Jews and Arabs alike. There was sharp criticism in the British Parliament, and only the grave international situation gave the government the needed majority; Labor and some 20 Conservatives (including Churchill) voted against it. The strongest words came from the Mandates Commission of the League of Nations, which stated unanimously that the policy "was not in accordance with the interpretation which . . . the Commission had placed upon the Palestine Mandate." The matter was to come up before the Council of the League of Nations, due to meet in September, since a change in the terms of the Mandate called for the council's consent. The war started before it met, and the British government considered itself free to act. In the meantime, the extremist Arabs found themselves leaderless as al-Husseini and some of his associates were not allowed to return. This was used by the Arab moderates who saw a chance to gain both the leadership and a compromise that would give the Arabs most of what they wanted. The Jewish leaders in Palestine and abroad refused to cooperate with the British administration, and some extremist elements, mainly the underground Irgun Ẓeva'i Le'ummi (I.Ẓ.L.), soon turned to the use of force. The Zionist Congress which met in Geneva on the very eve of World War II avoided taking dramatic decisions. With armies massing all over Europe and with the signature of the Molotov-Ribbentrop Pact, it was realized that both valor and wisdom would be needed in the coming struggle.

War and Holocaust. Even before the initial Axis successes brought a direct military threat to Palestine in 1940, tragedy befell European Jewry—the Holocaust. Its unbelievable dimensions did not become known until later, but there were already large numbers of Jews fleeing from death and trying to reach Palestine. The immediate task was to help in their escape. Next to it was the need to mobilize the *yishuv* for the war. As had been the case a quarter of a century earlier, the British were reluctant to accept Jewish volunteers. Only the early defeats in North Africa weakened this reluctance, and by 1940 many thousands of Palestinian Jews enlisted. The *yishuv*'s economic potential also gradually became a factor of considerable value. The British did not forget their White Paper, however, and in February 1940 introduced crippling regulations concerning land transactions, which caused another bitter outburst on the part of the Jews. The immigration problem had taken on a different character. The British aim was to spread out the use of the 75,000 "certificates" over five years and—if possible—until the end of the war (although nobody could know when that would be). In any case, regular immigration was unlikely to continue under war conditions. Indeed, less than 20,000 immigrants—authorized and unauthorized—entered during the years 1940–42. Furthermore, the fact that the Chamberlain government fell in May 1940 and another administration took over, headed by Churchill and including a number of other friendly ministers, was bound to influence the general political climate.

As to the Arabs, the initial military successes of the Axis made them stake their future on its victory, and many were ready merely to wait for it. Hence the failure of al-Husseini's call for an open rebellion. The fall of France in 1940 turned Syria and Lebanon into bases of subversion and February 1941 brought about a pro-German putsch in Iraq. Allied countermeasures prevented further deterioration. Al-Husseini turned up in Rome and Berlin in the autumn of 1941, and some Egyptian sympathizers of the Axis (including the future president of the UAR, Anwar Sadat) plotted with Axis men in North Africa. A slight change took place after Rommel's defeat in 1942. British efforts were largely directed at exploiting the improved situation, and in due course a policy of unifying the Arabs evolved, which led to the organization of the Arab League in 1945. Palestine Arabs were granted a voice in the league itself when it was organized, their cause having been included in its charter.

Among the Jews there was a feeling that somewhat friendlier winds were imperceptibly blowing in London. The immediate peril to the *yishuv* had receded, but the dimensions of the tragedy that befell European Jewry were gradually emerging. The need for immigration, and immigration itself, were again coming to the fore. Internal pressures were building up; the wartime "truce" between the British authorities and extremist elements was coming to an end, and violence erupted again in Palestine, this time initiated by the I.Ẓ.L. The Zionist leadership found it necessary to clarify its own position and seek clarification of the position likely to be taken up by the Churchill government. Much of the thinking harked back to the Royal Commission's proposals, but the formulation adopted at a conference called by American Zionists at the Biltmore Hotel in New York in May 1942 claimed "that Palestine be established as a Jewish Commonwealth." This was later approved by the appropriate Zionist bodies in Jerusalem over the opposition of some of the former anti-partitionists. Outbursts of terror from Jewish extreme underground organizations, including the murder in Cairo of the British minister for the Near East, Lord Moyne, by members of Loḥamei Ḥerut Israel (Leḥi), again increased the feeling of impending crisis.

YEARS OF DECISION. The end of the war in Europe in May 1945 was followed by the fall of Churchill. Labor, which replaced him, had in the past displayed great sympathy for Zionism, and its party conference had just confirmed its promise to help the development of the National Home by making room for it through "extending the present Palestinian boundaries, by agreement with Egypt, Syria, or Transjordan." The urgent need for action soon became clear with the disclosure that it was necessary to aid in the rehabilitation of hundreds of thousands of survivors of Nazi camps. This could only be done through Anglo-American cooperation. The United States had already become a factor in Middle Eastern affairs, militarily and economically. Now, because of its friendly ties with both Jews and Arabs, it was beginning to become involved politically as well.

In the days immediately following World War II, the voice of the American Jewish community on its own government carried much weight in Washington. This was the culminating point of a generation of sporadic political endeavor by the Zionist movement in America, which had resulted in 1924 in the U.S. government's formally approving the League of Nations Mandate for Palestine and its guarantee of Jewish national rights. Every president of the United States after Woodrow Wilson had made declarations favorable to Zionist aspirations, and the majority of Congress was moved several times to declare its pro-Zionist views, both officially in joint resolutions and informally. With the rise of Nazism, Zionist membership in the United States grew rapidly and the Zionist organizations became a prevailing influence in the community while also widening the circle of friends and supporters in the general community. During

World War II there was lively and even bitter disagreement between those Zionists who followed Stephen S. Wise in being ready to rely on the goodwill of President Roosevelt and were therefore willing to remain relatively quiescent and those led by Abba Hillel Silver, whose orientation was toward the opposition Republican Party and who believed public opinion had to be organized against the government in order to both save Jewish lives in Europe and realize Zionist aims after the war. These forces paved the road to the adoption of the Biltmore platform in 1942, which postulated Jewish independence as the Zionist war aim. Distrust in the goodwill of others and the desire for independence deepened while the news of the Holocaust continued to seep out of Europe. By the winter of 1943 Abba Hillel Silver replaced Stephen Wise as the head of Zionist political affairs and public relations in the United States. With the help of Emanuel Neumann and a number of others, the American Zionist Emergency Committee, which Silver led, mounted a political offensive throughout the United States and prepared the grounds both in the public mind and in political circles for U.S. support of Zionism against the continuing White Paper policy of the British government and for the establishment of a Jewish state. The Zionist forces had a substantial impact on the White House and on Congress, which were responsive to public protest and pressure mounted within the democratic process, and they thus managed (1947–48) to influence the policy of the U.S. government, despite the continuing opposition of the State Department.

The United States also had to shoulder most of the burden of aid to the vast numbers of Displaced Persons in Europe. The Jewish Agency asked for an immediate grant of 100,000 immigration permits, but Britain, embroiled in a fierce election campaign, was incapable of acting. Two months earlier, a change of leadership had also taken place in the U.S. Roosevelt's successor, President Truman, was anxious to help, and one of his first steps was the dispatch of an envoy to D.P. camps. The latter recommended resettlement of 100,000 stateless Jews found in the western zone of occupied Germany, and pointed out that "Palestine is definitely . . . the first choice." This recommendation, with Truman's backing, was sent to London, but the new prime minister, Attlee, could not see his way to accepting it, proposing instead a joint Anglo-American investigation of the entire problem. This was agreed upon in October 1945.

Uncertainty and conflicting pressures had their most damaging effect in the Middle East itself. The Arabs saw new danger to their hopes, raised high by the 1939 White Paper. A reorganized Arab Higher Commission was soon established. The Arab states' position as founding members of the new United Nations gave them a feeling of being able to sway political developments. Now they were incensed by America, even more than by Britain. There were violent demonstrations and attacks on Jews and foreigners. On the other hand, the *yishuv* also found new strength in its very despair. Some 20,000 Jewish troops were beginning to return, well trained, many with war experience, having seen with their own eyes what happened to their brethren in Europe. They, and others in the *yishuv,* vowed "never again!" Acts of violence were becoming widespread. The Haganah, which in the past had concentrated on defense and on preparations for the day of decision, undertook action of its own. Soon the government, with all the forces at its disposal, found itself at war with the *yishuv.* The only respite came during the work of the Anglo-American Committee of Inquiry, whose prospects, however, were prejudiced in advance by the new British foreign secretary Ernest Bevin, who from the outset left little doubt of his hostility. The Labor government inherited a crushing burden of problems of which the Middle East was only one. Britain became unable to continue its imperial role. It was necessary to cut losses and safeguard only the most vital interests. Soon India was to be independent, after being split into two states, and other parts of the empire were to follow. So was Palestine, but at the end of 1945 and beginning of 1946 a way was still being sought to keep Britain in control. Under pressure of immigration needs, a

The Anglo-American Committee of Inquiry regarding the problems of European Jewry and Palestine arriving in Jerusalem, March 6, 1946. 1) Sir John Singleton (British chairman), 2) Judge Joseph C. Hutcheson (American chairman), 3) Frank W. Buxton (U.S.), 4) William Phillips (U.S.), 5) W. F. Crick (Britain), 6) Sir Frederick Leggett (Britain), 7) Bartley C. Crum (U.S.), 8) Frank Aydelotte (U.S.), 9) James G. McDonald (U.S.), 10) R. E. Manningham-Buller (Britain), 11) R. H. S. Crossman (Britain). The twelfth member of the committee was Lord Morrison (Britain). Courtesy Central Zionist Archives, Jerusalem.

provisional monthly "schedule" of 1,500 permits had been decided upon for the duration of the discussions and it was stated, for the first time, that any proposed settlement would be brought before the United Nations.

The work of the Anglo-American Commission, which started in Washington in January 1946, continued in London and in other places in Europe, then in Jerusalem, Cairo, and a number of other Arab capitals, and ended in Lausanne in March. It was conducted in a highly charged atmosphere. Large numbers of Jewish survivors of the Holocaust were being intercepted on the high seas by the British navy as "illegal" immigrants. Acts of violence in Palestine became a daily occurrence. So did Arab threats, especially after Husseini escaped from Germany on the eve of its surrender and appeared in Cairo. The Palestine Arabs mainly relied on the influence of the Arab states, whose willingness to assist them was proclaimed daily. It was inevitable that the inquiry should seek a compromise, and the final report turned not to partition but to its alternative: a bi-national Palestine state based on parity and under a United Nations trusteeship. To help in meeting pressing needs, 100,000 immigration permits were to be issued, if possible in 1946, and future immigration was to be based on compromise.

With the exception of Washington, no interested party approved the recommendations. Britain's equivocations found expression in official statements and, even more, in Bevin's speeches. The Arabs saw their hopes for Arab rule in Palestine dashed. The Jews, though pleased by the opportunity of rapidly bringing in a large number of Displaced Persons, feared the prospect of unending strife with the Arabs and with the "Trustee," which they expected would be Britain. The breaking point was reached in June 1946, when, in a retaliatory action, Palmaḥ units destroyed a number of rail and road bridges in sensitive points, and the British government hit back by imposing a virtual siege on the *yishuv:* mass searches for arms and incriminating documents were carried out in hundreds of buildings, including the offices of the Jewish Agency; over 2,000 people, among them the members of the Jewish Agency and Va'ad Le'ummi executives, were arrested. The life of the *yishuv* had been dislocated. In time, some of the detainees were freed, but over 700, including Agency and Va'ad Le'ummi leaders, were interned. A short time later, I.Z.L. blew up a wing of the King David Hotel in Jerusalem, housing offices of the government secretariat. The casualties, belonging to all communities, were heavy. The *yishuv* was shocked, and the Jewish Agency condemned the deed. Meanwhile attempts were made in Washington and London to proceed with discussions about the results of their joint inquiry. Another committee, headed by Henry F. Grady (U.S.) and Herbert Morrison (Britain), found it more advisable to go back to the principles of territorial division. It suggested the establishment of a Jewish sector, an Arab sector, and a British sector, including Jerusalem and the Negev, as an intermediary stage that could eventually lead either to a unitary state, to a bi-national one, or outright partition. Administration of common interests such as defense, foreign relations, communications, etc., was to remain in the hands of a British high commissioner. During the initial five years, he was also to appoint presidents of the legislatures of the Jewish and Arab sectors, and his approval would be needed for new legislation. Immigration would also remain under his control after the agreed 100,000 were brought in with American help. The implementation of the scheme as a whole was made conditional on American participation and Arab-Jewish consent.

There was little to recommend this latest compromise, which contained most of the drawbacks of earlier suggestions. Washington withdrew from it almost immediately, and there was much criticism in London. The Arabs insisted on all their original demands, and the Jews refused to accept the plan. Again, London proposed a conference. The Jewish Agency was ready for it but not on the basis of the Morrison-Grady plan. The Arab Executive refused because its conditions (including the participation of Amin al-Husseini) were rejected. Thus, when the conference convened in September 1946 the main parties to the dispute were absent and only the British and Arab governments were represented. No progress could be made, and Britain suggested that the discussions be temporarily suspended for a further attempt to bring in the parties concerned. This was to take place at the beginning of 1947 in order to enable the Jewish Agency to bring the matter before the forthcoming Zionist Congress. To make things easier, the interned Zionist and *yishuv* leaders and a number of other internees were released. By then the Jewish Agency had again disassociated itself from the acts of violence, which were continued, however, by I.Ẓ.L. and Leḥi. Simultaneously, a number of Husseini's men were allowed to return to the country.

When the Zionist Congress met in December 1946 in Basle, it revealed a significant change in the internal situation. The Labor wing of the movement lost some ground, and within its ranks the activist elements had the upper hand. The American Zionists were led by Abba Hillel Silver, a supporter of a more determined policy. Furthermore, the Revisionists rejoined the Zionist Organization. As a result, the Congress refused to participate in the London talks, albeit leaving the door slightly ajar for later reconsideration. The idea of partition had enough support, but no initiative was to come from the Jewish Agency. Finally, the post of president had been left vacant, thus demonstrating the rejection of the Weizmann line. It was the absence of the Zionists that helped the Arab League persuade the Palestine Arab leaders to take their seats at the second round of the London talks in January 1947. An amended version of the Morrison-Grady scheme was put forward by Bevin, designed to meet some of the earlier criticism: cantonal self-government, for instance, in place of provincial authority; a shortened period of trusteeship; 100,000 immigrants in two years instead of one; and no partition. The Arab reply, however, was nevertheless a resounding no. This left things in a worse state than ever because it became obvious that the 1939 White Paper was also dead, a victim of the Holocaust, determined Jewish opposition, Arab conduct during the war and, finally, United States intervention. Left without an official policy, London turned to the United Nations on April 2, 1947. The purpose of this step was made clear in a statement before the House of Commons: "We are not going to the United Nations to surrender the Mandate. We are going to the United Nations setting out the problem and asking their advice as to how the Mandate can be administered. If the Mandate cannot be administered in its present form, we are asking how it can be amended."

THE UNITED NATIONS INVESTIGATES. Though this was the first time that the United Nations was to deal with the Palestine problem, the latter was not unknown to it. Preliminary skirmishes on the subject took place at the San Francisco Conference in 1945 and at the first session of the General Assembly in 1946, when Arab representatives attempted in vain to obtain decisions prejudicial to the Jewish position. The first special session of the General Assembly met between April 28 and May 15, 1947, with the purpose of "constituting and instructing a Special Committee to prepare for the consideration of the Question of Palestine at the second Regular Session" (scheduled to open September 16). The five Arab delegations tried to alter the very purpose of the deliberations on the eve of the session by requesting to amend the subject of discussions by adding to the agenda an item entitled: "Termination of the Mandate over Palestine and declaration of its independence." As before, the Assembly rejected their request; it also refused to exclude from its discussions the problems of displaced Jews in Europe.

For the first time, representatives of the Jews and of Palestine Arabs were heard by the United Nations. When the question arose whether their spokesmen should be heard at a plenary meeting or at a meeting of the Assembly's political committee, Czechoslovakia and Poland, backed by the U.S.S.R., urged for a hearing in the plenary, while Britain and America viewed the committee as the appropriate place for statements by delegations that did not represent member states. The latter view prevailed. The Jewish Agency spokesmen were Ben-Gurion, Silver, and Shertok (Sharett). The Arab Higher Committee was represented by E. Ghouri and H. Kattan.

The burden of the Jewish case was summarized by Ben-Gurion, who told the committee: " . . . in Palestine you are faced not merely with a large and growing number of Jews, but with a distinct Jewish nation. There are Jews and Jewish communities in many countries, but in Palestine there is a new and unique phenomenon—a Jewish nation, with all the attributes and aspirations of nationhood." The Arab case was presented not only by the spokesmen of the Higher Committee but also by the five Arab member-states and it was summarized by Ghouri: "We only request the application to us of the principles of the democracies. We are only asking for our national rights. It is . . . the determined and unequivocal will of the Arabs to refuse to consider any solution which entails or even implies the loss of the sovereignty to the whole or to any part of the country, or the diminution of such sovereignty in any form whatever."

Much of the discussion was procedural, and the great majority of the delegates avoided anything that could be seen as clear commitment to one side or the other. The representative of India (a Muslim) was one of those who did not conceal his leaning to the Arab side, nor did the representative of Turkey. The delegate of China spoke with feeling of "the tragedy of the Jewish people" which contributed so much to the world and which "deserves a national home of some sort, deserves a place it can call its own, in which it can live in happiness, free from social and political discrimination and free from the eternal fear of persecution." Sympathy for Jewish aspirations was expressed by Czechoslovakia and Poland, but the chief surprise came when the Soviet delegate explained the stand of his government. The Soviet regime had long been known for its extreme hostility to Zionism, but the opportunity to hasten the removal of Britain from an area of special interest to the U.S.S.R. was far too important to let that stand in the way. While supporting the Jewish Agency's request for a hearing, Andrei Gromyko spoke of the sufferings of the Jewish people in Europe and said that it was "beyond description." "The fact that not a single Western European state" came to the help of the Jews "explains the aspirations of the Jews for the creation of a state of their own . . . It is impossible to justify a denial of this right of the Jewish people." The Mandate had failed; both Jews and Arabs called for its liquidation. The best solution would be "the establishment of an independent, dual, democratic, homogeneous Arab-Jewish state," but if that proved impossible "in view of the deterioration in the relations between the Jews and the Arabs," it would be necessary to consider "the partition of Palestine into two independent autonomous states, one Jewish and one Arab."

The divergent views led to dissensions concerning the composition of the proposed UN mission and its terms of reference. Talk of "neutrality" and "impartiality" was found to be of little help. But it was agreed that the UN Special Committee on Palestine (UNSCOP) was to have "the widest powers to ascertain and record facts, and to investigate all questions and issues relevant to the problem of Palestine" and it was to conduct "investigations in Palestine and wherever it may deem useful." It was asked to "give most careful considerations to the religious interests in Palestine of Islam, Judaism, and Christianity" and present its report by Sept. 1, 1947. The only votes against the decision were those of the Muslim states. As to the composition of UNSCOP, it was agreed to make it fully representative of all regions of the world, and to exclude the permanent members of the Security Council and the Arab countries. Two Muslims (from India and Iran) were included as well as delegates from Australia, Canada, Czechoslovakia, Guatemala, the Netherlands, Peru, Sweden, Uruguay, and Yugoslavia.

Arab dissatisfaction with these decisions found its immediate expression in a boycott by the Arab Higher Committee. The Arab League left the question of its cooperation open in the hope of persuading the mission not to visit refugee camps in Europe. The investigators did, indeed, postpone their decision on the subject until after the hearings in the Middle East. The latter started in the middle of June in an unusually tense atmosphere caused by numerous acts of violence, hangings, and retaliations. It also coincided with the dramatic developments concerning the fate of the refugee ship *Exodus 1947* with over 4,500 men, women, and children who sailed in it to Palestine only to be returned to Germany after a bloody encounter with British forces in Haifa harbor. Nevertheless UNSCOP (presided over by Swedish Chief Justice Emile Sandström) heard Jewish and British representatives, official and unofficial, and visited Arab areas of the country, as well as Jewish ones, spending over five weeks in Palestine. The Arabs who met the UN envoys privately repeated the demands already heard in New York. The Jewish Agency efforts were now clearly directed at achieving partition on fair terms. On its way back, UNSCOP members visited Lebanon, Syria, and Transjordan and heard representatives of the Arab states, who warned against any solution but the one proposed by them. Upon arriving in Geneva, UNSCOP decided to have a subcommittee visit Jewish refugee camps in Germany and Austria, and by the end of August it completed its work.

The UNSCOP report contained 12 general recommendations (11 of them adopted unanimously), a majority plan, and a minority plan. The majority plan, presented by Canada, Czechoslovakia, Guatemala, the Netherlands, Peru, Sweden and Uruguay, called for the partition of Palestine into an Arab state, a Jewish state, and an internationalized Jerusalem, the three to be linked in an economic union. The Jewish state was to include eastern Galilee, the Coastal Plain from a point south of Acre to north of Ashdod, and the Negev. The Arab state was to

Moshe Shertok (Sharett) giving evidence before the United Nations Special Committee on Palestine (UNSCOP), Jerusalem, 1947. Courtesy Central Zionist Archives, Jerusalem.

include western Galilee, central Palestine, and the Coastal Plain from Ashdod to the Egyptian border. The Jerusalem-Bethlehem area was to be administered by the United Nations under a permanent trusteeship. The Mandate was to come to an end, and from Sept. 1, 1947, Palestine was to be administered by Britain for another two years, alone or with the participation of one or more UN members, under UN auspices. The political regimes in the new states were to be "basically democratic." The holy places and access to them were to be safeguarded according to existing rights. Furthermore, the UN was to make speedy arrangements to solve the problem of a quarter of a million Jewish refugees in Europe. With two dissenting votes, UNSCOP also expressed its view that "any solution for Palestine cannot be considered as a solution of the Jewish problem as a whole." The argument of the minority report, concurred in by India, Iran, and Yugoslavia, with Australia abstaining in the vote on both plans, was based on the assumption that "the well-being of the country and its peoples as a whole" outweighed "the aspirations of the Jews." It suggested a federal regime comprising an Arab state and a Jewish state with Jerusalem as capital of a central government in charge of defense, foreign relations, and immigration. There was to be a bicameral legislature based on parity in one house and on proportional representation in the other, and all legislation would require majority support of both. Jewish immigration into the Jewish state was to be allowed for three years within its absorptive capacity. Arbitration was to help in overcoming any deadlock between the states. These proposals were made by less than one-third of UNSCOP and the division of views between the majority and the minority reflected the division within the UN itself, as was to be confirmed three months later.

THE UN DECISION. The UNSCOP report occupied the center of the stage when the regular General Assembly met in New York on Sept. 16, 1947, although there were other important items on the agenda as well. The preliminary discussion on the report took place at an Ad Hoc Committee representing all member states, whose number had increased in the meantime: Yemen and Pakistan had been admitted to the United Nations, thus strengthening the Arab and Muslim front. Apart from that, no new alignments of forces were to be seen during the opening stages of the debate that lasted for over three weeks and was characterized by confusion. The main shift that soon became noticeable was in the tactics of the British delegation, which openly and actively canvassed for the rejection of partition. Arab delegations also increased their pressure. They were outspoken in their threats to Western, and particularly American, interests in their lands, and there were powerful economic and military factors in the United States, Britain, and France which could be—and were—activated in order to defeat the UNSCOP proposals. Indeed, initial American remarks on the subject were reserved and hesitant. On the other hand, threats voiced by the Arab Higher Committee to the effect that what will happen to the Jews in Palestine if the UNSCOP proposals were adopted would "exceed the horrors of Genghis Khan" had the opposite effect. It became clear to a growing number of UN members, and to great sectors of the general public opinion, that decisions must be taken which would prevent these threats being carried out. The Jewish Agency announced acceptance of the majority plan early in the debate. Weizmann's speech before the committee left a profound impression. His role in realizing the ultimate decision of the United Nations in favor of partition and the creation of a Jewish state was of prime importance. Though out of office, for the Zionist Congress in 1946 did not reelect him as president, thus symbolizing its commitment to a more activist policy, Weizmann continued to work both in London and in New York for the creation of a Jewish state. He was particularly successful in moving and impressing President Harry Truman, from whom he secured the binding promise to support the partition proposal, including an outlet on the Red Sea for the proposed Jewish state.

As the discussions progressed, attitudes began to crystallize. The United States and the Soviet Union came out openly for partition. After that, the prospects of the majority plan gaining the necessary two-thirds of the votes grew. More attempts were made to find a compromise, in subcommittees and in the corridors, but the persistent Arab demands for the establishment of what could only be an Arab state with a Jewish minority at the mercy of its adversaries led to the failure of all such efforts. An ominous warning also came from Britain: while accepting UNSCOP's unanimous opinion that the Mandate be terminated, it would take no implementation of a decision that was not acceptable to the parties. This meant noncooperation. The question of implementation became of utmost importance, especially after the British refused to extend their stay in Palestine even for a few weeks beyond May 15, 1948, or to help in the transfer of power to the authorities that were to be established in the Jewish and Arab states. The readiness of the Mandatory power to act in a way that was tantamount to sabotaging an international design for relieving it of a responsibility that had become too great to bear also had an opposite effect. It stiffened resistance to those who refused to accept the majority view. A vote in the Ad Hoc committee on November 24 rejected an Arab proposal for a unitary state by 29 to 12. On November 25 a vote was taken on the partition plan, somewhat amended by a subcommittee, and it was approved by 25 to 13. This was not yet the two-thirds majority needed in the plenary. Both sides were by now making exerted efforts to gain their objectives. After one or two postponements, which further increased the tension, the decisive vote came on November 29, and it was 33 for, 13 against, and 10 abstentions.

The wave of emotion which followed gave abundant evidence that not only the Jewish people saw the UN verdict as truly historic, but many other nations found in it an expression of the wish to right some of the wrongs of which Jews were victims, particularly the Nazi Holocaust. There were also grave warning signs. Arabs of Palestine reacted by widespread attacks on Jews; large numbers of armed men were coming in from across the borders to participate in those attacks; and Arab governments made no secret of their preparations for large-scale military action on the day of Britain's withdrawal. The UN appointed a small Palestine Commission to help in an organized transfer of power to provisional councils of government in the two proposed states, but the British refused to cooperate with it or even allow it to enter Palestine before the month of May. The commission also reported that while Arab and Jewish police supernumeraries were being organized in towns and villages, only the Arabs were getting arms from the British. Furthermore, while the British continued to supply arms to Arab governments, the United States imposed an embargo on all such supplies to the area, thus forcing the Jews to seek other sources, mainly in Eastern Europe.

A sense of frustration and helplessness was gradually enveloping the UN which saw the danger that its first major decision might end in failure. While the UN machinery was going through the motions (the Trusteeship Council, for instance, prepared a draft statute for an international administration of Jerusalem), reports from Palestine spoke of mounting disorder, of fighting and casualties, and of British preparations to leave in an atmosphere of what was then called "planned chaos." The implementation commission made partial progress in one sector only: in cooperation with the Jewish Agency for the establishment of the necessary authorities in the future Jewish state. The situation was repeatedly discussed in the Security Council, which had been told by the commission (February 1948) that it would not be able to fulfill its task without armed assistance. A debate started within the Council concerning its own authority: while it was agreed that it may use force for the preservation of peace, there was less agreement about the same right in respect to the enforcement of UN decisions. U.S. views were negative, and they were strongly criticized by the Soviet Union. On March 19 the United States proposed that the work of the Palestine Commission be suspended and a temporary UN trusteeship over the country be established. The proposal had been made by the State Department in Washington without the knowledge of President Truman, as he later explained. The State Department had also been strongly urging Zionist leaders to postpone action on the establishment of the Jewish state for at least a few months, a suggestion that was turned down by the majority of the Jewish Agency members. Furthermore, the U.S. proposed to call another special session of the Assembly to discuss the trusteeship idea.

The new session met on April 16, 1948, and was immediately bogged down in a procedural debate. The United States presented a working paper outlining details of a temporary trusteeship, providing for a government and essential public services in Palestine pending further negotiations. At the same time, the Trusteeship Council was asked by the General Assembly to study measures for the protection of Jerusalem, where fighting was then going on almost without interruption. On April 28 the Council came to an understanding with the parties concerned about a truce in the city, but reports from Jerusalem spoke of continued firing. On May 5 the Council recommended that before the Mandate expired on May 15, a special municipal commissioner for Jerusalem should be appointed by the Mandatory with Jewish and Arab consent. The candidate for the post never went to Jerusalem, as the Arabs refused to cooperate with him and there was no truce. On May 14, the last day of the Mandate, a Franco-American proposal to establish a temporary international regime in Jerusalem failed to get the necessary support. It had also become clear that the idea of a trusteeship over the whole of Palestine stood no chance. The only outcome of the discussions on that day had been the disbanding of the Palestine Commission and the decision to appoint a mediator, for which task Count Folke Bernadotte of Sweden was later chosen. With the hands of the clock moving toward 6 P.M. in New York (midnight in Palestine and the end of the Mandate), the struggle was still on. But even before the hour came, the United Nations was informed that the establishment of the State of Israel had already been proclaimed in Tel Aviv. A few minutes after 6 P.M. it was announced by the White House that President Truman recognized its provisional government as the de facto government of the new state. Soviet de jure recognition followed a few days later. On May 15, regular forces of Egypt, Syria, Lebanon, and Iraq, including Saudi Arabian contingents, and the Arab Legion of Transjordan with its British officers, invaded Israel, and its newborn defense forces took the field against them.

8 ZIONIST ORGANIZATION

History. The Zionist Organization was founded at the First Zionist Congress (convened by Theodor Herzl in Basle, 1897) as the structural framework of the organized Zionist movement, "comprising all Jews who accept the Zionist program and pay the shekel." The biblical name shekel was given to the membership fee of the Zionist Organization.

Though a rudimentary framework of a popular movement had been established by the Ḥibbat Zion, it was only through the foundation of the Zionist Organization that Zionism became a modern, democratic, mass movement, based on a worldwide interterritorial organization and equipped with instruments for political, settlement, and educational activities on a large scale. The most important of these instruments were created during Herzl's presidency (1897–1904): the Jewish Colonial Trust, to serve as the Zionist bank (1899); the Jewish National Fund (1901), for the acquisition of land as the inalienable property of the Jewish people; and *Die Welt* (1897), as the official organ of the organization.

Herzl died in 1904 before attaining his primary political aim, the Charter, i.e., the grant by the Ottoman authorities of political autonomy in, and the right of settlement of, Ereẓ Israel. The conflict over the Uganda Scheme at the Sixth Zionist Congress (1903) led to a split in the Zionist Organization. When the Seventh Congress (1905) rejected any settlement activities outside the Land of Israel, the Territorialists seceded from the Zionist Organization and founded the Jewish Territorial Organization, which, however, failed to play a significant part in Jewish life and, after the Balfour Declaration, disappeared from the public scene.

The growth of the Zionist Organization is best illustrated by the increase in the total number of shekels distributed: in the two-year period ending with the Eighth Zionist Congress (1907; for the former period, only the sums of the shekel revenues are available) there were 164,333; at the 11th Congress (1913) the number of shekels was 217,231; it steeply rose to 855,590 at the next Congress in 1921, the first to be held after World War I and the Balfour Declaration (although at that time most of Russian Jewry, the mainstay of Zionism, had already been cut off from the main body of the movement); at the 21st Congress, on the eve of World War II (1939), the number of shekel holders exceeded 1,000,000; and at the first postwar and last pre-state gathering, the 22nd Congress in 1946, the shekel figures indicated that 2,159,840 Jews were organized in the Zionist Organization. After Herzl's death, the seat of the organization was transferred from Vienna to Cologne, the residence of Herzl's successor, David Wolffsohn (1905–11). When Otto Warburg headed the organization (1911–20), Berlin became the Zionist capital, but World War I isolated it from the Zionists in the Allied countries, whose activities were centered in London. The purpose of the Zionist Liaison Office set up in 1915 in neutral Copenhagen was to facilitate the contact across the war fronts between the two sections of the organization. London was the capital of the Zionist world during the presidencies of Chaim Weizmann (1920–31 and 1935–46) and of Nahum Sokolow (1931–35), but in 1936 the center was transferred to Jerusalem, although London remained the seat of its president and of some members of the Executive.

When the 18th Congress (1933) had resolved that "in all Zionist matters the duty of discipline in regard of the Zionist Organization must take precedence over the discipline to any other body," the majority of the Zionist Revisionists, led by Vladimir Jabotinsky, seceded from the Zionist Organization and set up the New Zionist Organization, while a minority of Revisionists, under Meir Gross-

The Eighteenth Zionist Congress, Prague, 1933. Courtesy J.N.U.L. Photo Collection, Jerusalem. Photo Neckar, Prague.

man, remained in the ranks as the Jewish State Party. The split lasted until 1946, when the Revisionists returned to the parent body and renewed their participation in the Zionist Congresses.

The First Congress laid down only a rough outline of a few organizational rules. It was the Third Congress (1899) that adopted the first complete Constitution (Organisations-Statut) which, substituted by a more elaborated text adopted by the Fifth (1901) and the Tenth Congresses (1911), remained in force until 1921, when a thorough revision of the text and its adaptation to the changed conditions was effected by the 12th Congress. Minor amendments were adopted by each of the subsequent Congresses. In 1960 an entirely new Constitution came into force and thoroughly changed its structure (see below). The 25th and 26th Congresses (1960, 1964) made efforts to broaden the basis of the Zionist Organization by the admission of associate members, i.e., Jewish bodies which endorse the Zionist program without obliging their members to be organized Zionists. These efforts were initiated and supported by the fifth president of the Zionist Organization, Nahum Goldmann (1956–68), who assumed

Vladimir Jabotinsky, head of Betar, presenting the flag to the Kovno unit of the Revisionist youth movement, 1933. Courtesy Jabotinsky Institute in Israel, Tel Aviv.

the presidency after the office had been vacant for ten years.

The 27th Congress (1968) adopted the greater part of the recommendations submitted by the Commission on Reorganization, which had been set up by the preceding Congress, and resolved to amend the Constitution accordingly. These amendments, however, affected details like Congress elections or the participation of youth in Zionist territorial organizations, rather than the general pattern and basic provisions of the Constitution.

STRUCTURE. Before the Zionist Organization was divided into parties, it had been organized on a purely territorial basis. According to its early Constitution, the members were organized in local societies that were grouped into regional units, which were in turn subordinated to territorial committees in charge of Zionist affairs in the country concerned. With the emergence of ideological trends and groupings, a type of dualism became characteristic of the structure of the Zionist Organization. According to the Constitution of 1921, the Zionist Organization was structured both horizontally and vertically: on the one hand, there were countrywide organizations comprising all Zionists without regard to their views on special issues—Zionist territorial unions with local branches; on the other, Zionists subscribing to a certain ideology, or, as the Constitution put it, "representing a special point of view," were, under certain conditions, given the privilege of forming a separate union (Sonderverband) which set up territorial branches. The first separate union was the Mizrachi (1902); the Po'alei Zion followed in 1907; Ha-Shomer ha-Ẓa'ir and the Jewish State Party were founded as separate unions after World War I. The Ancient Order of Maccabeans, established in Britain at an early stage of the movement, soon became defunct.

During the first decades of activity, the separate unions represented only a small minority of the membership. At the 12th Congress (1921) the delegates affiliated with the territorial unions numbered 376, while those of all separate unions totaled only 136. The membership and strength of the separate unions steadily grew, however, and at the last Congress before World War II (1939) the proportion was reversed: the delegates of the territorial unions numbered 171 and those of the separate unions 386. Furthermore, at the beginning the members of the Zionist territorial unions were called General Zionists, simply denoting all those who did not belong to any separate union; but a tendency rose and finally prevailed within the General Zionists to adopt an ideology of their own and to transform themselves into a party like the others. Furthermore, this group often split into two wings, at first called Groups A and B, and since the 24th Congress (1956) known as the Union and the Confederation of General Zionists, respectively. On the other hand, the difference between the separate unions and parties not registered as such became blurred and, apart from a few purely formal privileges of the former, ceased to exist for all practical purposes. Because of this differentiation between territorial and separate unions, the Zionist movement in some countries almost disintegrated into several independent parties without common framework, apart from joint committees established for special purposes like the shekel and election boards. As a reaction to this "atomization," several Congresses declared that a United Zionist Federation, based on individual membership and comprising all parties and groups, be compulsory in every country. These and later resolutions, which again made the establishment of a joint territorial framework obligatory, but were content with the collective membership of parties in so-called Zionist Federations, largely remained unimplemented.

The structure of the Zionist Organization underwent a profound change with the promulgation of a new Constitution in 1960. It introduced a new official name, the World Zionist Organization (although the traditional one, Zionist Organization, is still more frequently used); the shekel remained in existence as a token of Zionist allegiance and voting card, but members of the Zionist Organization were no longer individual shekel-payers but collective bodies only, namely Zionist territorial organizations and Zionist territorial and interterritorial associations. The former are either Zionist unions based on the membership of individual Zionists (like that of the Netherlands), or Zionist Federations based on the collective membership of Zionist bodies (like that of Belgium), or mixed Zionist Federations based on the membership both of bodies and individuals (like that of France). Examples of Zionist territorial and interterritorial associations are Hadassah and WIZO (incidentally, the two largest Zionist bodies in the world).

The Constitution of 1960 introduced a far-reaching reform of decentralization. According to the legal construction underlying the Constitution, the Zionist Organization is the "body authorized by its members to act for and on behalf of the movement and all the members for the implementation of the Zionist program." Emphasis is placed on the autonomy of the members: "Every member shall determine the conduct of his affairs, the form of his organization and procedure." Bodies that were affiliated with the Zionist Organization when the new Constitution came into force were considered members under its

Mizrachi conference in Lida, Poland, 1903. Among those present are: 1) Isaac Rabinowitz, 2) Jacob Moreno, 3) Mordecai Dov Judilovitz, 4) Moses Cohen, 5) Zisel Rubinstein, 6) Jacob Berman, 7) Rabbi Esterson, 8) Rabbi Stern, 9) Nahum Greenhaus, 10) Judah Leib (Fishman) Maimon, 11) Rabbi Bramson, 12) Joseph Lamdan, 13) S. J. Drozed, 14) Isaac Jacob Reines, 15) Pinḥas Rosovsky, 16) Rabbi Bernstein, 17) Rabbi Amitin, 18) Jacob Greenberg, 19) Samuel Alexandrov, 20) Samuel Waltesman, 21) Pesaḥ Friedland, 22) Abraham Saul Gusman, 23) Abraham Jacob Slutzky, 24) Ephraim Moshevitsky, 25) Zalman Kleinman, 26) Rabbi Melamed.

provisions. New members may be admitted by the Congress or General Council, provided they comply with a number of conditions laid down in the Constitution. One of these provisions is that the body "has regard to the protection of the requirements of all its members and to the fundamental principles of justice." (On the membership of national and international Jewish bodies, see above.)

GOVERNING BODIES. The pattern of internal organization very much resembles that of a sovereign state: the shekel payers are comparable to citizens, the Congress elected by them—and to a certain degree also the General Council—is similar to a parliament, the Executive resembles the government or administration of a country, and the Congress Tribunal and the attorney of the Zionist Organization are its "judicial branch." On the other hand, the Zionist Organization differs from a state in two important respects: it is an interterritorial body and not limited by national frontiers; and it is built on a purely voluntary basis, with no means of enforcing its decisions. The ultimate and gravest sanction it may impose is expulsion from its ranks.

THE ZIONIST CONGRESS. The Congress is the supreme organ of the Zionist Organization. It legislates, receives and considers reports from other organs, determines the financial policy, and elects the president, Executive, General Council, Congress Tribunal, attorney, and comptroller. Until the 26th Congress (1964) the shekel payers chose the Congress either by direct elections or by "unopposed elections," by means of a "united slate" arrived at through interparty agreements. The 27th Congress (1968) was not based on elections but, in accordance with special regulations enacted after the Six-Day War (1967), had the same composition as its predecessor. It decided that future Congresses should not be elected according to a uniform election system, but that each country should itself determine the method of elections of its Congress delegates, provided it does not conflict with generally accepted democratic principles. Until the 24th

WIZO delegation to the Twelfth Zionist Congress, Carlsbad, 1921. Left to right: Miriam Marks, Miriam Sacher, Edith Eder, Rebecca Sieff, Mrs. Weisberg (standing), Lady Samuel, Romana Goodman, Esther Feiwel, Henrietta Irwell, Ethel Solomon. Courtesy Central Zionist Archives, Jerusalem.

Congress (1956) the number of delegates allotted to an election area (country) was in direct proportion to the number of shekels sold there. Under the Constitution of 1960, however, the size of the representation is fixed by a special commission "having regard to the size of the Jewish population and the totality of the conditions and activities of the Zionist movement in the country concerned."

In Herzl's time Congress met every year (apart from 1902); until 1939 it convened once every two years (with the exception of World War I). The Constitution of 1960 legalized the practice of a four-year inter-Congress period.

THE GENERAL COUNCIL. The longer the intervals between Congresses, the greater the importance attaching to the Zionist General Council, also known by its original name of Herzl's times as Actions Committee. During the inter-Congress period, it has not only legislative functions, but "shall consider and decide upon all matters relating to the Zionist Organization and its institutions." The number of Council members with voting rights in 1968 was 110, compared with 25 in 1921. The Council meets at least once a year no later than March, since the budgetary year of the Zionist Organization terminates on March 31 and one of the Council's prerogatives is to decide on the budget in years when no Congress is held. It discharges this function either itself or through its Permanent Budget and Finance Committee. It has become general practice that the Congress or the Council fixes the framework of the budget, while the details are determined by the committee acting upon the proposals of the Executive. In the course of years the importance of the Council has grown because "delegated legislation" has become increasingly frequent, i.e., the Congress has authorized the Council to make decisions or take steps within the jurisdiction of the Congress. Thus, even the Constitution of 1960 was adopted by the Council and not by the Congress. The Council's membership exactly reflects the composition of the Congress, each grouping being represented by a number of members equal to a fifth of its Congress delegation. Apart from these members with full rights, the Constitution provides for members in an advisory capacity who are entitled to speak but not to vote in the Council's sessions, such as the members of the Executive or Zionist personalities who have been granted seats as "virilists" (i.e., veteran Zionists who are given a seat for their personal merits).

During World War II and up to the 22nd Congress (1946), an Inner General Council in Jerusalem composed of 31 members exercised all functions of the full Council, which could not meet. The presidium of the General Council, consisting of its chairman and 18 members, conducts the meetings of the Council, represents it in external and internal matters, and discharges various duties "imposed by law or referred to by Congress or Council."

THE EXECUTIVE. According to the Constitution of 1960, the Executive, elected by the Congress, is "its executive organ charged with the implementation of the decisions of Congress and Council and responsible to these bodies." Its seat and head office is in Jerusalem, but the Executive may "establish one or more divisions abroad." The branch in London was abolished shortly after the proclamation of the State of Israel (1948), but there is a New York section whose members join their Jerusalem colleagues several times a year for plenary sessions at which general policy is formulated. Day-to-day matters are handled in the almost weekly meetings of the Jerusalem Executive. The Executive acts through its departments, generally headed by one or more of its members. In 1972 the following main departments were in existence: Immigration and Absorption, Youth Aliyah, Youth and He-Ḥalutz, Settlement, Organization, Information, External Relations, Education and Culture—and Torah Education and Culture—in the Diaspora, Treasury, and Administration. Over the years no other governing body of the Zionist Organization has grown in size as much as the Executive, which, originally called the Small Actions Committee, initially numbered five and after Herzl's death seven members. The Executive elected at the first post-World War I Congress (1921) had only 15 members, but that appointed by the 23rd Congress (1951) numbered 19 members and two deputies, while that elected in 1966 included 26 regular members (one without voting rights—WIZO) and one deputy. The 27th Congress (1968) reversed this trend, reducing the number of the Executive members to 14 (among them one representative each of the WIZO and the Sephardim) and empowering the General Council to co-opt up to 5 nonparty Zionist personalities.

THE PRESIDENT. The president elected by the Congress is "the head and chief representative" of the Zionist Organization. He has the full rights of an Executive member. The actual standing of the president is determined less by his constitutional status than by his personality and activities. No president was elected at the 22nd Congress (1946) and until 1956 Nahum Goldmann and Berl Locker co-chaired the Executive. In 1956 Goldmann was elected president of the Zionist Organization until 1968, when, at the 27th

Congress, no president was elected, but Louis Aryeh Pincus was chairman of the Executive from 1965.

THE JUDICIAL ORGANS. The judicial organs of the Zionist Organization are the Congress Tribunal and the attorney. According to the Constitution of 1960, the Congress Tribunal combines the functions of the former Congress Court and Court of Honor. It consists of a maximum of 25 members including the chairman and up to five deputy-chairmen. The Congress Tribunal had jurisdiction to interpret the Constitution; to examine the legality of decisions of central Zionist bodies; to determine disputes between one central Zionist body and another or an individual—except in financial matters; to deal with objections to a postponement of the Congress or a Council session; to verify Congress elections; to deal with appeals from territorial judicial bodies and against decisions of the committees determining the number of Congress delegates and the system of Congress elections; to deal with complaints that the Constitution was infringed or that the interest and prestige of the Zionist Organization damaged. The attorney of the Zionist Organization (formerly Congress Attorney) is charged with representing the interests of the organization before the Congress Tribunal and advising central Zionist bodies in legal matters.

THE COMPTROLLER. The comptroller and his office are a counterpart to the state comptroller of Israel or the comptroller and auditor general of Great Britain. The comptroller's task is to "inspect the financial and economic activities of the Zionist Organization and its institutions and officers of every kind."

ZIONIST ORGANIZATION AND THE JEWISH AGENCY. The term Jewish Agency for Palestine was coined by the Mandate for Palestine promulgated by the League of Nations in 1922, whose article 4 made provision for "the recognition of an appropriate Jewish Agency as a public body for the purpose of advising and cooperating with the Administration of Palestine in such economic, social, and other matters as may affect the establishment of the Jewish

National Home and the interests of the Jewish population of Palestine." The Mandate designated the Zionist Organization as the Jewish Agency it envisioned, and until 1929 it functioned in that capacity, i.e., the Zionist Organization and the Jewish Agency were one and the same body. The position changed when at Weizmann's initiative the enlarged Jewish Agency was established at the 16th Zionist Congress (1929) "for discharging the functions of the Jewish Agency as set forth in the Mandate," on the principle of parity between Zionists and "non-Zionists," i.e., Jewish persons and bodies supporting the building of the National Home, without identifying themselves with the political aspirations of Zionism. Thereafter the Zionist Organization and the Jewish Agency were two different bodies, though headed by the same president. When the last "non-Zionist" member of the Jewish Agency Executive, Werner Senator, resigned in 1947, the complete identity between the Executives of the two institutions was reestablished. This identity existed until 1971. It was confirmed and stressed in the Israel Law on the Status (see below). In that period the difference between the two bodies was one of terminology rather than substance. In practice the name Zionist Organization indicated the activities and functions in respect to the Diaspora, while the designation Jewish Agency was mostly used in connection with work in and for Israel.

After the Six-Day War, when formerly uncommitted sections of the Jewish people identified themselves with the State of Israel to an unprecedented extent, the proposition to enlarge the Jewish Agency and reinstate its separation from the Zionist Organization was again put forward. The 27th Zionist Congress in 1968 authorized the Executive to initiate negotiations with "fund-raising instruments for Israel" with a view to "establishing a direct relationship between the Jewish Agency and such bodies." A year later the General Council approved the principles of the enlargement; in August 1970 the "Agreement on the Reconstitution of the Jewish Agency" was initialed, and on

June 21, 1971, it was signed. Since then the World Zionist Organization and the Jewish Agency have again been two independent and separate bodies, although—similar to the pattern of 1929—50% of the members of the governing bodies of the Jewish Agency are designated by the World Zionist Organization, the chairman of the Zionist Executive is chairman of the Assembly and of the Executive of the Jewish Agency, and they have in common a treasurer and comptroller. The agreement included a division of functions between the Jewish Agency and the Zionist Organization, according to which the latter will "continue as the organ of the Zionist movement for the fulfillment of Zionist programs and ideals." Its main field of activity is the Diaspora, and it deals with Zionist organization, information, youth and He-Ḥalutz (pioneering movements), education and culture, external relations, and the activities of the Jewish National Fund, and also encourages and promotes *aliyah* from free countries.

Zionist Organization and the State of Israel. In April 1948, one month before the proclamation of the State of Israel, the Zionist General Council resolved that after the establishment of the Provisional Government of Israel, "the jurisdiction of the Zionist Executive should comprise settlement, immigration, and all related matters including Youth Aliyah, Zionist information, organization, propaganda and culture, education in the Diaspora, youth and He-Ḥalutz, the development of Jerusalem and the National Funds." This principle of separation of functions was confirmed in a somewhat modified form by the resolution of the subsequent session of the General Council in August/September 1948 and of the 23rd Congress in 1951. Accordingly, while some functions previously exercised by the Zionist Organization have naturally devolved on the government, other functions remained the sole responsibility of the Zionist Organization-Jewish Agency. In Israel law the mutual relations between the State of Israel and the Zionist Organization-Jewish Agency were put on a firm legal basis by the Law on the Status of the World Zionist Organization-The Jewish Agency—5713 (1952), article 4 of which declares: "The State of Israel recognizes the World Zionist Organization as the authorized agency which will continue to operate in the State of Israel for the development and settlement of the country, the absorption of immigrants from the Diaspora and the coordination of activities in Israel of Jewish institutions and organizations active in those fields." The details of this status and the forms of collaboration between the Zionist Organization-Jewish Agency Executive and the government of Israel were, as foreseen in article 7 of the law, determined by a "covenant" entered into by them in 1954. A special committee consisting of an equal number of government ministers and Zionist Executive members was set up to coordinate activities, but in practice the delineation of the functions of the Zionist Organization-Jewish Agency has remained in a state of flux. After the Six-Day War proposals were made to increase the government's responsibility for the integration of the immigrants and were widely discussed in Israel and the Diaspora. In June 1968 the government decided to create a special Ministry for Absorption, with the understanding that even after its establishment, certain aspects of absorption of immigrants would remain in the domain of the Executive of the Zionist Organization-Jewish Agency.

9 ZIONISM IN MANY LANDS

In Australia and New Zealand. Zionism developed more slowly in Australia than in other British dominions. An attempt by Leon Jona to establish a Zionist society in Adelaide after the First Zionist Congress (1897) failed. The first Zionist bodies in the Commonwealth of Australia were the Victorian Zionist League in Melbourne (founded 1907) and the Sydney Zionist Society (1908); from 1913 a West Australian Zionist Society (Perth) was also in existence. In Australia's sister dominion, New Zealand, there were Zionist associations at the time in Auckland and Wellington; the former had developed from a Ḥovevei Zion society founded as early as 1903. Nonetheless, as the Sydney Zionist Society, the most active of these bodies, wrote in a report to Zionist headquarters at Cologne in 1911, "there were comparatively few enthusiastic Zionists in Australia" and the attitude of the great majority of the Jewish community toward the movement was "apathy, though not hostility." In 1911 the first delegate from Australia, Salomon Pechter of Sydney, made his appearance at the Tenth Zionist Congress in Basle. During the so-called language conflict in Ereẓ Israel in 1914, the Zionist societies in Australia came out strongly in favor of Hebrew and against German as the language of instruction at the newly founded Technion of Haifa.

Efforts to bring all Zionist bodies in the various cities into the common framework of an Australian Federation had begun in 1908. Some bodies, like the Victorian Zionist Association, were directly affiliated with the Zionist Federation of Great Britain. It was only after World War I and the Balfour Declaration that the first all-Australian Zionist Conference took place in Melbourne (1927) and that the Zionist Federation of Australia and New Zealand was established, on the initiative of Alexander Goldstein. Although its name continued to include New Zealand, the Zionist Council of New Zealand has virtually become an independent organization (close cooperation with the Australian Federation notwithstanding) and has been represented by its own delegates at the Zionist Congresses.

Sir John Monash, who had been commander-in-chief of the Australian army in World War I, was elected honorary president of the Zionist Federation. However, the other most distinguished personality of Australian Jewry, Sir Isaac Isaacs, who had been chief justice and governor general of the Commonwealth, was an anti-Zionist, and during World War II he conducted a press campaign against the Zionists, charging them with disloyalty to Britain and denying the existence of a Jewish people. Rabbi Israel Brodie, later chief rabbi of the British Empire, served as president of the federation from its foundation until he left Australia in 1937.

During the economic depression at the beginning of the 1930s, the federation declined and its very existence was called in question, but it recovered again toward the end of that decade. During World War II its importance and prestige considerably rose as a result of its political and public relations work. The atmosphere for such activities was favorable because general public opinion in Australia was rather friendly to Zionism. Some strongly pro-Zionist Christian sects, like the Christadelphians, were active there. They even raised funds for Zionist causes. The pro-Zionist sentiment in the Commonwealth was also partly due to the excellent relations between the *yishuv* in Palestine and the Australian troops stationed there during both world wars. Australian statesmen Robert Menzies, Ben Chifley, and John Curtin (prime minister during World War II) were supporters of the Zionist cause. Particularly important was the role of Herbert Evatt, a personal friend of some Zionist leaders and an advocate of the idea of a Jewish state, who as foreign minister was elected chairman of the UN Palestine Ad Hoc Committee (1947). In this capacity he thwarted delaying maneuvers, and firmly directed the proceedings of the committee which culminated in the positive vote for the partition of Palestine in the General Assembly on Nov. 29, 1947.

Characteristic of Zionist life in Australia has been a certain competition, even to the point of rivalry, between the main Jewish centers: Sydney in New South Wales and Melbourne in Victoria. It has become traditional for the federation to transfer its seat periodically from one city to the other. Thus the 24th Australian Zionist Conference held in Melbourne in 1970 decided that the headquarters of the federation should be in Sydney for the next four years. Like the Commonwealth of Australia, the Australian Zionist Federation is organized on federative lines in state Zionist councils (New South Wales, Victoria, Queensland, West Australia,

Israel exhibition in Melbourne, Australia, 1952. Photo City Studio, Melbourne.

and South Australia) to which all Zionist societies, bodies, and groups of the state are affiliated. There was a total of 60 such bodies in 1972. A distinctive feature of the Australian Zionist Federation is that it embraces all organizations and institutions which are in any way connected with the work for, and support of, Israel. The Jewish National Fund had remained very strong and popular, and Zionist influence is predominant in the Australian Jewish communal institutions.

While the beginnings of Zionism in Australia were slow and precarious, from the later 1960s this community was one of the most Zionist-oriented in the Diaspora. During the Six-Day War between Israel and the Arab states (1967), several hundred young Australian Jews registered as volunteers for Israel, but only a few managed to arrive there in time to aid the war effort. The Zionist Membership Drive 1970/71 resulted in about 13,000 members, i.e., almost 20% of the total Jewish population in the Commonwealth of Australia.

In Austria. Austria, as referred to in this article, is understood as the territory of the Austrian Federal Republic as it existed from 1918 to 1938 and again from 1945. The history of Austrian Zionism, in this territorial sense, is almost identical with that of Vienna, where more than 90% of Austrian Jews were concentrated.

Vienna, then the capital of the Hapsburg monarchy with a Jewish population of about two million, had been one of the centers of the nascent Jewish national movement even before Herzl's appearance on the stage of history. Several Jewish national student associations existed, the most notable being Kadimah (founded in 1883). Even the name Zionism was coined in Vienna by Nathan Birnbaum, the most prominent ideologist of these early Zionists. When Herzl published *Der Judenstaat,* he found enthusiastic followers among these forerunners of political Zionism and many other young Jews, particularly students, but met stiff opposition in the Jewish liberal bourgeoisie and the Jewish community establishment. Since Herzl was a resident of Vienna, that city was during his lifetime the capital of Zionism, i.e., the seat of the Zionist Executive (the Inner Actions Committee), the central Zionist organ *Die Welt,* and the Jewish National Fund. Viennese Zionists like Johann Kremenetzky, M. Schnirer, Alexander Marmorek, and Oser Kokesch occupied key positions in the Inner Actions Committee. It was also in Vienna that the first Zionist-Socialist movement, Aḥva, emerged in 1898, upon the initiative of Saul Raphael Landau.

After Herzl's death, Vienna lost its central position in the Zionist world movement, the central institutions having been transferred to Cologne, but Zionism remained a vibrant movement in Austria, albeit with a change of emphasis and leadership. The trend was now on practical Zionism, both in respect to settlement work in Ereẓ Israel and in Jewish national politics in the Diaspora ("Work in the present"), greatly invigorated after the introduction of universal suffrage in 1907. The leaders of the movement in the period prior to World War I were Adolf Boehm, Robert Stricker, and Jacob Ehrlich. In 1909, 25 Zionist societies existed in Austria, mostly in Vienna, organized in the Zionistischer Landesverband. The 11th Zionist Congress (1913) was held in Vienna. The great influx of refugees from Galicia during World War I and the obvious victory of the principle of national self-determination at the end of the war further strengthened the Zionist movement.

After the dismemberment of the multi-national Hapsburg monarchy and the establishment of the Austrian Republic, a Jewish National Council was established on Zionist initiative. In the first elections Robert Stricker was elected on a Zionist ticket to parliament and three Zionists to the city council of Vienna. But after some time there was a sharp decline in the Zionist following, mainly due to the attraction of the Social-Democratic Party, which had many Jewish leaders, almost all of them assimilationists and opponents of Zionism. Even in that period of decline there was,

Members of the Vienna students' Zionist association, Bar Kochba, 1905. Courtesy Central Zionist Archives, Jerusalem.

however, a bustling and very diversified Zionist activity going on. There were scores of Zionist associations, parties, youth movements, cultural clubs, sports associations, etc. Vienna was the most important transit place for immigrants to Palestine and, therefore, an important meeting place. Upon the initiative of Rabbi Ẓevi Pereẓ Chajes, who had been appointed chief rabbi of Vienna in 1918, a Hebrew teachers' seminary has been established, as well as a secondary school, bearing (after Chajes' death) his name.

From 1918 until 1927 a Zionist daily, the *Wiener Morgenzeitung,* appeared, as well as several weeklies. In 1925 the 14th Zionist Congress assembled in Vienna. In 1932 the Zionists succeeded in realizing Herzl's slogan of the "conquest of the communities," gaining 20 out of 36 seats in the Jewish community council. Desider Friedmann was elected president of the community. Zionists stood, therefore, at the helm of Austrian Jewry when the catastrophe befell them in 1938. From the Nazi conquest in March 1938 until the outbreak of World War II in September 1939, about one-half of Austrian Jewry succeeded in leaving the country, many of them for Palestine, mostly by "illegal" routes. Almost all of the remaining Jews fell victim of the Holocaust; among them were prominent leaders of Austrian Zionists, like Desider Friedmann, Robert Stricker, and many others.

After World War II Austria was the scene of great Zionist activity, being located on the main route of the *beriḥah*[22] and

[22]Escape movement from E. Europe en route to Palestine

Youngsters from *beriḥah* transit camps in Vienna dance the *horah* before leaving for Ereẓ Israel, 1946. Courtesy Ephraim Deckel, Tel Aviv.

harboring in its confines many camps of Jewish D.P.s. In the small reconstituted Jewish community of Vienna a diversified Zionist activity started, all Zionist parties reemerged, but for most of the postwar period the Zionists constituted a minority of the community, while the majority supported the non-Zionist, albeit not anti-Israel, Social-Democratic Bund werktaetiger Juden.

In Bulgaria. A large part of the predominantly Sephardi and Ladino-speaking Jewish community of Bulgaria was always strongly attached to Zionism, although enjoying full civic rights since the establishment of independent Bulgaria (1878). They were not under pressure to emigrate and suffered little from anti-Semitism. Even before Herzl's appearance, there were Zionist societies like Ezrat Aḥim in Sofia, Carmel in Plovdiv (Philippopolis), and Dorshei Zion in Khaskovo. Bulgarian Jews founded the settlement Hartuv in Ereẓ Israel as early as 1896, the same year in which Herzl was surprised and moved by the enthusiastic welcome accorded to him by masses of Jews when his train stopped at the Sofia railway station en route to Constantinople.

Bulgaria was represented at the First Zionist Congress (1897) by Ẓevi Belkovsky, Yehoshua Caleb, and Carl Herbst. Marcus Ehrenpreis, who became chief rabbi of Bulgaria, had taken a very active part in preparing the Congress and also attended it. The first Bulgarian Zionist Conference took place in 1898 in Plovdiv, which was the Zionist center before Sofia. The leader of political Zionism in Bulgaria during its first stage was, until his death (1899), Josef Marcou Baruch.

The rapid spread of Zionist societies encountered some opposition on the part of the assimilationists influenced by the French education in the Alliance Israélite Universelle schools, but they were less strong than in other countries. However, the Zionists quickly "conquered the communities," in accordance with Herzl's demand. In 1900 they initiated the convocation of the First National Congress of Bulgarian Jewry, which adopted statutes transforming synagogue groups into veritable communities. The second congress in 1920 already had a Zionist majority and proclaimed the religious and national solidarity of all Jewish inhabitants of the country, regardless of origin, language, or citizenship. Another congress took place in 1932. The publication of the central Zionist organ *Ha-Shofar* was started in 1901. Due to Zionist influence, in the 1920s Hebrew became the language of instruction (apart from subjects like Bulgarian history and literature) at all schools maintained by the Consistory, the central Jewish community organization, which were attended by the great majority of Jewish children.

Between the two world wars Alberto Romano, for many years chairman of the Zionist Federation of Bulgaria, and Ḥayyim Aaron Farḥi, chairman of the Consistory and member of the Bulgarian parliament, were among the most important figures in Zionist life. The movement became diversified, and parties and youth movements were set up. The Bulgarian WIZO was founded in 1923; in 1930 Maccabi had more than 3,300 members in 24 clubs; the number of shekel holders reached 8,000, a much higher percentage of the population than in most countries; He-Ḥalutz was training its members for *aliyah* in training farms, such as that near Pazardzhik. After the Revisionist secession from the World Zionist Organization (1935), the New Zionist Organization set up branches of the Betar movement. They issued their own weekly *Razsvet*. One of their leaders, Benjamin Arditti, was afterward a member of the Israel Knesset from the Ḥerut list.

Hundreds of Bulgarian Jews settled in Palestine during the Mandate period. Some of them established their own settlements, like the moshavim Kefar Ḥittin near Tiberias and Bet Ḥanan south of Tel Aviv. Members of Ha-Shomer ha-Ẓa'ir who settled in Palestine before 1935 founded five kibbutzim.

The Zionists of Bulgaria were active in organizing "illegal" immigration to Palestine before and immediately after World War

ивъ 9 ноемврий 1935 год. БРОЯ 3 ЛЕВА Брой 54

Ционизмътъ се стреми ... въ
Палестина едно гарантирано отъ публичното право убежище за еврейския народ. — Базелска

Masthead of *Ha-Shofar,* the Zionist weekly in Hebrew and Bulgarian published in Plovdiv, November 1935. Jerusalem, Yad Vashem Archives.

II. They also assisted Jews from other countries, who fled the Nazis or pro-Nazi regimes, to embark on "illegal" transports from Bulgarian ports to Palestine. All Zionist activities had to cease under the Fascist regime during World War II, but immediately after the country's liberation a Zionist Conference was convened (1944) and a Zionist organ *Zionisticheska Tribuna* published. In 1946 a United Zionist Organization was set up. In the same year more than 14,000 shekels were distributed and almost 9,000 voters took part in the elections to the 22nd Zionist Congress, at which Bulgaria was represented by four delegates.

The Communist regime, under Georgi Dimitrov, at first displayed sympathy for the newborn State of Israel and permitted all Bulgarian Jews who wished to go to Israel to do so without placing any obstacles in their way. Thus, in the years 1944–49, a real exodus of Bulgarian Jews took place, when 40,000 of them settled in Israel. However, in accordance with the policy of the Soviet bloc, this attitude changed, and in 1949 all Zionist bodies had to disband "voluntarily" and all Zionist activities ceased.

In Canada. In 1898, one year after the First Zionist Congress, a Zionist society, Agudat Zion, was formed in Montreal. One year later, five more societies came into existence in Quebec and Ontario and formed The Federation of Zionist Societies, electing Clarence I. De Sola as its first president. The number of Zionist societies increased gradually and conventions were held annually. With the outbreak of World War I, all Zionist work practically came to a standstill, as contact with the *yishuv* was severed; however, the Balfour Declaration revitalized the Zionist activities.

The year 1919 was a turning point in the affairs of the Zionist Federation; De Sola stepped down from the presidency and was succeeded by A. J. Freiman of Ottawa, and Lilian Freiman organized the Canadian Hadassah Organization. One year later, Keren Hayesod began its activities. Within the next four years the Labor Zionist Organization was formed. It sponsored a program for Palestine based on a synthesis of socialism and Jewish nationalism. During the same period the Mizrachi Organization was organized by religious Zionists. All these groups participated actively in the Keren Hayesod-United Palestine (Israel) Appeal and the Jewish National Fund (JNF). In 1924 the Labor Zionists added their own annual campaign, which was called the Geverkshaften (later Histadrut) Campaign; M. Dickstein played an important role in this activity. Each of the organizations also organized national women's branches—Hadassah (affiliated with WIZO), Mizrachi Women, Pioneer Women—each conducting active programs and substantial campaigns for institutions in Palestine and later also for Youth Aliyah. The parent bodies also organized youth movements: Young Judea was begun in 1916 by Bernard Joseph (who later, as Dov Joseph, was military governor of Jerusalem during the siege of 1948 and occupied important cabinet positions in subsequent Israel governments); the Habonim Labor Zionist organization and Junior Hadassah were formed later.

Organization. In 1966 the Federated Zionist Organization of Canada (F.Z.O.C.) was established to unify all the existing Zionist organizations into a single framework. It includes the following bodies: (1) The Zionist Organization of Canada, the oldest and largest of the Zionist organizations, which has branches in most of the sizable communities, as well as fraternal orders in the larger cities. It holds regional conferences regularly, and together with the women's organization, Hadassah (WIZO), and the other Zionist movements, influences the Canadian Jewish community in a large measure. (2) The Labor Zionist Movement, a federative structure of autonomous Labor Zionist bodies which embraces the United Labor Zionist Party (Po'alei Zion), now united with Aḥdut ha-Avodah; the Farband Labor Zionist Order; and the Pioneer Women of Canada; as well as Habonim Labor Zionist Youth; and the Israel Histadrut Campaign. (3) The Mizrachi-Ha-Po'el

Delegates to the convention of the Zionist Organization of Canada, Montreal, 1950. Left to right: Samuel J. Zacks, Meyer Weisgal (U.S.), Sam Schwisberg, Q.C., Justice Douglas Abbot, Edward E. Gelber, Justice Harry Batshaw, Leon D. Crestohl, Q.C Federal Photos, Montreal.

ha-Mizrachi Organization of Canada, which has three offices (in Montreal, Toronto, and Winnipeg) and a Mishmeret Ẓe'irah of young couples in these centers, as well as its youth movement and a women's division. (4) The Zionist Revisionist Movement of Canada, with its youth movement, Betar, and women's organization. (5) The Friends of Pioneering Israel, which is closely affiliated with Mapam in Israel.

The Federated Zionist Organization publishes a monthly entitled *The Canadian Zionist.* The United Labor Zionist Party (Labor Zionist Party and Aḥdut ha-Avodah-Po'alei Zion, affiliated in 1970) publishes *Dos Vort* in Yiddish and English, and a quarterly, *Viewpoints.* Hadassah publishes *Orah, Campaigns and Projects.* The United Israel Campaigns, which have been carried on annually, averaged $3,000,000–3,500,000 (Canadian) a year between 1960 and 1967. In the latter year a special Emergency Campaign brought in an additional $30,000,000. In addition, since 1953 there has been an annual sale of State of Israel bonds, initiated under the leadership of Samuel Bronfman and E. E. Gelber. In the first year there were over 10,000 subscribers, with a net sale of $4,500,000. Subsequently there was an annual sale of $3,000,000–3,500,000 up to 1967, which rose thereafter to $4,000,000–5,000,000 annually. The Jewish National Fund has been functioning since the beginning of Zionist activities in Canada. It has concentrated on "Traditional Funds," which link the fund with special occasions in Jewish family life, such as bar mitzvahs and weddings. In addition, it has initiated and sponsored special projects, such as the "Negev Dinners," for acquiring funds to plant forests and develop new land projects in Israel. These projects have brought in considerable sums of money over the years.

In 1927 Canadian Zionists bought a tract of 30,000 dunams on the shores of the Mediterranean for $1,000,000, and it was developed as Emek Ḥefer. In 1952 a convention of Canadian Zionists undertook to redeem an area of 50,000 dunams in the western Negev. In 1955 the JNF of Canada began a project to plant 500,000 trees at Ein Kerem in the Judean Hills, to be known as the Canadian Forest. Canadian Hadassah has sponsored such projects as the Agricultural School for Girls at Nahalal; the Hadassim Children's Village; a hydrotherapy pool for crippled children at Sarafand; a child guidance clinic in Jerusalem; baby crèches; and "Canada Hall" at the Hebrew University. Likewise, the Histadrut Campaign has sponsored a number of special Canadian projects in Israel, particularly the Amal vocational schools. The Pioneer Women have established Omna, a children's home in Haifa, and a community center at Migdal ha-Emek and have helped maintain the many institutions of the Mo'eẓet ha-Po'alot (Working Women's Council in Israel). In 1955, the Mizrachi Organization began to raise funds for the new Bar Ilan University, and the Mizrachi Women have sponsored a number of their own projects. The Zionist Revisionist group and their women's organization, Jordania, also have special projects. In addition, the Friends of the Hebrew University was organized in 1944 under the national chairmanship of Allan Bronfman. There is also a Canadian Technion Society, led by D. Lou Harris until his death in 1972, as well as a group interested in the Weizmann Institute at Reḥovot, in which Samuel J. Zacks, a past president of the Zionist Organization of Canada, was very active during his lifetime.

The various Zionist organizations have summer camps for youth. In the 1970s the Zionist Organization of Canada operated eight youth camps between Halifax and Vancouver, with an enrollment of 1,700 youngsters. The Mizrachi-Ha-Po'el ha-Mizrachi ran a Hebrew camp for over 500 youngsters. The

Labor Zionist Movement operated a youth camp near Montreal and Camp Miriam at Vancouver. The Keren ha-Tarbut, Hebrew department of the Zionist Organization of Canada, is active in the larger cities (Montreal, Toronto, Winnipeg, and Vancouver). It carries on special programs, such as Hebrew courses, "Hebrew-on-the-air," and *ulpanim,* particularly for those planning to settle in Israel. The Labor Zionist Movement was influential in helping to establish the Canadian Jewish Congress and has been active in that organization throughout the years. The Zionist organizations also assist indirectly in Jewish education. The Labor Zionist Movement is directly affiliated with the Folk Shule and Peretz schools in Montreal and the Bialik Hebrew Day School in Toronto. The public relations department of the Zionist Organization of Canada operates an ongoing program, supplies speakers for the Jewish and non-Jewish service clubs, and assists in the work of the Canadian Israel Association, a non-Jewish organization which has been in existence and active since 1947. Together with the Canadian Jewish Congress and B'nai B'rith, the Zionist Organization of Canada operates a Canadian-Israel Public Affairs Committee.

Aliyah and Settlement in Israel. The first Canadian *ḥalutz,* Ya'akov Pruzhansky, who later changed his name to Aḥvah, arrived and settled in Ereẓ Israel in 1913. During World War I more than 200 Canadians volunteered as members of the Jewish Legion and fought under General Allenby; a fairly large number remained in Palestine. In 1948, during Israel's War of Independence, about 250 young men volunteered their services in Maḥal, and a certain number remained on after the state came into being. The Six-Day War of 1967 evoked an unparalleled response of identification with Israel. Financial contributions were made freely and spontaneously; demonstrations for Israel took place throughout the country; delegations of prominent Canadian Jews visited the prime minister and urged that the Canadian government take a positive stand in favor of Israel's position; blood and plasma was volunteered for shipment to Israel. Over 10,000 volunteers offered themselves and, in spite of traveling difficulties at the time, about 400 left Canada and by devious means reached Israel. Of these, 228 went with the direct aid of the Zionist Organization of Canada and many of them remained and settled permanently.

Even before 1967, but particularly from then on, there has been a steady flow of tourists, students, temporary settlers and many who have made their permanent home in Israel, among them prominent Zionist leaders. It was estimated that in 1972 there were about 3,500 former Canadians residing in Israel.

In Czechoslovakia. *Before the Establishment of the Czechoslovak Republic (1918).* The growing tension between Czechs and Germans in Bohemia and Moravia aroused the sensitivity of the Jews to the nationality problem and a positive disposition toward the Zionist idea. Several Jewish nationalist societies were established even before the appearance of Theodor Herzl, especially in Czech provincial cities. The first Zionist society was established in 1893 in the town of Horaždōvice in Bohemia. The appearance of Herzl aroused a strong response, especially in the communities of Moravia, due partly to the fact that many of the youth of these communities had come into contact with Herzl and Zionism while studying in Vienna. In 1900 the first Zionist weekly, the *Juedische Volksstimme,* was founded in Brno (Bruenn). Berthold Feiwel and Robert Stricker, among the first Zionist students from Moravia, rose later to leading positions in the world movement. Zionist societies were also established in Prague and the cities of the Sudeten. In the final decade before World War I, the Zionist student association Bar Kochba, led by Shemuel Hugo Bergman, was outstanding for its high intellectual level. This group adopted not only the political program of Zionism but aimed also at a return to the sources of Jewish spiritual creativity and found contacts with the Jewish cultural and social way of life in Eastern Europe. Their goals blended into the great educational task designed to "renew the image of Jewish man." On the whole this group supported the outlook of the Democratic Fraction within the Zionist Organization and cultural Zionism; later on it leaned toward the ideas of A. D. Gordon[23]. Its initiative led to the publication of the Zionist weekly *Selbstwehr* (1907) and the anthology *Vom Judentum* (1913). From Bar Kochba emerged many Zionist leaders in Czechoslovakia and beyond, S. H. Bergman, Hugo Hermann, and Robert Weltsch. With the expansion of the movement among Czech-speaking students, another, parallel group was founded under the name Theodor Herzl (1909). The student Zionist society Barissia, founded in 1903, supported militant political Zionism. In the last two years before the outbreak of World War I, the first youth movement, Blau-Weiss, was established. Maccabi and other sports organizations were also established in many communities, as were women's organizations.

In Slovakia, then part of Hungary, Zionism penetrated only into communities in the western areas, which maintained closer contact

[23]Thinker in Palestine who advocated the "philosophy of labor"

with Jewry in Vienna and Moravia. The founding world convention of Mizrachi was held in Pressburg (Bratislava) in 1904. Although World War I interrupted the organizational work of the Zionist Organization, it also widened and deepened the national feelings by bringing Jewish soldiers from the West to centers of Jewish life in Eastern Europe, on the one hand, and many thousands of Jewish refugees from Galicia to communities in Moravia and Bohemia, on the other.

In the Republic of Czechoslovakia (1918–39). The establishment of the Czechoslovak Republic signified a victory for the principle of national self-determination, which was also supported by the Zionist movement. The establishment of the new, democratic republic also appeared to be the great hour of the Zionist movement, as the leader of the new state, the philosopher and humanist T. G. Masaryk, had fought against anti-Jewish blood libels, was a great admirer of Aḥad Ha-Am, and was supported in his struggle for national independence by Zionist leaders in the United States and Great Britain. The Jewish National Council was founded on the initiative of Zionists and was headed by the leader of the Prague Zionists, L. Singer, aided by Max Brod, Emil Margulies, chief rabbi Chaim Brody, and others. The council's program aimed toward achieving national, political, and cultural autonomy, built upon the communities as autonomous cells. The movement achieved recognition for the Jewish nationality in the constitution of the republic and protection for the rights of a national minority and also succeeded in building a network of Hebrew and Jewish schools—especially in the eastern areas of the republic, but it never achieved the full realization of Jewish cultural autonomy.

The stress on Diaspora work met with opposition in the Zionist movement, and at the second national conference, held in Brno in 1921, a new leadership was chosen for the Zionist movement. It was headed by Joseph Rufeisen, who advanced practical activities toward the upbuilding of Ereẓ Israel as the central platform of the Zionist program. The center of the Zionist movement was set up in Ostrava and remained there until 1938. The Zionist Organization in Czechoslovakia, headed by Rufeisen, was outstanding in its efforts for settlement work in Ereẓ Israel, Hebrew and Jewish education, and training of *ḥalutzim,* while the Jewish National Council and the Jewish Party (Zidovská Strana) handled local political matters. On Zionist policy, the majority supported Weizmann's line and based itself on the close cooperation between the General Zionists, headed by Rufeisen, and the Labor Zionists; the

Revisionists and Mizrachi also developed substantially.

The Zionists had decisive influence in the communities in Slovakia and Sub-Carpathian Ruthenia. Their opponents were the Czech assimilationist movement, and most fiercely the Communists on one end of the spectrum and the ultra-Orthodox on the other. A pioneering He-Ḥalutz movement had existed since the establishment of the republic and succeeded in founding a number of collective settlements and moshavim in Palestine. Various youth movements were active in the spirit of pioneering and *aliyah*. Zionist influence was also decisive in the sphere of education and in the 1930s in the area of social welfare, especially for the Jews of Sub-Carpathian Ruthenia and the refugees of Nazi persecution. Three Zionist Congresses were held on Czechoslovak territory: the 12th Zionist Congress (1921) and 13th Zionist Congress (1923) in Carlsbad and the 18th Zionist Congress (1933) in Prague.

The Holocaust and After. The destruction of the Czechoslovak Republic, after the annexation of Austria, came in several quick stages: the annexation of the Sudetenland to Germany (October 1938), giving over certain areas to Hungary and Poland (November 1938), the establishment of "independent" Slovakia (March 14, 1939), the conquest of Bohemia and Moravia by the German army turning them into the "Protectorate" (March 15, 1939), the annexation of the remainder of Sub-Carpathian Ruthenia by Hungary (March 16, 1939). These were also the stages of the destruction of Czechoslovak Jewry, while the Zionists played central roles in attempts to save it. They increased their efforts toward facilitating *aliyah* and emigration. About 15,000 Jews from Czechoslovakia succeeded in reaching Palestine between the autumn of 1938 and the end of 1939, the overwhelming majority by means of "illegal" immigration. Zionists remained in most positions of community leadership both in the "Protectorate" and Slovakia. Under the leadership of the Zionists Jacob Edelstein, Franz Kahn, Otto Zucker and Hannah Steiner, together with the leaders of the pioneering movement, the Zionists preserved their sense of cooperation, national loyalty, and Jewish values in the Theresienstadt concentration camp and even in Auschwitz. They organized means of escape from Slovakia, where the head of WIZO, Gisi Fleischmann, initiated the Europa Plan to save European Jewry, and many Zionist youths took part in the partisan uprising in Slovakia in the summer of 1944.

The few who survived the Holocaust tried to reestablish the Zionist movement after the war and save the survivors through *aliyah* and settlement in Ereẓ Israel. Zionist activity was renewed in all parts of the republic. Czechoslovakia was a major transit country for the flow of the *beriḥah* from Poland. During the Israel War of Independence (1948), Czechoslovakia was a major source of arms' supply to the new state. Emigration to Israel was permitted, and more than 20,000 Jews, about 40% of the Jewish community, settled there. After a short while, however, the sympathy of the new Communist government in Czechoslovakia for Israel evaporated. Zionist activity was forbidden, and after a time emigration was also halted. In 1952 the Communist government staged a show trial against "Zionism" (the Slánský Trial). During the short period of the "Prague Spring" in 1968, under the leadership of Alexander Dubček, expression of sympathy for the State of Israel was again permitted and even *aliyah* was renewed, but organized Zionist activity did not resume and the invasion of the Warsaw Pact armies in August 1968 ended this period of relative improvement.

In France. *Early History.* The Jewish community of France occupies an important place in the early history of Jewish settlement in Ereẓ Israel, due to the initiative of the Alliance Israélite Universelle and of Baron Edmond de Rothschild. The Alliance set up a network of elementary and vocational schools there, the first of which was the Mikveh Israel agricultural school, founded in 1870. Although these activities were similar to Alliance projects in other parts of the Ottoman Empire, this interest in Ereẓ Israel was undoubtedly influenced by the discussions of Joseph Natonek and Moses Hess with Alliance directors in Paris in 1866. Rabbi Samuel Mohilewer, accompanied by young settlers from Rishon le-Zion, paid a visit to Edmond de Rothschild that served to move him to increase financial, technical, and administrative assistance to new Jewish agricultural enterprises in Ereẓ Israel. Rothschild's intervention was crucial in saving the struggling villages from ruin and in facilitating the development of budding Jewish agriculture. Despite the philanthropic character of Rothschild's undertakings, his paternal attitude, and outbursts of indignation against political Zionism, his contribution was substantial and at a certain stage decisive for the continuation of settlement work.

Paris can also be considered the cradle of political Zionism. It was while in Paris as a correspondent for the *Neue Freie Presse* that Theodor Herzl conceived his Zionist idea and wrote *Der Judenstaat*, and it was in Paris that Max Nordau lived from 1880 to the outbreak of World War I. Among the early Zionists in France were Alexander Marmorek and his brothers Oscar and Isidore, the writer Bernard Lazare, Miriam Schach, and the sculptor S. F. Beer. Zadoc Kahn, France's chief rabbi, supported Zionism and Herzl, but abstained from publicly expressing his support. The Fédération Sioniste de France was established in 1901 and its president until his death in 1923 was Alexander Marmorek. In 1899 he founded the journal *L'Echo Sioniste* which appeared from 1899 to 1905 and again from 1912 to 1914. In 1916 it reappeared under the title *Le Peuple Juif* and remained in existence to 1921. In 1914 the federation had five groups in Paris, one in Nice, and two in Tunis. The great majority of native-born Jews and the official communal bodies, however, were indifferent, if not hostile, to the Zionist program, fearing that their status acquired in the great Emancipation would be placed in jeopardy. This hostility to Zionism did not subside with the Balfour Declaration, although the French minister for foreign affairs, Stephen Pichon, afforded French assent to the declaration. During the Peace Conference at Versailles (1919), two French representatives, the poet André Spire and Professor Sylvain Lévi, were members of the committee established by Chaim Weizmann together with N. Sokolow and M. Ussishkin, to present the Zionist views to the conference delegations. Lévi, however, who was president of the Alliance, clashed with the committee, since, in his view, the Zionist objectives conflicted with French interests in the Middle East.

Zionism in France appealed mainly to Jewish immigrants from Central and Eastern Europe who arrived there beginning in the 1880s. Thus, the successive leaders of French Zionism were Israel Yefroykin, Marc Jarblum, and Joseph Fischer (Ariel). Fischer founded a bimonthly journal, originally as the organ of the Jewish National Fund, *La Terre Retrouvée* (published from 1928). Jarblum, a leader of Labor Zionism, was its spokesman in the Socialist movement of France and Belgium. He had influence with such men as Léon Blum, Emil Vandervelde, and Camille Huysmans. However, a small number of leading French-born Jews also supported Zionism, among them the poets Edmond Fleg and André Spire. The latter's Zionist writings caused him to split with Charles Péguy and his circle of *Cahiers de la Quinzaine*. In 1915 a group of Jewish and non-Jewish intellectuals established the Ligue Franco-Sioniste, and in 1917 André Spire published *Les Juifs et la guerre*, which dealt with the problem how to present the idea of the Jewish state to the future peace conference. In the same year he established the Ligue des Amis du Sionisme, of which he was the secretary general, and its organ *La Palestine Nouvelle*.

1917–1939. In 1917 a Zionist youth movement was established in Strasbourg, from which the bulk of French immigrants went to Palestine prior to World War II. In 1920 a Zionist students' club was founded in Paris, and in 1921 a Mizrachi group was established with its center in Strasbourg. In 1925 the Union Régionale des Sionistes de L'Est de la France was founded by Léon Metzger and Robert Lévy-Dreyfus. This union was the strongest Zionist organization in France before World War II, and up to the conquest of France by the Nazis in 1941 it retained a separate identity. In 1923 a women's group was founded by Mrs. Richard Gottheil; it later merged with the Women's International Zionist Organization (WIZO). In 1929 French Jews accepted Weizmann's invitation to join the "enlarged" Jewish Agency, and Léon Blum, Leo Zadoc-Kahn, and Henri Lévi represented French non-Zionists in the founding meeting in Zurich in August 1929. In the 1930s the following Zionist organizations existed: Po'alei Zion (Left), founded in 1922; the Union of Zionist Revisionists, founded in Paris in 1925 and becoming the center of its world movement; Po'alei Zion-Hitaḥadut, which included a League for Labor Palestine and the Jewish People's League; Organisation Sioniste de France, founded in 1933, an organization of General Zionists; and the Jewish State Party, founded in 1936. Mizrachi also had a certain following in France, including a group called Yavne and a Yiddish-language journal. In the same period branches of many Zionist youth movements were formed: Bleu-Blanc (General Zionists), Betar (Revisionists), Berit ha-Kannaim (Jewish State Party), Deror (Po'alei Zion-Hitaḥadut), Ha-Shomer ha-Ẓa'ir, Ẓe'irei ha-Mizrachi, Ha-Po'el ha-Mizrachi, and Ha-No'ar ha-Ẓiyyoni. In 1937 the Féderation de la Jeunesse Sioniste et Pro-Palestinienne was founded as a result of the merger between the Jewish scouting movement and a few Zionist youth groups, with a total membership of 5,000.

World War II. From the German occupation in 1940, Zionist activities were centered in the southern area known as Vichy France. In 1941, at a secret conference in Lyons, initiated by J. Fischer (Ariel), a new Zionist leadership embracing all groups was established under the chairmanship of Leonce Bernheim, former chairman of the Zionist coordination committee. At another meeting in Vichy in the same year, the Mouvement de la Jeunesse Sioniste, embracing all youth organizations, was created under the direction of Simon Lévitte and Jules Jefroykin. Both frameworks engaged in educational work, such as the teaching of Hebrew, Jewish history, etc., but devoted their energies mainly to smuggling Jewish refugees into Switzerland and Spain. Young Zionists also played a leading part in organizing Jewish armed resistance to the Nazis.

After World War II. Immediately after World War II, leading French Jews, such as André Blumel, were active in aiding the "illegal" immigration and the *beriḥah* movement to Palestine through French ports. With the establishment of the State of Israel, Jewish community officials in France adopted an attitude of sympathy, putting an end to their previous hostility. In 1947 the Union Sioniste Française was founded, uniting all Zionists in France and North Africa, led for some time by André Blumel. The transformation of French Jewry by the influx of North African, particularly Algerian Jews, also influenced the Zionist movement there. Migration to Israel increased steadily. French Jewry demonstrated its solidarity with Israel before and after the Six-Day War (1967), and Chief Rabbi Jacob Kaplan voiced Jewish disapproval of De Gaulle's anti-Israel policies. All traditional Jewish bodies began openly to support Israel, and a Comité de Coordination des Organisations Juives en France, headed by Guy de Rothschild, was specially created in 1967 for financial aid and information services for Israel. Groups for *aliyah* to Israel were formed, among them Oded, comprising young intellectuals from North Africa. All Zionist parties and most world organizations collecting funds and selling bonds for Israel have branches in France, many of them publishing their own journals, such as the French *Amitiés France-Israel* (since 1953) and the Yiddish daily *Unzer Vort* (since 1945) and *Tsionistishe Shtime.*

In Germany. The First Zionist Congress (1897) was attended by more than 40 delegates from Germany, not all of them natives of that country. (The delegation included four representatives from Ereẓ Israel, one of whom, Heinrich Loewe, was a founder of a Zionist group in Germany even before the appearance of Theodor Herzl.) There were, however, a few bodies in Germany that could be regarded as forerunners of modern Zionism: the Esra society in Berlin (founded 1883) tended to the Ḥibbat Zion; the Russian Jewish Scientific Society in Berlin (1889) which was composed almost exclusively of "Eastern Jews"; the Association for the Promotion of Agriculture and Crafts in Palestine, founded in Cologne in 1892 by Max Bodenheimer and David Wolffsohn,

The Jewish students' society of Berlin University, the first university Zionist group in Germany, 1895. Courtesy Central Zionist Archives, Jerusalem.

was in 1897 transformed into the Nationaljuedische Vereinigung and demanded, before the Basle Program, nothing less than a Jewish state. As early as October 1897 the Zionistische Vereinigung in Deutschland (Z.V.D.), a roof organization of all Zionist societies, was set up. The Zionist movement in Germany was distinguished by quality—especially excellent organization and harmonious internal relations—rather than by quantity, since, to quote Richard Lichtheim: "nowhere was the opposition of Jews to the new movement so widespread, principled, and fierce as in Germany." Herzl's original plan to convoke the First Congress in Munich failed because of the hostility of the German rabbis; the board of the Union of German Rabbis issued a proclamation against the Congress and Zionism (hence Protest Rabbis).

The slow but steady growth of the Z.V.D. is reflected by the following figures: in 1912 it had 8,400 members and in 1927 some 20,000, 2,000 of whom were members (or "old boys") of the Zionist students' associations organized in the Kartell juedischer Verbindungen; in the same years the number of local branches doubled from 100 to 200. The year 1902 saw the establishment of two Zionist institutions whose influence reached far beyond the borders of Germany: the Zionist weekly *Juedische Rundschau* and the publishing house Juedischer Verlag. Special importance is attached to the Zionist territorial conference of 1912 because it adopted a resolution obliging every Zionist "to include *aliyah* in the program of his life" or at least to connect his personal fate with that of the national home by means of economic interests.

The influence of the Zionist Federation of Germany was particularly strong during the 15 years in which the headquarters of the World Zionist Organization were in Germany: in Cologne during the presidency of David Wolffsohn (1905–11) and in Berlin during that of Otto Warburg (1911–20), all the more so as one of the chairmen of the Z.V.D., Arthur Hantke, was a leading member of the Zionist Executive. It was largely due to the fact that the Zionist headquarters remained in Berlin during World War I, although some Executive members went abroad, and that German Zionists continued to hold key positions in the world movement, that German representatives in Turkey exerted their influence in favor of the *yishuv* and helped to mitigate its persecution. Leaders of German Zionism like Felix Rosenblueth (later Pinḥas Rosen, Israel's first minister of justice), Richard Lichtheim, and Kurt Blumenfeld held highest office in the world movement even after its seat had been transferred to London.

During the Weimar Republic (1918–1933) the Zionists in Germany continued to be an elite rather than a mass movement. Shekel figures moved round 20,000, and it was only after the Nazis had seized power that the Zionistische Vereinigung in Deutschland reached its maximum membership of 35,000. It always embraced all Zionist parties—with the exception of the Revisionists, who seceded in 1932. When the ascent of the Nazis had conclusively proved the bankruptcy of assimilation, Zionism became the dominant force in German Jewry. The courageous and dignified article of the *Juedische Rundschau,* "Wear the Yellow Badge with Pride," by its editor Robert Weltsch, which was the Zionist reply to the anti-Jewish boycott of April 1, 1933, made Jewish history. The main efforts of the Z.V.D. were now directed at the preparation and promotion of *aliyah* and *hakhsharah* (youth training). Through the Ha'avarah, the transfer of Jewish assets to Palestine, some £6,000,000 were saved and infused into the economy of Ereẓ Israel to its great benefit. After the Nuremberg Laws in 1935 the Z.V.D. was subjected to increasing restrictions and in 1938 was dissolved by the authorities.

Immediately after World War II a United Zionist Federation was established by the Displaced Persons. It was very active, but after most of the D.P.s had left, mainly for Israel, it was dissolved. In 1954 the Zionist Organization in Germany was established, against considerable opposition in the world movement, but when two delegates from Germany were admitted to the 24th Congress (1956), this federation, with its seat in Frankfort, gained official recognition. Due to the small number of Jews in Germany and to other factors, the scope and quality of its activities fall necessarily short of those of the former Z.V.D., but it is doing useful work in particular in the fields of fund raising and public relations.

In Great Britain. There were many Jewish and non-Jewish forerunners of the Zionist idea and supporters of Jewish settlement in Palestine, as well as an active group of Ḥovevei Zion (the Ḥibbat Zion), in Great Britain. Thus, political Zionism appeared on the British scene very early. It was in London that Theodor Herzl made his first Zionist speech (at the Maccabean Club in November 1895) and outlined his program in an article in the *Jewish Chronicle,* in January 1896, before the publication of *Der Judenstaat.* He was received with great reservations not only by the Jewish establishment, but even by some of the Ḥovevei Zion. On his next visit, in July 1896, he addressed a mass meeting in the East End and received an enthusiastic response. Among his first supporters and followers were the Sephardi Haham Moses Gaster, the Hebrew teacher Ephraim Ish-Kishor, the already famous writer Israel Zangwill, and Jacob de Haas, followed soon after by Joseph Cowen, Leopold Greenberg, and Leopold Kessler. In March 1898 Ḥovevei Zion in Britain joined the Zionist movement mainly under the influence of Herbert Bentwich and Albert Goldsmid. As a consequence, the Second Zionist Congress (1898) was attended by 15 delegates from Britain, compared to eight at the First Congress. In January 1899 the English Zionist Federation was founded, with Sir Francis Abraham Montefiore, a grand-nephew of Sir Moses Montefiore, elected the first president of the Federation. Herzl, who from the beginning believed in British support for Zionism, registered the Jewish Colonial Trust as a British corporation (1899), and in 1900 convoked the Fourth Zionist Congress in London, the only Congress during his lifetime not held in Basle. "From here the Zionist idea will soon soar higher and higher," Herzl declared in his opening speech. Most British Zionists supported Herzl in the controversy over the Uganda Scheme, while Jacob K. Goldbloom, one of Herzl's first followers, led the opposition. The Zionist movement in Britain suffered a severe blow when Zangwill seceded, in 1905, and founded the Jewish Territorial Organization.

In 1904 Chaim Weizmann settled in England, having received a position at the University of Manchester, and soon gathered around him a group of devoted Zionists who later distinguished themselves in the British and world movement, notably Simon Marks, Israel Sieff, Harry Sacher, and Leon Simon. In 1914 Weizmann became vice-president of the Zionist Federation (under Joseph Cowen as president). World War I opened new political perspectives. An advisory committee on Zionist political activity was formed, composed of Nahum Sokolow and Yeḥiel Tschlenow (members of the world Executive who had moved to London), Cowen, Weizmann, Gaster, and Bentwich. The Zionist Federation became an important factor in these activities. In 1915 it organized a petition demanding "the establishment of a publicly recognized and legally secured Home for the Jewish people in Palestine, as formulated by the Zionist Congress in Basle in 1897." The petition was signed by 77,000 adults out of a total Jewish population of about 300,000. In January 1917 Cowen resigned from the presidency of the Zionist Federation to make way for Weizmann.

In their struggle for British support for the Zionist goals, the leaders of the movement were enthusiastically supported by the federation and advised and supported by Zionists from abroad who spent the war years in London, like Aḥad Ha-Am and Vladimir Jabotinsky, as well as by some British Jews of high social standing, most notably Herbert Samuel and Lord Rothschild. Chief Rabbi Joseph Herman Hertz came out as a supporter of Zionism, in remarkable contrast to his predecessor Herman Adler, who had denounced Zionism as a fantasy. Still, anti-Zionist sentiments were so strong in the Jewish establishment that the presidents of the Board of Deputies and of the Anglo-Jewish Association, D. L. Alexander and Claude Montefiore, respectively, publicly repudiated Zionist aims in the name of their organizations. The sharp protest by the fohowers and sympathizers of Zionism forced Alexander to resign. Lord Rothschild accepted the honorary presidency of the Zionist Federation and so became the addressee of the Balfour Declaration. At the first Zionist World Conference after the war, held in London in 1920, Weizmann was elected president of the World Zionist Organization and the seat of the Executive and of the main instruments of the movement was formally established in London, which thus became the capital of world Zionism.

Zionist rally in protest against the Passfield White Paper, London, 1930. On the platform, left to right, are: Rebecca Sieff, Leib Jaffe, Maurice Perlzweig, J. K. Goldbloom, Vera Weizmann, Chaim Weizmann, Naḥum Sokolow, Lavy Bakstansky, Selig Brodetsky, Morris Myer, A. Marcus, Lazar Barth, Berthold Feiwel, Yoseph Sprinzak. Courtesy Central Zionist Archives, Jerusalem.

During the 30 years of British administration in Palestine, the activities of the Zionist movement in Great Britain were of utmost importance for the work and struggle of the Zionist Executive, by providing mass support in the political, financial, and cultural fields. Zionist influence within British Jewry increased. In 1929 the Board of Deputies joined the enlarged Jewish Agency for Palestine as a constituent body. In 1939 Selig Brodetsky, a member of the Zionist Federation, was elected president of the Board of Deputies, and since then only Zionists or staunch supporters of Israel have served in that capacity. Zionist youth movements developed, and there was a significant *aliyah* from Britain. At the 21st Congress (in 1939) Great Britain was represented by 15 delegates, eight representing the Federation (General Zionists), three Po'alei Zion, three Mizrachi, and one the Jewish State Party. The Revisionists, who at that time had already seceded from the World Zionist Organization, also moved their headquarters to London, which was the seat of the Zionist-led European Executive of the World Jewish Congress, as well. In 1944 the Board of Deputies embraced the Biltmore Program by adopting a resolution calling for the establishment of a Jewish state in undivided Palestine, hopefully within the framework of the British Commonwealth. During the years of the struggle and resistance of the *yishuv* after World War II, preceding the independence of Israel, British Zionists took a courageous stand against their government.

After the establishment of the State of Israel, Great Britain naturally lost its central position in the Zionist world, but British Zionists—under the direction of Lavy Bakstansky—continued to distinguish themselves by their generous support of Israel and their increasing influence within the Jewish community of Great Britain. The achievement of raising £11,000,000 in the Emergency Campaign of 1967 (as compared with £2,600,000 raised the year before), as well as the fact that within a few days about 10,000 volunteers for Israel enlisted, about 2,000 of whom actually arrived in Israel, is worthy of note. The most impressive achievement within the framework of the community is the establishment of a network of Zionist day schools since 1953. In 1969 ten schools were operating with an enrollment of over 5,000 pupils.

In Holland. The Zionist Federation was established in Holland in 1899 under the name of Nederlandse Zionistenbond. Among its founders was the young banker Jacobus H. Kann, who was a close collaborator of Theodor Herzl. The members of the organization were mainly middle-class intellectuals, and for about 30 years the Zionist movement of Holland was unsuccessful in attracting a wider following among the Jewish proletariat. The movement also encountered violent opposition from Orthodox circles. The chief rabbi of Amsterdam, J. Y. Duenner, supported the Zionist movement from the start and some of his close friends founded the Mizrachi movement, led by S. Ph. de Vries. But his colleagues and almost all of his disciples rejected Zionism, and in 1904 the Council of Chief Rabbis (which Duenner refused to join) forbade the Jews to join the Zionist movement. The Eighth Zionist Congress, which was held in The Hague, led to an awakening of the movement. An attempt to establish a Zionist youth movement during that period ended in failure, but the official Zionist organ, *De Joodse Wachter*, founded in 1905, which in time became a weekly, stood its ground.

In 1912 Nehemiah de Lieme was elected president of the Nederlandse Zionistenbond, and S. A. van Vriesland (who was later to become treasurer of the World Zionist Organization) was elected its secretary. De Lieme consolidated the organization's special character by establishing several principles: the negation of any Zionist work for Diaspora Jewry *("Gegenwartsarbeit");* sound economic management in the upbuilding of Ereẓ Israel; the exemplary organization of the Zionist movement in the Diaspora. In Holland, the organization made the following demands: prohibition of the sale of the shekel for obtaining the right to vote at elections to the Zionist Congresses (therefore Holland's representation at all the Congresses fell below the organization's actual strength); membership to be registered personally (not through Zionist parties); insistence on Zionist principles in propaganda as well as fund raising for Ereẓ Israel. De Lieme exerted tremendous influence on his friends and followers, among them S. Hoofien, later director of the Anglo-Palestine Bank in Palestine, Abel Herzberg, author and politician, and others. In 1914 the world headquarters of the Jewish National Fund were transferred to The Hague, and de Lieme headed the fund for seven years and formulated its principles. In 1920 he was elected to the Executive of the World Zionist Organization, but resigned when his principles were not accepted. After de Lieme's resignation, he returned to the leadership of the Nederlandse Zionistenbond and developed a stance of opposition to the Executive of the World Zionist Organization. Pereẓ (Fritz) Bernstein also extended this opposition to the political line of Chaim Weizmann, and in his capacity of editor of *De Joodse Wachter* and later as president of the organization, he left his imprint on the movement. Only a small group of Dutch Zionists countered the de Lieme-Bernstein line, among them David Cohen and the Po'alei Zion, founded in 1933 by S. de Wolff. There was also a small Revisionist group which would not gain much influence because of the anti-Weizmann stance of the whole Zionist Federation.

During World War I the arrival of refugees from Belgium (all of whom were Jews of East European origin) added an important element to the movement. The study of modern Hebrew developed and several newspapers included a Hebrew supplement. In 1917 an organization of Zionist youth groups, Joodse Jeugdfederatie, was established with the moral support of the Zionist leadership and under its aegis. The Jeugdfederatie encompassed many groups throughout the country and held independent activities (publications, lectures, conventions). After about ten years, it was headed by young people, mostly students, who had emerged from its own ranks.

The rise of anti-Semitism in Germany was a cause for much agitation in Holland, and the 30,000 German Jewish refugees who arrived in the country highlighted the problem. The influence of the Zionist movement increased, and although it had no more than 4,000 registered members, many beyond its ranks accepted the Zionist ideology. Anti-Jewish trends then began to grow in Holland and the local Zionist leadership was inclined to conceal the Jewish national character of Zionism. In opposition to this tendency, a trend calling itself "Radical Zionism," greatly influenced by Lion Nordheim, developed within the youth movements and among the students. It clashed sharply with the Zionist leadership, especially over the following points: the Joodse Jeugdfederatie demanded of its members complete identification with the Jewish people and public detachment from the Dutch nation; it stood for the safeguarding of Jewish national values and traditions and for Jewish education, thus opposing the prohibition of *"Gegenwartsarbeit";* it propagated the ideal of *ḥalutziyyut* (pioneering) among its members. The rift within the youth movement (which also encompassed religious and labor groups and commanded a membership of 2,000 in 40 branches) reached its climax in 1940. With the German invasion, however, it was decided to establish a joint leadership of all the Zionist organizations in Holland, and this body administered the affairs of the Nederlandse Zionistenbond until its dissolution.

Immediately after World War I, many *ḥalutzim* from Eastern Europe had arrived in Holland to complete their agricultural training with Dutch farmers. During the 1930s *ḥalutzim* also emerged from the ranks of the Joodse Jeugdfederatie. They established three organizations: Ḥevrat Olim (the adherents of Bernstein), Berit Ḥalutzim Datiyyim (religious) and He-Ḥalutz (composed mainly of *ḥalutzim* from other countries, including German refugees). As Holland was not considered to be a danger zone, not even by the World Zionist Organization, over 800 *ḥalutzim* were trapped there for many years. Many of them perished during the war, but 444 were saved, mainly due to the activity of the Westerweel group. After World War II the Dutch Zionist movement was dominated mainly by the radical trend. Its slogan, which called for massive *aliyah,* led to considerable success. Out of the 25,000 Jews who survived in Holland, some 4,000 settled in Israel between 1948 and 1969, a higher percentage than from any other Western country. During this period most of the Zionist leadership itself migrated to Israel, and the Nederlandse Zionistenbond lost its central position within the remnant of Dutch Jewry. Zionist periodicals in Holland included, apart from *De Joodse Wachter, Tikvath Jisrael* (from 1917), monthly of the youth movement; *Mizrachie* (from 1932), monthly of the Mizrachi movement; and *Jaarboek van de Nederlandse Zionistische Studentenorganisatie* (since 1909).

In Hungary. Two strong and opposing forces were influential among Hungarian Jewry from the 1840s: on the one hand a desire to assimilate linguistically and culturally into the Magyar nation, and on the other extreme religious conservatism. In addition, Ḥasidism exerted a substantial influence, particularly in the northern part of the country. These three phenomena were an obstacle to the proliferation of the Zionist idea at the end of the 19th century. Nonetheless, the difficult and extended struggle of the Zionists succeeded in spreading the Zionist idea among relatively small groups throughout the country. During the period of the Ḥovevei Zion a number of enthusiastic supporters of this movement in Hungary maintained ties with other Ḥovevei Zion beyond the borders. However, even the fact that Theodor Herzl was a native of Budapest and was bound to Hungarian Jewry through familial ties did not facilitate the development of the

Young Zionists dancing the *horah* outside the Lekstraat synagogue in Amsterdam after a meeting in support of a Jewish State, 1945. Courtesy Central Zionist Archives, Jerusalem.

Zionist movement in Hungary. On a number of occasions Herzl himself declared that Zionism would reach Hungary, but only later on.

In spite of strong opposition to Zionism in religious circles, some Orthodox Jews from Hungary participated in the founding of the world religious Zionist movement. Some Hungarian Jews also settled in Ereẓ Israel during the 19th century and became an important element in the old *yishuv*, but as a rule they bore no ties to Zionism. Representatives from Hungary participated in the First Zionist Congress (1897). One of them, János Rónai, delivered a speech at the Congress and pointed to the normal condition of life of Hungarian Jewry, but he expressed the fear that this situation would deteriorate and predicted that Hungarian Jewry would then join the Zionist movement. Immediately after the Congress, Rónai, an attorney from Transylvania, began to engage in varied organizational activities, establishing branches of the Zionist movement, heading the national efforts at organization, and being elected first chairman of the Hungarian Zionist Organization. In preparation for his appearance at the Congress, he wrote an ideological pamphlet in German entitled *Zionismus in Ungarn* (1897), in which he engaged the arguments of both the assimilationist and religious opposition. Another central figure was Samu Bettelheim, who was active in Bratislava. Bettelheim was a religious Zionist, and upon his initiative the first world conference of Mizrachi was convened in his city in 1904. The number of local Zionist groups began to increase, and at the Second Zionist Congress (1898) 32 branches of the Hungarian Zionist Federation were in existence.

In 1908 the Hungarian authorities became aware of the movement and prohibited collecting money for the Zionist funds. Local Zionists alerted the president of the World Zionist Organization, David Wolffsohn. He visited Budapest and was received by the minister of interior, Count Gyula Andrássy, who displayed understanding and even friendship toward the Zionist movement but explained to Wolffsohn that the problem of minorities was very disturbing in Hungary and he could not afford to allow the creation of yet another national minority, the Jewish nation. This approach continued to characterize the position of the Hungarian authorities vis-à-vis Zionism.

At the beginning of the 20th century, some of the students at the University of Budapest became Zionists. In 1903 they founded a society called Makkabea, which played a central role in the propagation of the Zionist idea in the capital and the provinces until World War II. The Zionist press was also established by the initiative of this society. The first Zionist organ was *Zsidó Néplap,* which was published from 1905 to 1907. In 1911 another organ, *Zsidó Szemle,* began to appear under the editorship of Jozef Schőnfeld. These papers, however, did not succeed in penetrating into wider Jewish circles. A Jewish quarterly called *Mult és Jövo* began appearing in 1911 under the editorship of Joseph Patai. Although this literary and artistic periodical was not an official organ of Zionism, it clearly identified with the Jewish nationalist and Zionist trend and achieved great popularity (publication ceased during the Holocaust). Zionists were also active in the establishment of Jewish sports organizations that maintained ties with similar groups in Austria.

Feeble attempts were made at the beginning of the century to establish Po'alei Zion in Hungary, but the Jews among Hungarian Social Democrats opposed this idea. The Jewish Territorial Organization (I.T.O.) also set up a branch in Hungary in 1912. Local Zionists became involved in a difficult struggle with the I.T.O., which was also supported by the non-Zionist Jewish press. In spite of all these difficulties, however, on the eve of World War I there were branches of of the Hungarian Zionist Organization in many cities throughout Hungary, and 20 delegates from Hungary participated in the 11th Zionist Congress (1913).

During World War I many active Zionists were mobilized into the army, and some who were captured came into contact with Russian Jews and Zionists. These contacts proved to be very fruitful. During the last months of World War I and the period of the Russian Revolution, Zionists, and especially demobilized officers, organized into self-defense units and in a number of places overcame mob attacks on the Jews. The first short-lived Communist regime in Hungary (1919) displayed open hostility to Zionism, prohibited organizational activities, and forced the Zionist organ to close down for a period.

In the peace treaty that ended World War I, Hungary was divided up, and the Zionist activity in areas annexed to Rumania, Czechoslovakia, Austria, and Yugoslavia began to develop independently of the Hungarian Zionist Organization, whose headquarters were in Budapest. Zionist activities continued in the limited area of Hungary, where one of the central problems was the extended struggle to acquire government authorization for the Zionist Organization. The leaders of the Neolog Jewish community also opposed the granting of such authorization, since they regarded Zionism as a breach of Hungarian patriotism. Legalization was finally achieved in 1927, with the Hungarian Zionists receiving strong political support from the Zionist Executive in London. The Pro-Palestine Association exerted influence among those Jews who did not formally join the Zionist Organization.

By the 16th Zionist Congress (1929) many youth movements had already been formed in Hungary, including He-Ḥalutz. A great step forward was the enlargement of the Jewish Agency and the seating of the Hungarian Zionist Joseph Patai, and the chief rabbi of Szeged, Immanuel Löw, who was considered a non-Zionist, on its General Council. In 1937, 17 local branches of the Zionist Organization and 3,600 members existed in Hungary. The number of youth movement members was also substantial. The year 1937 was the last before the cancellation of equal rights for Hungarian Jews (the Hungarian parliament had already begun deliberating the law to reduce their rights, which was passed in 1938). The first anti-Jewish law, the restrictions on Jewish economic activities, and the proximity of German Nazism—after Germany had annexed Austria—increased the interest of Hungarian Jewry in the Zionist movement. Zionist cultural activities expanded, especially those of the youth movements. The number of Jews who wished to go to Palestine, as well as the number of those who realized their desire, was on the rise.

Jewish refugees from Austria, Poland, and other places began arriving in Hungary, and aid was extended to them principally through the framework of the Zionist movement. Efforts to move refugees to Palestine through "illegal" channels were made under Zionist auspices, particularly through the youth movements. With the annexation of northern Transylvania to Hungary in 1940, a group of Transylvanian Zionist leaders experienced in public and political life arrived in Budapest. Among them were Rezső Rudolf Kasztner and the newspaper editor Ernő Marton. The Zionist Socialist movement was further strengthened during this period, and Béla Dános, its leader, also took upon himself varied activities. Youth leaders arrived from Slovakia and other parts of former Czechoslovakia, bringing with them strong Zionist views. The movement in Hungary was then headed by Ottó Komoly. Those who came from the annexed provinces, as well as active Zionists who had fled from other countries, were aided by, and extended aid to, the rescue activities of the Zionist movement and to some degree the Aid and Rescue Committee set up for that purpose. The Aid and Rescue Committee established contact with Adolf

Eichmann to discuss rescue plans and sent Joel Brand, one of the active Zionist Socialists, on his tragic mission. During World War II Hungarian Zionists were active mainly in rescue activities.

After World War II, in 1945, the Zionist Organization in Hungary was reconstituted. Zionist youth movements directed many young people to Ereẓ Israel. The new government displayed hostility toward the Zionist activities from the very start and tried gradually to liquidate the movement. In 1949 the Zionist Organization and all Zionist activities were formally prohibited. A number of trials, directed specifically against Zionists, were later held by the government, and in other trials, including that of László Rajk, some of the defendants were accused of "conspiring with Zionists." The 50-year history of the Zionist movement in Hungary thus came to an end.

In Italy. Because of the small number of Jews in Italy and the fact that they were largely assimilated, Zionism could penetrate only slowly and with difficulty and for years retained an exclusive character. Among the Jewish periodicals, the first to express Zionist ideas at the end of the 19th century was *Il Corriere Israelitico,* which was published in Italian but appeared in Trieste (then under Austrian rule). No Italian delegates were present at the First Zionist Congress in 1897. The Second Congress (1898) was attended by the rabbi of Naples, Joseph Sonnino, who was chosen as delegate without formal elections. He represented the first Zionist groups that had been formed in Italy in Ancona, Rome, Leghorn, Florence, and Naples. Also present at the Second Congress was Felice Ravenna, who was to become the head of Italian Zionism and was to remain its leader for many years, representing it at the Third Congress in 1899, together with two other delegates. It was only in 1901 that the Italian Zionist Federation was formed. Its conventions originally took place every two years in various towns. In 1901 the first Zionist periodical, *L'Idea Sionista,* was founded and survived for ten years; in 1908 the more penetrating *L'Eco Sionista d'Italia* appeared.

At that time Italian Zionism had no important political scope and was troubled by various controversies; its nature was mainly philanthropic. Due to the intervention of some of its exponents, however, Theodor Herzl was received in January 1904 by King Victor Emmanuel III and by Pope Pius X. On that occasion, Herzl had an interview with the Italian minister for foreign affairs and later sent him a written statement. From the beginning, the most active and penetrating Zionist writer and journalist was Dante

Lattes. After Herzl's death the movement experienced a period of decline, and the center of its activities was transferred to Florence, under the leadership of Alfonso Pacifici. In 1916 the weekly *Israel* was founded there and remained the center of Zionist activity, although it carried no Zionist label.

Immediately after World War I an Italian Jew, naval captain Angelo Levi-Bianchini, was sent by the government as Italian military attaché to General Allenby's General Staff. Under the influence of Chaim Weizmann, he became an ardent Zionist. He was killed in a Bedouin ambush in Syria in 1920. In 1922 Weizmann went to Italy and made his first close contact with Italian Jewry, defining it in his autobiography as follows: "The Italian Jewish community seemed to be a community of *sujets d'élite.* And the *élite* of that community were turning their eyes to Palestine." During the early years of Fascist rule, the relations between the Italian government and the Zionist Organization were so good that in 1928 the Comitato Italia-Palestina was formed to facilitate the contact between Italy and Palestine. Personalities of high standing in politics and literature were among the members of this committee. There had even been talk in 1931 of holding the 19th Zionist Congress at Abbazia (now Opatjai, Yugoslavia). The Zionist Revisionist movement was also in touch with the Italian government. Its leader, Leone Carpi in Milan, published the periodical *L'Idea Sionistica.* The Revisionists founded a naval school at Civitavecchia for the world Betar movement that was several times visited by Vladimir Jabotinsky.

Although the attitude of Mussolini's government became increasingly pro-Arab, Zionism remained active for some years. It maintained agricultural training centers *(hakhsharot);* encouraged contributions to the Zionist funds, which showed increases; replied firmly to controversies in newspapers; and regularly sent delegates to the Zionist Congresses. Following the introduction of the racial laws in 1938, the position of Italian Jewry rapidly deteriorated. The existing Jewish periodicals were ordered to stop publication, the Zionist organizations were dissolved, and Jewish life, with the exception of religious and charitable functions, had to be carried on in secret. This period marked the beginning of a considerable *aliyah* from Italy, whose first pioneers and standard-bearers had been Enzo and Ada Sereni.

After the interval of World War II, marked by deportations and ruin, particularly during the German occupation, Jewish and Zionist life slowly revived in Italy. Immediately after World War II

Parade of Zionist youth in Port of Spain, Trinidad, May 16, 1948, in honor of the establishment of the State of Israel. Courtesy Central Zionist Archives, Jerusalem.

Italy became a center of widespread and feverish underground activities in the organization of "illegal" immigration of Jewish survivors from Central and Eastern Europe to Palestine (directed by Ada Sereni) and also of secret arms transports for the Haganah. Italian Zionist and communal leaders, among them Raffaele Cantoni, played a major role in these operations. These facts, as well as the presence of the soldiers of the Jewish Brigade Group from Palestine, created a climate of deep identification of Italian Jewry with the struggle for Jewish independence in Palestine.

Numerous Zionist conventions took place in Italy from 1947 onward and *aliyah* increased considerably. Jewish education, e.g., the great Jewish school in Milan, became Hebrew-and Israel-oriented. Italian Zionism, which is numerically still very small because of the limited size of the Jewish community, is now more politically conscious and has more cultural and personal ties with Israel than ever before.

In Latin America. The Zionist movement in Latin America grew with the development of the continent's Jewish communities. In most countries Jewish communal and Zionist institutions collaborated from the start, and from the time of the struggle for independence and the establishment of the State of Israel the activities of the Zionist movement have expanded to continental proportions. The movement has sponsored such major continental gatherings as the first Zionist congress in Montevideo (1945); the second Zionist congress in Buenos Aires (1950); the first Jewish Latin American youth convention (Montevideo 1961); a conference convened after the Six-Day War that brought together 527 delegates from Argentina, Uruguay, Chile, Paraguay, and Peru (Nov. 1967); and a South American encounter for the new Zionist generations (Buenos Aires, April 1970).

Argentina. Zionist groups arose in Buenos Aires and in the interior simultaneously with the organization of the First Zionist Congress in Basle. The oldest group (established 1897) was Sion. The Dr. Theodor Herzl League was also influential for several years. As the movement grew, its activities were coordinated by a Federación (established 1904), a central institution which was an extension of the Herzl League. In 1908 it was replaced by Tifereth Zion. The movement's leadership developed within the framework of the Federación Sionista Argentina (established 1913), whose first leaders were Jacobo Joselevich, Nathan Gezang, and Solomon Liebeshutz.

During the early stages of its development, the movement did not tend toward internal political polarization. There were, however, lesser organizations which espoused particular ideological trends: Ḥerut, Socialist Territorialists (established 1905); S.S., Socialist Zionists (established 1906); and a Borochovist group, Po'alei Zion (est. 1909), and Ẓe'irei Zion (1918). The two last groups united in 1932 to form Po'alei Zion-Ẓe'irei Zion and its periodical *Di Naye Tzait,* established 1918, still exists. The other major local party is the General Zionists, whose official publication is *El Estado Judío.* Ha-Shomer ha-Ẓa'ir, particularly active after World War II, publishes the *Nueva Sion* (established 1947). The Revisionist party (established 1930), which increased its organizational cadres during the struggle of the *yishuv* against the British administration in Palestine, puts out *La idea Sionista.* Mizrachi was established in 1940 on the foundations of previously organized smaller groups.

These parties have sponsored the creation of youth movements which have made significant contributions in the areas of Jewish education and *aliyah.* Women's organizations of each party, as well as WIZO, are also active. The Consejo Central Sionista (established 1948), in which all local Zionist institutions are represented, arose from the reorganization of the Zionist parties and the creation of a Comisión Coordinadora (established 1940).

The League for Ereẓ Israel Labor at the Jewish settlement in Bernasconi, La Pampa province, Argentina, celebrating the harvesting of a crop for the benefit of Palestine, 1934. Courtesy C.A.H.J.P., Jerusalem.

As of 1951 it has undertaken functions previously carried out by the Jewish Agency (established 1937, for Argentina and Latin America). Delegates from Argentina have attended Zionist Congresses since 1925; their presence in previous years had been sporadic. The Zionist Organization of Argentina became one of the central organizations of Argentine Jewry.

Brazil. The first Zionist organizations, Tifereth Zion and Ahavath Zion (1916–17), sprang up in São Paolo and Rio de Janeiro. Smaller centers were also established in the northern provinces. With the founding of the Zionist Organization (1921), a degree of coordination was attained, including collaboration between Ashkenazim and Sephardim. During World War II, when Brazil imposed legislation restricting the internal development of national minorities, the Zionist movement was officially closed down (1938), but it nevertheless continued its activities on a limited scale until 1945, when its legal status was renewed. The reorganized Zionist political parties coordinated into the United Zionist Organization (established 1945). The most influential of these parties were Mapai (organized in the 1920s), General Zionists (since 1947), and the Revisionists. The Keren Hayesod was reorganized in 1946.

The movement encountered difficulties which derived from the complex internal organization of the Jewish community; local autonomous trends and a division according to countries of origin interfered with its collaboration with a centralized communal organization. Nevertheless, communal institutions in the state of São Paolo consolidated their activities with the Zionist Organization in support of the Jewish state and to aid European Jewry. The assimilation of Jewish sectors into Brazilian society, a growing manifestation during and subsequent to World War II, was a contributing factor to the limited influence of the movement during those years. There has been an upswing in the local Zionist movement since the 1950s, particularly after the Six-Day War (1967).

Colombia. The communal life of this small Jewish community, composed of Sephardim who emigrated from Palestine during the crisis years of the 1920s, German-speaking Ashkenazi immigrants arriving since World War I, and refugees from Nazi persecution, was organized with difficulty. The Zionist movement also had a slow beginning due to the restrictive measures adopted by the authorities to prevent the formation of "ethnic islands." The Federación Sionista, together with the Comité Central (established 1936), adopted measures against anti-Semitism and racial discrimination.

Ecuador and Paraguay. The respective organizations of Ecuador and Paraguay enjoy a limited membership, and they work together with communal institutions. Paraguay, whose minute Jewish population is preponderantly pro-Zionist, has seen an increase in activities in the wake of the Six-Day War.

Chile. Chile's flourishing Jewish community has attained a strong internal organization in which the Zionist movement wields authority and influence. The earliest Zionist initiatives were sporadic. The first stable group was formed in 1911 by members maintaining contact with the Argentinian Zionist movement. An influential figure during this early period was Mauricio Baltiansky. From the first Zionist convention in 1919, the movement became more firmly established. The major blocs were Po'alei Zion (established 1916) and the General Zionist Party (1947). Since the 1930s all Zionist parties and factions have increasingly polarized within the local movement. These include the Pro-Palestine Labor League (1931), the Revisionists (1932), and Mizrachi. Smaller groups such as the Folksfarband and the Grupo Hebraista formed the opposition. Active pioneer organizations are Ivriah (1930), Betar (1933), Benei Akiva (1940), Kadimah (1944)—from which Ha-Shomer ha-Ẓa'ir grew—Deror-He-Ḥalutz, and Iḥud ha-No'ar ha-Ḥalutzi (1950) of the Po'alei Zion-Hitaḥadut. Zionist women's organizations are WIZO (1926) and Pioneer Women (1949).

The firmly organized Zionist Federation of Chile (established 1919) incorporates all political and Zionist organizations, the United Jewish Appeal, and every institution which, if not specifically Zionist, nonetheless identifies with the movement's objectives. Together with the Jewish representative body, the Comité Representativo, it engages in nationwide Jewish education, is involved with cultural activities, and participates in the Central Committee for Jewish Education (established 1946). It sponsors the Instituto Chileno-Israelita de Cultura (established 1950), which is associated with the Comisión de Cooperación Intelectual of the University of Chile. It has also carried out an intensive campaign of political explanation within non-Jewish circles, particularly since World War II and the creation of the State of Israel.

Peru. The Zionist movement in Peru, established at the end of World War I, encountered initial resistance on the part of the Bund and other leftwing groups in the communal institutions and in the Jewish press. After its establishment (1925) the Zionist Federation collaborated closely with the Unión Israelita del Peru, an Ashkenazi community functioning since 1924, and with the Sociedad de Sociedades (1942), representative of the community. Together with the latter, the Zionist Federation sponsors the León Pinelo school (inaugurated 1946). Jewish public opinion in Peru today is preponderantly pro-Zionist. Jewish university students are organized in the Centro Universitario Peruano-Israelita (established 1960-61), which was reorganized in 1969 as the Movimiento Universitario Peruano-Israelita. An independent youth group, Kinneret (est. 1962), sponsors immigration to Israel and local communal activities. The Zionist Federation has collaborated with the Comité Pro-Palestina (1945) and works with the Instituto Cultural Peru-Israel.

Mexico. Despite the divergencies between Zionists and sectors identified with the non-Zionist left, the Zionist movement exerted increasing influence from the 1920s onward. Both blocs collaborated in certain communal activities, particularly those pertaining to education. Prior to institutional Zionist organization, activities were sporadic (i.e., on behalf of the Balfour Declaration (1917), a

Keren Hayesod campaign (1923), etc.). The first organized group was the Po'alei Zion (1923), which published the first Yiddish publication, *Unzer Vort*. Groups with divergent leanings and bereft of specific partisan character collaborated in the Federación Sionista (1925), which later became affiliated with General Zionism. Fragmentation into specific parties and Zionist institutions—according to countries of origin or youth and women's sectors—began during the years immediately preceding World War II: Liga Pro-Palestina Obrera (1934), Pioneras (1935), Revisionists (end of the decade), Organización Sionista Sefardí (1936, functioning jointly with the Sephardi community), WIZO (1938), Ha-Shomer ha-Ẓa'ir—the first pioneer organization (1940)—Mizrachi (1942), Betar (1946), Benei Akiva (1946), Ha-No'ar ha-Ẓioni (1948), Habonim (1948), Mapam (1948). The youth organizations centralized their activities in the Federación Juvenil Sionista (1943). Each of the trends had its own publication: *Dos Wort* (1947, Po'alei Zion), *Ha-Shomer ha-Ẓa'ir* (1942), *La Voz Sionista* (1948, General Zionists), *Unidad Juvenil* (Po'alei Zion youth), *Avangard* (1948, Mapam), *Unzer Tribune* and *El Heraldo* (Revisionists), *Mizrachi Leben* (religious). The overall organized movement formed the Federación Sionista de Méjico (established 1950), which has since undertaken central leadership tasks, including those of a local communal nature. An index of the movement's scope are the following figures: approximately 400 organized institutions cooperated in the Emergency Palestine Committee of 1946; in 1954 90% of the Jewish population considered itself Zionist, 8% non-Zionist, and 2% anti-Zionist. The Federación collaborates with the Comité Central Israelita, a representative communal institution, and with the Instituto de Relaciones Culturales Méjico-Israel.

Uruguay. This community of strong Zionist leanings had evolved from groups which have collaborated since the earliest stages of their development. In the first group, Agudath Zion, Israel Tschlenow (1914) brought together Zionists of no particular political leanings. The Sephardim founded the "Dr. Herzl" group in 1918; Po'alei Zion was established in 1917. Various trends took shape during the 1930s, and the movement expanded. All the Zionist parties and their pioneer movements and women's institutions are locally represented. The Organización Sionista Territorial, which encompasses the Federación Juvenil Sionista, cooperates closely with the Comité Central Israelita, a representative communal institution. It also collaborated with the Comité

Central committee of the Zionist Organization in Montevideo with Alexander Goldstein of the Keren Hayesod during the Uruguay appeal for the fund, 1921. Courtesy Central Zionist Archives, Jerusalem.

Uruguayo Pro-Palestina (1940) and later with the Comité Cultural Uruguay-Israel.

Venezuela. The Zionist Organization has been the most active and influential institution of this small community since its reorganization in 1949. It works together with the Ashkenazi and Sephardi sectors, as well as with B'nai B'rith and the Jewish National Fund. Despite their limited number, the following youth movements also operate: Ha-Shomer ha-Ẓa'ir, Benei Akiva, Unión de Jovenes Hebreos (est. 1955), which form the Federación Universitaria Sionista Sudamericana. WIZO maintains branches in the capital and in the interior of the country. Affiliation with the Federación can also be individual. It collaborates with the Instituto Cultural Venezuela-Israel.

Central America. Despite their small size, the Jewish communities of Guatemala, Honduras, Nicaragua, Costa Rica, El Salvador, and Panama have organized Zionist institutions. In El Salvador they have functioned since 1946 and enjoy the cooperation of non-Jewish intellectuals and government figures. In Panama and Costa Rica, Zionist activities have found support among the political non-Jewish personalities who have also sponsored relations with the State of Israel. The Zionist movement in the region has increased its activities since 1965 in the wake of the formation of the Federación de Comunidades de America Central, in which the Zionist Organization is also represented.

In North African and Asian Countries. The attachment of oriental Jewry to Ereẓ Israel was a messianic-religious one, expressed in prayers and aspirations and at times in going to Ereẓ Israel to die and be buried there. Until the 1880s migration to Ereẓ Israel was an individual matter and was not undertaken by organized groups.

Organizations. In the late 19th century the European Zionist movement attracted followers and sympathizers in all the oriental countries, with the exception of remote and backward Yemen. The first African and Asian countries in which Zionist movements were founded were Algeria, Tunisia, and Egypt. As early as 1898 communities from these three countries sent two delegates to the Second Zionist Congress, convened at Basle. Later on, Zionist organizations were established in Iraq, China (Shanghai), Turkey, and Morocco and afterward in Libya, Syria, India, and Singapore. At first groups were set up to read Zionist journals and literature from Europe. Later on, organizations were founded, sometimes several in the same city. Most of these groups were not registered officially, either because registration was not required by law or because Zionist organizations were not permitted, such as in the Ottoman Empire. From the late 19th century to the 1930s these organizations had a limited membership. The few active members devoted most of their time to Zionist fund raising, and not enough attention was given to strengthening Hebrew and Zionist education.

After World War I, though in some places only after the 1930s, an important change took place in the development of Zionist organizations in oriental countries. Zionist youth movements were established and directed by *sheliḥim* (emissaries) from Ereẓ Israel, for the most part independent of the adult Zionist organizations. The youth movements were generally more successful than the adult organizations for several reasons: they were organized and run by young people who were sent especially for this task and devoted all their time to it; the emissaries were not interested in collecting funds, but engaged in Hebrew and Zionist education; and they even dared to establish underground organizations when Zionist activities were prohibited. When necessary (in Iraq, Egypt, and Libya), the emissaries also established paramilitary underground self-defense organizations in which hundreds of young Jews were trained in the use of weapons in case of anti-Jewish outbursts.

In 1972 when most of the African and Asian Jewish communities had ceased to exist, Zionist organizations survived only in Iran and in Turkey, where young people are active in Hebrew and Zionist education.

Financial Contributions. Large sums were contributed to the Jewish National Fund by Iraqi and Shanghai Jewry only in the early 1920s. However, most of the money contributed to the JNF between 1920 and 1923 (£36,500 out of a total of £38,470) was given by a Jew who wished to commemorate his brother, and his contribution enabled the establishment of the moshav Kefar Yeḥezkel in the Jezreel Valley. The rest of Iraqi Jewry contributed only £1,970 during that time. Shanghai Jewry contributed over £21,000 from 1911 to 1926, a rather large sum for a Jewish community in that area.

The contributions to the Keren Hayesod were not large, and the number of shekels (i.e., the dues paid for membership in the World Zionist Organization) acquired by the members of these communities was small. During the 1940s a relatively large number of shekels were acquired in the North African and non-Arabic countries in Asia, as shown in Table 1.

From 1951 fewer shekels were acquired by Jews in the Eastern countries in the wake of the mass *aliyah*. The weakness of Zionist activity in these countries may be explained by the lack of strong communal organizations. The wealthy and the notables in the community were not attracted to Zionism. As the authorities in

Table 1. Shekels in Muslim and Asiatic Countries, 1922–50

	1922–33	1946	1949–50
Tunisia	7,857	13,296	32,202
Morocco	5,602	11,982	58,339
Algeria		8,100	26,652
Syria, Turkey, Iran Iraq	4,302 4,557	4,536	20,613
Egypt	6,724	7,541	—
Libya	?	1,963	7,000
Other Asiatic countries	?	4,325	2,574
Total	30,000	51,743	147,380

several Arab countries prohibited Zionist activity, there was no choice but to establish underground organizations. Indeed, it was impossible to conduct either oral or written Zionist education and propaganda. Therefore, the fund-raising campaigns also suffered.

In Poland. *1897–1918.* Prior to the restoration of Polish statehood, Poland's territory remained divided into three sections: one under the administration of Germany, the second of czarist Russia, and the third of the Austrian monarchy. In the German part of former Poland, the very limited Jewish population (no more than around 50,000 at the beginning of the century) was thoroughly assimilated into German culture and displayed little interest in Jewish affairs in general and in Zionism in particular. However, two prominent forerunners of Zionism, Ẓevi Hirsch Kalischer and Elijah Guttmacher, both lived in that part of Poland and there published their pamphlets calling for redemption of Zion, but their appeal had no influence upon the community, neither did the first conference of the Ḥovevei Zion movement, which took place in 1884 in the German part of Poland.

The development of Zionism was also slow among the great masses of the Jewish population in the Polish territories of czarist Russia, around 2,000,000 people at that time. A distinction should be drawn between the province of Congress Poland and other parts of the territory. In Congress Poland, which was one of the richest and economically most developed parts of the Russian Empire, the local Jewish population was somewhat influenced by the Polish assimilationist ideology and, on the other hand, the anti-Zionist Orthodoxy. It therefore had to be won over to Zionism with considerable effort. The standard-bearers of Zionism in that part of the country were the so-called "Litvaks," i.e., immigrants who came from Lithuania and the neighboring provinces, who were strongly imbued with Jewish nationalism and ideology and influenced other groups of the Jewish population. Quite different was the situation in other provinces, whose Jewish population was deeply rooted in Judaism, which was much nearer to the idea of Jewish nationalism and adopted the Zionist program with enthusiasm.

These initial differences disappeared in the course of time, however, as the movement conquered growing parts of the Jewish population. It was not particularly disturbed by the authorities, who were inclined to see in Zionism a means of reducing the danger of revolutionary propaganda among the Jews, or by the Polish population, which initially favored the idea of a movement likely to enlarge the scope of Jewish emigration. This situation changed considerably, however, when the Zionist movement proclaimed as a part of its immediate aims the struggle for civic and national rights for the Jewish population, as formulated in the Helsingfors Program of 1906. The reaction of the authorities was a marked reduction in tolerance toward Zionist activities and anti-Semitism spread among the Polish population, leading even to an economic boycott of the Jews, which continued until the outbreak of World War I.

The number of adherents of the Zionist movement and the scope of its influence nevertheless grew from year to year. At the beginning the membership was limited mainly to people from the middle class, but the movement subsequently won many adherents among the workers. Although a few groups broke away and joined the territorialist Zionist-Socialist Workers' Party (S.S.) or the party supporting Jewish autonomism (the "Sejmists), the other groups within the Polish Zionist movement remained concentrated around the Po'alei Zion Party and tried to combine their socialist ideology with the Zionist program. On the other hand, many groups of Orthodox Jewry had already supported the Ḥovevei Zion, joined the Zionist movement, and decided to establish a special faction of religious Zionists, the Mizrachi. The various groups cooperated closely, although the Po'alei Zion, influenced by the Russian branch with its strong proletarian class character, soon tended to proclaim its organizational independence, stressing the special interests of the Jewish workers.

The situation differed in many respects in Galicia, the Polish part of the Austrian monarchy. The roots of Jewish nationalism and Zionism were much deeper there than in Congress Poland. Not only did the movement of Enlightenment, which considered Jewish nationalism self-evident and whose most prominent representatives lived in Galicia, leave its deep impression on the area, but the organized Zionist movement appeared there years before the First Zionist Congress (1897). The Zionist movement drew its supporters mainly from among the university students and the large groups of the Jewish intelligentsia. It is not surprising, therefore, that Herzl's call was responded to by the masses of the Jewish population, despite the opposition of rather small, if vociferous, groups of assimilationists, the extreme adherents of Ḥasidism, and the unfriendly attitude of the authorities, who were opposed to Jewish nationalism. This opposition grew much stronger when the Galician Zionists conducted a vigorous and relatively successful struggle for civic and national rights for the Jews, whose platform was formulated at the Cracow Conference (1906). In the first election to the Austrian parliament, after universal suffrage had been granted (1907), the Zionists acquired three seats in Galicia. One after another, various groups of the population joined the movement: members of the middle class, considerable groups of wage earners (especially the commercial employees), university and high school students, etc. It was an authentic popular movement, trying simultaneously to satisfy both the cultural needs of the population, through a network of Hebrew schools, and the economic needs, especially by establishment of credit unions in the poor and neglected province of the Hapsburg monarchy. Adolf Stand and Osias Thon were the prominent leaders of Galician Zionism in that period.

In Independent Poland. The Zionist movement suffered strongly during World War I, especially in the province of Galicia, which was occupied for almost a year by the Russian army. After the war it was faced with a new situation and new tasks in the reconstituted Polish republic. It emerged as the strongest force in Jewish public life, challenged only by the anti-Zionist Orthodoxy, the Socialist Bund, and for a certain period also the movement of "Folkists" (the Folkspartei). At the same time, it was faced with the task of merging into one the movement throughout the various parts of the country now united within the borders of the reconstituted Polish state. This task, however, could be accomplished only to a very limited degree. The religious and socialist factions within the Zionist movement developed into full-fledged parties, independent of the mother body, which thus became one party among several others. The religious Mizrachi Party consolidated quickly and established its countrywide organization irrespective of the former territorial division. The labor movement, on the other hand, suffered for years from extreme differentiation and many splits, until at the beginning of the 1930s the main groups united in the Po'alei Zion–Hitaḥadut. The left Po'alei Zion remained aloof and outside the World Zionist Organization, which it joined only shortly before World War II. At the other extreme, the Revisionist Party developed, from the second half of the 1920s, to considerable strength. When the Revisionists broke away from the World Zionist Organization in 1935, a minority group split away from them, constituting the Jewish State Party, which remained within the ranks of the World Zionist Organization. Some of these parties were organized on a national basis, comprising the whole of Poland, whereas others, although ideologically united, stuck to the previous territorial division. Only the center party of General Zionists was divided both on territorial and ideological grounds. In Congress Poland they split into the progressive, pro-labor Al ha-Mishmar faction, led by Yizḥak Gruenbaum, and the outspokenly middle-class Et Livnot faction, led by Leon Levite; in Galicia they were divided into the West Galician Federation, under the leadership of Osias Thon and later of Ignacy Schwarzbart, and the East Galician Federation led by Leon Reich, Fishel Rotenstreich, and Emil Schmorak.

The process of internal disintegration and dissent frequently weakened the influence of the Zionist movement. This was especially felt in the field of national and local politics, the main bone of contention between the rival factions. Activities in this field were very pronounced, frequently taking first place in the program of various parties. The Zionist representation in the Polish Sejm grew considerably, especially in the first three parliaments, reaching its climax in the second Sejm with 32 Zionist deputies out of a total of 47 Jewish deputies. It fell considerably, however, in the following parliaments, with the progressing degeneration of democracy in the life of the country, but it still continued to lead the struggle against the ever-growing wave of anti-Semitism. In the municipalities and the administration of the Jewish communities, however, Zionist influence was overshadowed by that of other political groups, especially the Bund and various Orthodox groups on the right.

In spite of external difficulties and internal frictions, Zionist activities continued with increasing intensity throughout the entire period, securing for Polish Zionism the first place within the world movement, especially in the field of *aliyah* to Ereẓ Israel, and strongly influenced all facets of Jewish life in the country. Polish Jewry was strongly represented in the waves of migration to Palestine between the two world wars, both by worker pioneers and the middle class. The membership of the various pioneering youth movements exceeded 100,000 in the 1930s, with 20,000 in active training *(hakhsharah)* for future life in Ereẓ Israel. Not all of them succeeded in emigrating, as the number of immigration certificates was severely limited by the Mandatory government of Palestine. As a consequence, Polish Jewish youth was also strongly represented in the "illegal" immigration, especially in the later 1930s. Jewish life in Poland during that period can hardly be imagined without *aliyah* as its focal point.

 No less felt was the influence of Zionism on cultural life in all its

Lag ba-Omer parade of the Zionist-Socialist youth movement, Ha-Shomer ha-Ẓa'ir, in Kletsk, Poland, 1925. From *Pinkas Kletsk,* Tel Aviv, 1959.

forms. Jewish literature, press, and artistic life all remained under the strongest influence of Zionist ideology. One of the most outstanding fields of activity was education. Of the 250,000 students in Jewish educational institutions in Poland in the 1930s, those in institutions under predominant Zionist influence took first place. This was especially true for the network of the Tarbut schools (around 40,000 students), with Hebrew as language of instruction, but other networks, such as those under the influence of the Mizrachi and of the Po'alei Zion, as well as the officially nonpartisan organization of Jewish secondary schools in Poland, also actually remained under the overwhelming influence of Zionism, despite assimilationist pressures from the Polish authorities. Zionist influence was also dominant in the press. In the period before World War I special importance may be attributed to the Hebrew daily *Ha-Ẓefirah,* the Yiddish periodicals *Dos Yidishe Vort* and *Tagblat,* and the Polish periodical *Wschód.* In the period between the two world wars virtually all Jewish dailies and periodicals, with the exception of those published by Bund or by Agudat Israel, were either openly Zionist or influenced by Zionist ideology, including the leading Yiddish dailies *Haynt* and *Moment,* the dailies in Polish *Nasz Przegląd, Nowy Dziennik,* and *Chwila,* and many weeklies and other periodicals, issued by various Zionist parties and youth movements.

There was hardly any other Jewish community in the world before World War II, with the possible exception of the relatively small communities of the Baltic countries and Bessarabia, in which the influence of Zionism was so strongly felt. All this broke down with the destruction of Jewish life in Poland during World War II. Various Zionist groups, especially groups of Zionist youth, tried for a period to continue their activities underground. They took the lead in the clandestine struggle against the Nazi occupation and in the ghetto uprisings. Zionists who succeeded in escaping from Poland established centers for rescue beyond the border, the most important of them in Vilna until its annexation to the Soviet Union and later the German invasion of the U.S.S.R. in 1941. Zionist refugees participated actively in the political and rescue activities of various Jewish bodies, notably the World Jewish Congress. Ignacy Schwarzbart in his capacity as member of the Polish parliament in exile represented the Jewish minority before the Polish government in London. The second representative was a non-Zionist, member of the socialist "Bund" Party. Emil Sommerstein in his capacity as chairman of the Jewish Central Committee represented the Jews before the Polish authorities established in the Soviet Union. But all these efforts could not arrest the course of events: the extermination of the great Jewish community of Poland. After the war surviving Zionists, and especially Zionist youth movements, established escape routes to and from Poland (the *beriḥah*), assembled children who had been hidden in monasteries and in gentiles' homes, and reorganized Jewish education. But after a short period of transition all Zionist activity within Poland was finally liquidated by the Communist regime.

In Rumania. The Jews from the principalities of Moldavia and Walachia had rooted religious ties with Ereẓ Israel. In Jerusalem, Tiberias, Safed, and Hebron there were groups of Jews who had emigrated from these two Rumanian principalities, whence they received aid. At the middle of the 19th century the first modern pre-Zionist ideas arose in Rumania. Israel Benjamin, known as Benjamin the Second, a native of Falticeni (Moldavia), advocated Jewish agricultural settlement in Ereẓ Israel in his travel memoirs, which were published in 1856.

The first pre-Zionist groups were established starting in 1873, with the trend for the participants to emigrate to Ereẓ Israel and dedicate themselves to agriculture. The initiative began that year from Nicoresti with a group of 100 families, joined by other families from Tecuci, Ivesti, Galati, Piatra Neamt, Bacau, and Jassy. In 1875 a group from Moinesti sent a delegate, David Schub, to Ereẓ Israel to study the possibilities of settlement. The war between Russia and Turkey in 1877 hindered the continuation of that movement.

The Yishuv Ereẓ Israel Movement. In 1880 Eleazar Rokeaḥ arrived in Rumania from Ereẓ Israel to collect funds for an agricultural settlement, Gei Oni, near Safed. He also unexpectedly found candidates for *aliyah* partly because of the difficult living conditions of the Jewish population after the Congress of Berlin (1878). One year after Rokeaḥ's mission, groups that called themselves Ḥevrat Yishuv Ereẓ Israel al yedei Avodat Adamah (Society to Settle Ereẓ Israel by Working the Land) existed in 30 Rumanian towns. The members of these groups decided to emigrate with their families. The publisher and editor in chief of *Ha-Maggid,* David Gordon, suggested the creation of a central committee, and on Jan. 11–12, 1882, the first meeting of 32 branches from throughout the country took place in Focsani. The president of the meeting was Samuel Pineles. It was decided that the first group of 100 families was to leave for Ereẓ Israel before Passover, and resolutions were adopted in order to subsidize the settlement. Among the leaders of the movement were R. Avner Kasvan, Karpel Lippe, the Hebrew writer Israel Teller, and others. The central committee was in Galati, and Pineles was secretary.

In February 1882 the Rumanian parliament discussed the "creation of the Palestinian Kingdom," and Prime Minister I. C. Bratianu declared that the Rumanian government would give its wholehearted support to this plan. In May 1882 the second meeting with delegates from 28 localities took place in Jassy, with the visit of Laurence Oliphant. The English gentile spoke at the meeting and promised financial aid from non-Jews. Meanwhile Pineles negotiated with the Turkish consul in Galati and, with the approval of the Turkish ambassador in Bucharest, obtained the assurance that Rumanian Jews would be able to settle in Ereẓ Israel, except for the Jerusalem region, in groups of 50 to 100 families. At the same time a delegation sent from Bucharest to Constantinople was received by the sultan, the vizier, and the minister of the interior. As a result of these audiences, a decision favorable to the settlement of Rumanian Jews was adopted at the meeting of the Turkish cabinet. The sultan, however, refrained from giving his own approval because of the events in Egypt.

The Beginnings of Settlement. While negotiations were taking place, from the spring of 1882, delegates left Rumania for Ereẓ Israel in order to buy land there, and, from towns such as Moinesti, Barlad, Bacau, Bucharest, Tulcea, dozens of families had already emigrated. The group from Moinesti had sent their own delegate, David Schub, who in the summer of that year had bought the lands at Gei Oni, where a previous settlement of Jews from Safed had failed. In August 1882 the first organized 39 families (228 persons) emigrated; the nucleus of this group was formed by those from Moinesti who founded the village of Rosh Pinnah. The central committee also purchased another 6,000 dunams, and Zikhron Ya'akov was founded with 386 settlers. The creation of these two colonies gave an impetus to the *aliyah,* and until the end of 1882 a total of 1,322 settlers had left Rumania. In the summer of the same year a movement for agricultural training was started on estates leased by Jews. At the same time, a number of youth organizations held a joint meeting at Galati in December 1882 with delegates from 12 towns and founded Aẓilei Benei Israel. In April 1883 a second meeting of the youth organizations took place at which the integration with the Yishuv Ereẓ Israel movement was decided upon. On Sept. 17, 1883, the third meeting of the Yishuv Ereẓ Israel movement took place in Galati, and it was decided that the administration of Zikhron Ya'akov would be handed over to Baron Edmond de Rothschild, since the central committee in Rumania could not provide sufficiently for the economic needs of the village. In November 1883 Rosh Pinnah, which was in the same situation, also passed to Rothschild's administration. The 60 branches of the movement were dissolved one by one. The central committee ceased its activity in 1884. The pre-Zionist movement was resurrected again in Rumania under the influence of the movement in Russia. Between 1890 and 1892, branches of Ḥovevei Zion were formed in some towns. By 1895 such branches existed in 31 towns and two conferences had been held. A central committee was elected under the management of Pineles, and once again groups of potential settlers organized. A plot of 11,000 dunams was acquired in Brustras and a group of 80 families from Jassy, together with another 16 families from Bulgaria, acquired another 18,000 dunams on the east side of the Jordan. Herzl's *Der Judenstaat* was published in 1896, and by the end of that year the first Rumanian translation appeared in Botosani. Pineles started to collect the signatures of those who wished to settle in Ereẓ Israel. Some 50,000 Rumanian Jews signed the petition. Shortly before the

First Zionist Congress in Basle (1897) the third meeting of Ḥovevei Zion took place in Galati, expressing support for Herzl's political Zionism. The First Zionist Congress was opened by a speech of the oldest delegate Karpel Lippe. Pineles was elected vice-president of the Congress. During the fourth conference of Ḥovevei Zion in 1898, the Basle Program was unanimously accepted. The number of Zionist groups increased from 26 in 1897 to 136 in 1899.

The deadlock in which the World Zionist movement found itself caused the number of active Rumanian Zionist groups to decrease from 136 in 1899 to 56 in 1911. An additional reason for the decline was the creation of the Union of Native Jews (U.E.P.) in 1910. The Union, which dedicated itself to the fight for local Jewish emancipation, attracted the active participation of many Zionist leaders. But the younger generation of Zionists wanted a Jewish national emphasis within the movement for political emancipation. A group of young scholars, directed by Jacob Nacht, fought against the trend toward assimilation in the U.E.P. by encouraging Jewish cultural activities, e.g., Rumanian translations of Hebrew and Yiddish literature and the introduction of Hebrew as a living language in schools. In this spirit the weekly paper *Ha-Tikvah*, edited by Leon Gold, was published in Galati in 1914. It had a great influence on Jewish life in Rumania and included among its contributors A. L. Zissu, Mattathias Friedman, and J. Nacht, as well as almost all the more important Jewish writers of Rumania.

Between the Two World Wars. In March 1919 the Zionist leadership of Galati published a program of Jewish demands to be presented at the Versailles peace negotiations. It demanded complete political, cultural, and religious autonomy for Jews as a national minority. Under the influence of the young Zionist leaders, the U.E.P. rejected the attempts of the Rumanian government to evade again the problem of Jewish citizenship by involved juridical proceedings, as was the case after the Congress of Berlin in 1878. The Jewish population followed the instructions of the U.E.P. leaders and boycotted the government's equivocal laws on Jewish citizenship. Rumanian Zionists, together with delegates from the U.E.P., were included in the Comité des Délégations Juives at the Versailles Peace Conference. After the Jews finally obtained collective naturalization in 1920 as a result of the Versailles peace treaty, there remained the problem of Jewish participation in elections and in the political life of the country. The U.E.P. supported the idea of Jewish candidates. Therefore, in the next year, the U.E.P. joined the Zionists in presenting a separate Jewish list. Because of fraudulent election procedures, not one Jewish deputy was elected. It was only in 1926 that the first Jewish national deputies entered parliament, but they were representatives of territories annexed by Rumania after the war: Bessarabia, Bukovina, and Transylvania.

The Zionist Organization in the rest of Rumania went on with its policy of neutrality in internal politics. In 1919, at a Zionist conference in Bucharest, it was decided to transfer the central headquarters from Galati to Bucharest and to draw the leadership more and more from the younger generation. In the new era after the Balfour Declaration, Zionism became a mass movement whose principal activity was the collection of funds. In 1924 the Zionist group Renaşterea Noastrã ("Our Revival") was created, many of whose members had belonged to the student association Hasmonaea. Later, Renaşterea became affiliated with the radical Zionist faction. In 1930, as a result of Renaşterea's initiative, the Jewish Party was created in Muntenia and Moldavia; it included Zionists, especially from the intellectual younger generation. Along with the Jewish-national deputies elected from the annexed territories, S. Singer and Mişu Weissman were elected to parliament from Muntenia and Moldavia in 1931 and 1932, respectively. At the same time such Zionist groups as Ẓe'irei Zion, Po'alei Zion, Mizrachi, and the Revisionists were formed. Zionist leadership had been drawn from the ranks of the General Zionists until 1930, when the first coalition of radicals and Ẓe'irei Zion was elected to the leadership. The Zionist youth movements remained organized along the traditional lines existing in the World Zionist Organization.

In 1920 Rumania's Zionist Organization tried to create a school for teachers of Hebrew at Jassy, but it only functioned one year because the Rumanian authorities refused to authorize it. In 1925 a *hakhsharah* farm to train *ḥalutzim* (pioneers for Palestine) was created in Jassy. Between the two world wars Zionist organizations functioned in 71 Rumanian towns, and a central Zionist Council was established in Bucharest. WIZO, which had 5,000 members in its branches in 33 towns, set up 17 kindergartens in which the language of instruction was Hebrew. It also established the agricultural and housekeeping school Ayanot at Nes Ẓiyyonah in Palestine. On Mt. Carmel between 1922 and 1925, 3,500 dunams (875 acres) of land were acquired by a Rumanian group and given the name Aḥuzah (actually Aḥuzat Herbert Samuel), on which some of its 1,000 members settled. Another Rumanian society bought land in the Haifa Bay area.

The Zionist Press. During the interwar period, many Zionist magazines were issued in Rumanian. Among the more important publications were: *Ştiri din lumea Evreiască* ("News from the Jewish World"), the official organ of the Zionist Organization; *Renaşterea Noastră* ("Our Revival"), the organ of the radical group, which also expressed the point of view of the Jewish Party; *Drumuri Nouă* ("New Roads"), first the Revisionist organ, then the organ of the Jewish State Party; and *Tribuna Evreiască* ("The Jewish Platform"; Jassy). In addition, the monthly magazine *Hasmonaea,* organ of the Zionist students, was published regularly.

World War II Period. After the invasion of Poland in 1939, Rumania became a transit route for *aliyah* from Eastern Europe. Britain, however, pressured the Rumanian government to stop the flow of *aliyah* from and through the country. At the beginning of 1940 the collection of Zionist funds was forbidden, but it was authorized again on Feb. 26, 1940, under the condition that the Zionist leadership would not encourage emigration. In September 1940, however, the government of Ion Antonescu, which approved of Jewish emigration, came to power and negotiations were held between Zionists and the government on emigration plans. The Zionist Organization continued to work even after December 1941, when all other Jewish organizations were dissolved. The Zionist Organization was dissolved only in August 1942, by the order of Gustav Richter, Eichmann's agent in Rumania. However, the Zionist leadership and youth movements clandestinely continued their activities, while the semi-official organ of the German legation, *Bukarester Tageblatt,* carried on a defamatory campaign against the Zionists. The Rumanian government continued to negotiate with the Zionists about emigration, and at the same time a Jewish underground, in which Zionist leaders also participated, was formed. From the beginning of 1939 until the very capitulation of Rumania in August 1944, 31 ships with more than 13,000 emigrants, some of whom were refugees from Poland, Hungary, and Czechoslovakia, left from Rumanian harbors. The Palestine Office of the Zionist Organization in Bucharest succeeded in continuing its activity in the guise of a travel agency. Detecting these underground activities, the Germans initiated the imprisonment of the leaders of the Zionist Organization and the youth movements in January and February of 1944. Diplomatic intervention, especially by the International Red Cross, obtained their release, however. Imminent German defeat and the approach of the Allies allowed A. L. Zissu, a Zionist leader, to obtain from Rumanian ministers in June 1944 the authorization to create an emigration office which was to serve as a cover for the underground Zionist Executive. In order to report on the situation of Jews in Rumania, the Zionist leaders maintained contact secretly with the Jewish Agency in Jerusalem during the whole period of underground activity.

Post-World War II Period. Soon after the cessation of hostilities in Rumania in August 1944, the Zionist Organization resumed its legal activity and attracted many members because of the desire of most Jews to emigrate. The Zionist parties and youth organizations were reestablished, and Zionist weekly magazines began to appear. From 1944 to 1948 a Zionist publishing house, Bicurim, published about 80 volumes of translations from Hebrew literature and works of Zionist history and ideology. Although Britain continued to restrict Jewish migration to Palestine according to the White Paper of 1939, 30,000 Rumanian Jews entered Palestine "illegally" before 1948. After World War II the Jewish Communists founded the Jewish Democratic Committee, in which at first the Zionist Socialists also participated. But the latter were eliminated after the creation of the State of Israel as the Jewish Democratic Committee started an anti-Zionist campaign. As a result of the pressure exerted by the Jewish Democratic Committee, the Zionist Organization and its constituent parties were forced to dissolve at the end of 1948. During the summer of 1950 the leaders of the Zionists and the Zionist youth movements were arrested, tried, and condemned to prison. Some were accused of spying and others of inciting against the Communist regime. Finally, in 1955, under a general political amnesty, the leaders were liberated. (Three of them died in prison and some others soon after their arrival in Israel.) From the end of 1949 until the end of 1952 112,652 Rumanian Jews left for Israel. Then, for a period of ten years, emigration was effectively stopped, only to start again at various times since 1962. The Jewish Democratic Committee was dissolved in 1953. All in all, about three-quarters of the Rumanian Jews who survived the Nazi terror went to Israel.

In Russia. Theodor Herzl's activities engendered a revival within the Ḥibbat Zion movement in Russia, and large new groups joined the movement, which soon encompassed masses of people. The number of Zionist societies in Russia increased from 23 to 373 in 1897, the year of the First Zionist Congress. There were 877 societies by May 1899; 1,034 in 1900; and 1,572 in 1903–04. At the First Zionist Congress the Russian delegation accounted for one-third of all the delegates (66 out of 197), among them L. Motzkin, H. Schapira, M. Mandelstamm, V. Tiomkin, and M. M. Ussishkin, and four delegates from Russia were elected there to the Zionist General Council, each of them with a specific function. Y. Bernstein-Cohen of Kishinev headed the Zionist center of correspondence in Russia (the so-called "Post Bureau"), Mandelstamm was responsible for financial matters, Rabbi S. Mohilever of Bialystok headed the center for cultural activities, and Y. Yassinovsky of Warsaw headed the center for Zionist literature. For all practical purposes the "Post Bureau" became the organizational center of the Zionist movement in Russia until before the Fifth Zionist Congress (Basle, 1901), when it was replaced by the office of information headed by V. Jacobson. The delegates divided the country into districts and held district conferences. In 1898, prior to the Second Zionist Congress (Basle, 1898), the majority of the first Russian Zionists convened in Warsaw consisting of 160 delegates from 93 cities and towns, among them 14 Orthodox rabbis, supported the demand that the practical settlement activity in Ereẓ Israel continue, as against the position of the "political" Zionists, who supported Herzl's concept that small-scale "infiltration" into the country might harm the prospects of achieving the Charter. Eventually a compromise decision was formulated. The demand of the rabbis at the Zionist Congress to create a rabbinic committee to supervise Zionist cultural work was rejected. Rabbi A. E. Rabinowich of Poltava and other rabbis left the movement, became its opponents, and later organized in Kovno, together with other ultra-Orthodox rabbis, Ha-Lishkah ha-Sheḥorah ("The Black Bureau"), which published books and pamphlets against the Zionist movement.

Among the Russian delegates at the Second Zionist Congress were Chaim Weizmann, Nahum Sokolow, and Shemaryahu Levin, who played increasingly dominant roles in the Zionist movement. At the Fourth Zionist Congress (London, 1900) Russian Zionists were represented by more than 200 delegates, and at the Fifth Congress (Basle, 1901) the Democratic Fraction, headed by Weizmann, M. Buber, Motzkin, and B. Feiwel, was established. It demanded a much greater emphasis on Jewish education and culture on the part of the Zionist Organization. They were opposed by J. J. Reines and the Orthodox wing forming the Mizrachi movement, which opposed the anticipated secular character of

Zionist cultural activity.

The second All-Russian Zionist Conference was held in 1902 in Minsk. This was much larger, with the participation of 500 delegates, representing some 75,000 shekel holders. It was the only legal Zionist conference in czarist Russia and aroused much public interest. About 160 delegates represented Mizrachi and about 60 represented the Democratic Fraction. After a long and stormy debate on education, a compromise was reached recognizing both educational trends, the secular and the religious.

In 1903 the Russian delegation to the Sixth Zionist Congress (Basle) were the prime movers of the opposition to the Uganda Scheme, which was finally rejected (after Herzl's death) at the Seventh Congress (Basle 1905), where a minority group, the territorialists, seceded and created the Jewish Territorial Organization. While territorialism did not gain much ground among most Zionists in Russia, its influence grew in the budding Zionist labor movement. The Zionist Socialists (called S.S. according to their Russian name Sionisty Sotsialisty) repudiated the solution of the Jewish problem in Ereẓ Israel, devoting their main attention to Jewish migration, which they believed would eventually lead to settlement on a specific territory and thus solve the Jewish problem. Another group in Russian Jewry, known as the "Sejmists," rejected both Zionist and territorialist solutions and advocated instead the struggle for officially recognized Jewish national autonomy in the Diaspora countries. The Zionist Socialist movement Po'alei Zion, under the leadership of B. Borochov, emerged in 1905–06. Another movement of socialist-oriented moderate Zionists was Ẓe'irei Zion, which eventually became linked to Ha-Po'el ha-Ẓa'ir in Ereẓ Israel. These movements, which represented Labor Zionism in Russia, soon became popular among the younger generation and the intelligentsia. The main force opposing Zionism in Russian Jewry was also a social democratic party, the Bund, which regarded Yiddish as the sole national language of the Jews and fought against the Zionists and against the cultivation of modern Hebrew.

Prior to the 1905 Revolution, the Zionist movement in Russia abstained from any participation in Russian politics. This abstention was based on the original Zionist concept of "negation of the Diaspora" and rejection of the possibility of Jewish national existence in Russia. The 1905 Revolution brought a radical change in this position. An All-Russian Zionist Conference, known as the Helsingfors Conference (1906) formulated a new Zionist program,

The All-Russian Zionist Conference (the Helsingfors Conference), held in the Finnish capital in 1906, with Jehiel Tschlenow in the chair. Courtesy Jabotinsky Institute in Israel, Tel Aviv.

that of "synthetic Zionism," which combined the basic negation of Jewish future in exile with the struggle not only for equal rights in the existing Diaspora, but also for the right of self-determination as a national minority group (the Helsingfors Program). Consequently the Zionists nominated their own candidates in the election to the First Duma, and five out of 12 elected Jewish deputies were Zionists. In the Second Duma one of six Jewish delegates elected was a Zionist. When the czarist government renewed its political repression in 1907, the Zionist movement, like other political trends in Russia, became practically paralyzed.

Legal Status. The Russian Zionists did not request official permission to organize because they did not expect to receive such legitimation for a movement whose world center was located abroad. At first, although the authorities knew of the Zionist activities, they on the whole did not interfere. Later a change for the worse took place in the official attitude toward the Zionist movement and to Jews in general, which culminated in the spring of 1903 in the Kishinev pogrom. In June 1903 the czarist minister of the interior, Plehve, issued a directive prohibiting any Zionist activity in Russia. Herzl then traveled to Russia in order to influence the Russian government in favor of Zionism and to abolish the anti-Zionist decree. Plehve promised Herzl that the government would not interfere, provided that the Zionists did not engage in the organization of Russian Jewry on a national scale, but rather encouraged emigration.

The attitude of the authorities, however, did not improve substantially. The holding of public meetings was prohibited. The Zionists were able, however, to continue their educational and cultural activities, the collection of shekels, and the sale of shares of the Jewish Colonial Trust. Though in November 1904 a Zionist delegation learned from the liberal minister of the interior, Sviatopolsk-Mirsky, that the movement would not be persecuted, a turn for the worse took place again. The resolutions of the Helsingfors Conference increased the government's suspicions. The Zionist Organization was declared illegal. Licenses for local groups named "Palestine" were revoked, and activities on behalf of the Jewish National Fund (JNF) were prohibited (1907). Then David Wolffsohn, president of the World Zionist Organization, went to St. Petersburg (1908) and was promised that activity for the JNF and the Jewish Colonial Trust would be facilitated but the Zionist Organization would not be legalized. In 1910 the persecutions increased, and when the Zionist central committee of Russia met in Moscow with the Russian members of the Zionist General Council, some of them, including the editor of *Haolam*, A. Druyanow, were brought to trial. The central committee was then transferred to St. Petersburg and the editorial board of *Haolam* to Odessa (1912). The police did not harm the editorial board of the Zionist weekly *Razsvet* and Zionist leaders in St. Petersburg.

The Second and Third Aliyah. The pogroms in Kishinev and Gomel and other forms of oppression, together with the deep disappointment caused by the failure of the 1905 Revolution, stimulated a renewed movement of migration and settlement in Ereẓ Israel. Israel Belkind went from Ereẓ Israel to Russia seeking support to establish an agricultural school there for the orphans of the Kishinev pogrom. M. Ussishkin, in his pamphlet *Our Program,* and Josef Vitkin's call from Ereẓ Israel to Jewish youth in the Diaspora for *aliyah* and settlement contributed to a new wave of pioneering migration. Thus the Second Aliyah started, and it included members of different trends, such as Ẓe'irei Zion, Po'alei Zion, Bilu he-Ḥadash, etc. Among the pioneers were men like Berl Katznelson, David Ben-Gurion, Izhak Ben-Zvi, Joseph Sprinzak, and others who later became leaders of the *yishuv* and the Zionist movement during the Mandatory period and during Israel's independence. Middle-class settlers from Russia participated in founding a residential neighborhood near Jaffa, Aḥuzat Bayit,

Members of the Zionist women's association, Ha-Teḥiyyah, St. Petersburg, 1913. The group includes: 1) Zila Feinberg-Shoham, 2) Hannah Bielotzerkovski-Minkovitz, 3) David Bielotzerkovski, 4) Lea Zimmerman-Lichtenthal, 5) Dasha Knopper. Courtesy Central Zionist Archives, Jerusalem.

which became Tel Aviv. Settlement societies were founded in various cities in Russia. After World War I the Third Aliyah started as a movement of survivors of the pogroms in the Ukraine and of pioneers who followed Joseph Trumpeldor.

The Russian Revolution of February 1917 removed all the official obstacles from the Zionist movement, which immediately grew tremendously. An All-Russian Zionist Conference met in Petrograd on May 24, 1917, and its 552 delegates represented 140,000 shekel holders (in 1913 there were only 26,000 shekel holders). The conference reaffirmed the Helsingfors Program and succeeded in drafting a unified program of all Zionist groups for the forthcoming elections to the Russian Constituent Assembly. The newly elected central committee was instructed to take the initiative in convening an All-Russian Jewish Congress. This conference, the first after 1902, was attended by Trumpeldor, who spread his idea about creating a Jewish army to march through the Caucasus to Ereẓ Israel. About 20 delegates supported Jabotinsky's pro-British activity in establishing the Jewish Legion, but the overwhelming majority adhered to the official Zionist neutralism in the World War. The Balfour Declaration of Nov. 2, 1917, which put an end to this neutralist position, made Zionism the dominant trend in Russian Jewry, and in the elections to the All-Russian Jewish Congress the Zionists received the majority of votes. Wartime conditions made the meeting of the congress impossible, but a Jewish National Council was established in which the various Jewish parties were represented in proportion to the number of seats they had won in the elections to the congress. The Zionists also maintained the Tarbut organization with a network of more than 250 Hebrew-language schools and other educational institutions.

The October (Bolshevik) Revolution of 1917 did not, at first, affect Zionist activities. A Palestine Week, proclaimed in spring 1918, was successfully conducted in hundreds of Jewish communities. Palestine Offices were established in various cities, among them Petrograd and Minsk. Efforts were made to mobilize private capital for investment in Palestine, and various companies were established for the construction of residential and business premises, an oil refinery in Haifa, etc. Trumpeldor founded the He-Ḥalutz movement. A conference of 149 delegates from 40 Jewish communities in central Russia, which took place in Moscow in July 1918, had a Zionist majority. In the Ukraine, where the Soviet regime was finally established in February 1919, the Zionist movement was in 1918 the dominant force in Ukrainian Jewry. In the elections to Jewish community councils *(kehillot)* there, the Zionists received 54.5% of the vote, and in the elections to the provisional Jewish National Council of the Ukraine in November 1918, about 54% voted for Zionist candidates.

Liquidation and Resurrection in the U.S.S.R. Under Soviet rule Zionism soon became the object of repression and persecution. Zionist parties and organizations were outlawed, their clandestine meetings and regional conferences dispersed by force, and their participants and delegates arrested. The Hebrew language itself was gradually proscribed. Some underground Zionist activity continued, however, in the first decade of the Soviet regime, including the emergence of the pioneering youth movement Ha-Shomer ha-Ẓa'ir as an important factor among young Zionists striving to reach Palestine. In the forefront of the anti-Zionist campaign stood the "Jewish section" (Yevsektsiya) of the ruling Bolshevik Party, whose task it was to eradicate "clericalism" and "bourgeois nationalism" from Jewish life. Various attempts made in the 1920s to achieve a permissive, or at least tolerant, attitude to

Приказ Кіевскаго Исполкома.

В Кіевских „Извѣстіях" от 18 іюля был опубликован слѣдующій приказ.

На основаніи циркулярнаго распоряженія Наркомвнудела о закрытіи буржуазных сіонистских и клерикальных еврейских партійных, политических, экономических и культурно-просвѣтительных обществ и учрежденій, отдѣл управленія, с согласія президіума Губисполкома, постановляет:

1) Прекратить немедленно дѣятельность центральнаго и мѣстнаго комитетов партіи сіонистов и ея фракцій, выступающих под названіем „Мизрахи" „Цеире-Цион", „Дройр", а также клерикальной партіи „Ахдус" и еврейскаго національнаго секретаріата. Немедленному закрытію подлежат общество „Тарбут" и всѣ сіонистскія изданія.

2) Вмѣнить в обязанность всѣм членам комитетов и организацій, а также активным членам, в 7-дневный срок со дня опубликованія настоящаго постановленія, передать в отдѣл управленія подписку о полном прекращеніи дѣятельности упомянутых организацій, обществ и учрежденій.

3) Поручить представителям организацій К. П. У. и еврейскаго коммунистическаго союза, совмѣстно с представителем отдѣла управленія, провѣрить списки всѣх еврейских обществ и учрежденій, как представивших свои уставы к регистраціи, так и не представивших. Общества, организаціи и учрежденія, служащіе проводниками политических, сіонистских и клерикальных партій, должны быть немедленно закрыты и переданы в распоряженіе ликвидаціонной комиссіи по еврейским дѣлам.

4) Имущество всѣх ликвидированных учрежденій передать соотвѣтствующим отдѣлам Губисполкома по актам через ликвидаціонную комиссію по еврейским дѣлам. Капиталы внести в депозит центральной ликвидаціонной комиссіи Наркомвнудела.

5) Архивы сіонистских и клерикальных партій, организацій и учрежденій и всю проч. переписку опечатать и препроводить в центрально-ликвидаціонную комиссію по еврейским дѣлам при отдѣлѣ мѣстнаго управленія Наркомвнудела.

6) Предписать всѣм типографіям, под отвѣтственностью завѣдывающих, сообщить в отдѣл управленія о всѣх печатающихся произведеніях, относящихся по своему направленію и содержанію к сіонистским и клерикальным организаціям, таковыя изданія задержать выходом в свѣт и конфисковать.

7) За неисполненіе настоящаго постановленія члены указанных обществ, учрежденій, организацій и партій будут преданы Ревтрибуналу по всѣм строгостям закона военнаго времени. Равно подлежат преданію суду Ревтрибунала всѣ лица, стремящіеся и способствующія скрыть имущество клерикальных и сіонистских обществ и организацій.

8) Проведеніе в жизнь настоящаго постановленія возлагается на начальника городской милиціи и коммунальные комитеты.

9) Постановленіе вводится в жизнь со дня опубликованія.

Предсѣдатель коллегіи отдѣла управленія Кордовскій

Order of the Kiev local authority closing all Zionist organizations and institutions, July 18, 1919. Courtesy A. Rafaeli-Zenziper, Archive for Russian Zionism, Tel Aviv.

Four Zionist exiles in Siberia, part of a group of 15 subjected to revised and harsher sentences, awaiting transportation to prison in Tomsk, December 1925. Second from left is Aryeh Rafaeli-Zenziper.

some aspects of Zionist activity, mainly in the cultural field and emigration to Palestine (such as the semi-official negotiations of the member of the Zionist Executive, M. D. Eder, during his visit to Moscow in 1921 or the exchanges of a Moscow Zionist, Isaac Rabinovich, with high-ranking Soviet personalities in 1926) proved futile. However, until the late 1920s a number of Jews convicted for Zionist activities were allowed to leave for Palestine.

From 1949, and particularly in 1952–53, "Zionism" became an odious catchword in Stalin's anti-Jewish campaigns (e.g. Slánský Trials, Doctors' Plot). After Stalin's death this trend was dormant for several years, until it emerged again under Khrushchev in the 1960s and with particular virulence after the Six-Day War of 1967, when the almost daily attacks against "World Zionism" in the Soviet mass media and "political-education" system achieved an intensity similar to the anti-Semitic propaganda of czarist times. Meanwhile from 1948 Soviet Jews showed more and more signs of interest in, and attachment to, the State of Israel, demonstrating their sympathy for it and often their desire to migrate and settle there. These demonstrations took various forms, from many thousands of Jews attending synagogues when members of the Israel diplomatic mission came to pray or many young Jews who came to greet Israel delegations to international youth festivals, Israel sport teams, or folk singers visiting the U.S.S.R., to the famous mass gatherings of Jewish youth singing Hebrew songs and openly declaring their attachment to the Jewish nation and to Israel on the Simḥat Torah festival in and around synagogues of Moscow, Leningrad, and other cities.

This movement became more and more pronounced and daring from 1969, when an increasing number of Jews from various Soviet regions addressed fully signed petitions and protests to the Soviet authorities, the government of Israel, the United Nations, and even to Communist parties in the West, demanding their right—under the Universal Declaration of Human Rights signed by the U.S.S.R., and a convention including a clause that every person has the right to leave any country, including his own, recently ratified by the Supreme Soviet—to leave the Soviet Union for "repatriation to the Jewish ancestral homeland in Israel." There is evidence that this spontaneous movement—which can be defined as "neo-Zionist"—also encompasses private groups of young Jews studying Hebrew, Jewish history, about the State of Israel, etc. The Soviet authorities, particularly the security services, attempted to deter them by arrests, show trials, and other measures of intimidation, but the Jews maintained their campaign for the right to settle in Israel and an increasing number were permitted to leave.

In South Africa. The Zionist Organization found enthusiastic support in South Africa among the new immigrants, mostly from Lithuania, rather than among the Anglicized minority of the "oldtimers." The first Zionist associations were established in Cape Town (1897) and Johannesburg (1898). By the end of 1898, a dozen Zionist societies with some 5,000 members were already in existence. A year later the first women's Zionist association was set up in Pretoria. As early as December 1898, 12 years before the Union of South Africa came into being as a political entity, the South African Zionist Federation, including Zionist bodies on the whole South African subcontinent, was established. It was represented at the Third Zionist Congress in Basle (1899) by two delegates. After the Boer War, which impeded the growth of the movement, the Zionist Federation was recognized by the authorities as representative of South African Jewry and entrusted with official tasks, such as the repatriation of Jewish war refugees. Later, this official recognition was transferred to the general communal organization, the South African Jewish Board of Deputies, which, in the course of years, sometimes experienced competition and friction with the federation, but mostly worked in friendly cooperation with it.

In 1908 the *Zionist Record* was founded in Johannesburg as the official organ of the federation; it became the most important South African Jewish newspaper. The sympathies of the leaders of the Afrikaans community, like the generals Louis Botha and J. B. M. Hertzog, were conducive to the progress of Zionism and to its high standing in the country. Field Marshall Jan Christiaan Smuts was an avowed friend of Zionism and one of the architects of the Balfour Declaration. In later years the Zionist Federation secured his powerful support whenever a major crisis threatened the Zionist cause.

The financial contributions of South African Jewry to the Zionist funds have been outstanding. From 1926 South Africa occupied the second place in the world (after the U.S.) in fund raising for the Keren Hayesod; its per capita contribution—£1.16 in the 1920s—was by far the largest. The federation's growth is also reflected by the following figures: in 1921 there were 177 bodies affiliated with it, in 1930 about 200, and in 1949 no fewer than 350. Also the Rhodesias, Kenya, and even Belgian Congo then belonged to its jurisdiction. In 1932 the South African Women's Zionist Council was established to coordinate women's work for all Zionist purposes. It became affiliated with WIZO and in 1967 numbered some 16,000 members. The South African Zionist Federation also has a notably strong following among youth. A census taken shortly before the 30th South African Zionist Conference in 1967 showed that four youth movements affiliated with the federation numbered 6,800 active members, divided into 297 units throughout the country, and led by 556 youth group workers.

South African Zionists distinguished themselves as a highly efficient movement that succeeded in assuming and retaining leadership of the Jewish community at large. They have attained outstanding achievements in the fields of organization, financial support of Israel, the building up of an impressive network of schools, and in *aliyah*. About 6,000 Jews from South Africa settled in Israel, including members of collective settlements, men of private initiative, scientists, and public servants.

The South African Zionist Federation has been headed by able leaders, from S. Goldreich (first chairman) to H. Morris and N. Kirschner to B. Gering and I. A. Meisels. Under the successive direction of Jack Alexander, Zvi Infeld, and Sidney Berg, it gained a reputation for its organizational structure and efficiency. Divided geographically into provincial councils and functionally into some 20 departments, it covers a variety of Zionist activities, including fund raising, and embraces all the Zionists of the country, both party members and independents. Up to the early 1930s parties played no significant role in the federation; later the Zionist Revisionists and the Zionist Socialists became especially prominent. It was not until 1946 that the Executive of the federation was elected on a party basis, but it continued to include nonparty members. The number of shekel holders was exceptionally high; it sometimes approached and even exceeded 50% of the adult Jewish population (43,605 shekels in 1946 and 42,949 in 1960).

During World War II the federation also aided refugees passing through South Africa and accorded valuable material and moral support to the "illegal immigrants" who had been deported from Palestine and detained in Mauritius. In 1943 the federation arranged a "plebiscite," and its three points—to open the gates of Palestine to Jewish immigration, to set up a Jewish army, and to establish Palestine as a Jewish Commonwealth—were endorsed by 37,000 Jews. No fewer than 3,000 volunteers offered their services in the War of Independence (1948), and 700 were accepted and fought in Israel. During the period of the Six-Day War, 782 volunteers arrived in Israel from South Africa, but several times this number had registered.

In the United States. Jewish immigrants who came to the United States from Eastern Europe in the early 1880s brought the ideas of the Ḥibbat Zion movement with them, and by 1890 Ḥovevei Zion organizations existed in the large Jewish communities of New York, Chicago, Baltimore, Milwaukee, Boston, Philadelphia, and Cleveland. At the same time, newspapers propagating Ḥibbat Zion ideas appeared, two of which were *Shulamit,* edited by J. I. Bluestone in Yiddish, and *Ha-Pisgah* ("The Summit," 1888–89), a Hebrew paper edited by W. Schur. Following a mass meeting in New York on May 4, 1898, supporters of Zionism established an organization which *Die Welt* called the Zentralverein der amerikanischen Zionisten. Other Zionist organizations appeared in the months before the First Zionist Congress at Basle (1897). Opposition was expressed by upper-class Jews and Reform rabbis. The Central Conference of American Reform Rabbis passed a resolution in July 1897 denouncing Zionism in sharp terms:

Resolved that we totally disapprove of any attempt for the

establishment of a Jewish state. Such attempts show a misunderstanding of Israel's mission which, from the narrow political and national field, has been expanded to the promotion among the whole human race of the broad and universalistic religion first proclaimed by the Jewish prophets.

By 1898 two major Zionist organizations developed in New York City: the Federation of Zionist Societies of Greater New York, under the leadership of Richard Gottheil, and the League of Zionist Societies of the United States of North America, under Rabbi Philip Klein and Michael Singer. They united in February 1898 into the Federation of Zionists of Greater New York and Vicinity. Consolidation at the national level in July 1898 resulted in the establishment of the Federation of American Zionists (FAZ), under the presidency of Gottheil, with S. Wise as first secretary.

Despite initial progress, the FAZ encountered great organizational difficulties. Many Zionist organizations did not recognize its authority. The most recalcitrant were the scores of independent Zionist organizations in New York based on landsmanschaften and in Chicago on the Knights of Zion, who organized in October 1898 under the leadership of Leon Zolotkoff. Only in 1913 did the Knights accept the authority of the FAZ. Another obstacle to the growth of the FAZ was the opposition to Zionism from the left, i.e., from East European immigrants who adhered to socialist organizations and regarded socialism and trade unionism as the solution to Jewish problems as well. Difficulties were increased by the reluctance of the membership, which was primarily from Eastern Europe, to accept the leadership of "Germans," who differed from them in their way of life as well as social class.

In 1902 Jacob de Haas moved to the U.S. as editor of the FAZ's official paper, *The Maccabean,* and secretary of the organization. He tried to cope with the various organizational and administrative difficulties and to include more organizations under Richard Gottheil's leadership. De Haas instituted the "Shekel Day" and developed elaborate Zionist propaganda. Nevertheless, the FAZ was plagued by financial difficulties. In 1904 Gottheil resigned and Harry Friedenwald became president. In early 1905 de Haas also resigned and was replaced by Judah Magnes as secretary. With the two new leaders, the Zionist orientation of the FAZ changed. Gottheil and de Haas were "political Zionists" who supported Herzl on the Uganda issue, whereas Friedenwald and Magnes were "cultural Zionists" who tried to adapt Zionism to the

American scene. Other important cultural Zionists were Solomon Schechter, president of the Jewish Theological Seminary, and Israel Friedlander, also of the Seminary, a Bible scholar and communal leader. These "cultural Zionists" saw Zionism as a renaissance of traditional Jewish values and check on assimilation. Although Ereẓ Israel was for them a cultural center, they did not negate the Diaspora, which they viewed as equal in importance.

The first Labor Zionist (Po'alei Zion) organization was founded in New York City in March 1903. Its ancillary Jewish National Workers Alliance (Farband) was established as a benevolent organization in 1910, in part to attract members who might join the socialist, anti-Zionist Workmen's Circle. In its initial stages, Po'alei Zion was rejected by the socialists and regarded with suspicion by the Zionists. Labor Zionism combined Jewish national aspirations with a social philosophy dedicated to the establishment of a new political and economic order both in Ereẓ Israel and the Diaspora. During its first decade, the platform included as priorities: the furthering of Jewish settlement in Palestine, the struggle against assimilation, aid to Jewish workers, and the building of Yiddish folk schools. Its organs, *Der Yidisher Kemfer* (1905, with interruptions) and *The Jewish Frontier* (1934), exerted wide influence, especially in liberal and progressive circles outside Zionist ranks (the latter under the editorship of Ḥayyim Greenberg).

In 1911 a new FAZ administration whose members were mostly East European was elected. Friedenwald remained honorary president, but the affairs of the organization were handed to the chairman of the executive, Louis Lipsky. He shared the burden with his associates Abraham Goldberg, Bernard Rosenblatt, and Senior Abel, who founded the Yiddish organ of the movement, *Dos Yidishe Folk* (1909). Until World War I attempts were made to improve administration, notably by Henrietta Szold, who functioned as secretary between 1910 and 1911. Newly founded organizations gradually established ties with the FAZ: Po'alei Zion, Hadassah Women's Organization, founded by Henrietta Szold (1912), and the Mizrachi Organization of America (1914). The latter was established in 1911 by Meir Berlin (Bar-Ilan). In time it became the backbone of the World Mizrachi Organization by virtue of its numbers and resources.

World War I and After. Early in 1914 the Federation of American Zionists, and American Zionism, was small and weak; its membership was static and it was suffering from financial stress.

It did enjoy the support of the *Day* and *Morning Journal*, two leading Yiddish dailies. The *Forward*, however, was sharply anti-Zionist out of socialist conviction until it became more sympathetic during the 1920s. With the outbreak of World War I, international Zionist activity became largely centered in the U.S., where the Provisional Committee for General Zionist Affairs (PZC) was established. Louis D. Brandeis, who had his first contact with Zionism through Jacob de Haas, Nahum Sokolow, and Bernard Richards, accepted its chairmanship. He took up his role with great energy and drew to the Zionist movement Felix Frankfurter, Louis Kirstein, and Bernard Flexner, all of whom were also attracted by its democratic and progressive ideas. Under Brandeis' able leadership, the financial situation of the FAZ improved, and membership and political influence increased. Brandeis and his associates were influenced through Horace Kallen and others by the idea of cultural pluralism, the essence of which is that America is a nation of nations in which different cultures are blended. This theory served to reconcile "Americanism" with Zionism.

After Brandeis' elevation to the Supreme Court in June 1916, he resigned as active chairman but continued to lead the FAZ through his associates, notably de Haas. In 1916 the Po'alei Zion and Mizrachi organizations withdrew from the Provisional Zionist Committee, and in 1917 the federation reorganized all its branches into the Zionist Organization of America (ZOA), which was based on territorial districts. Brandeis became honorary president, Judge Julian W. Mack president, Stephen S. Wise and Harry Friedenwald vice-presidents.

After the war Brandeis visited Palestine and formed plans to build its future on the basis of large-scale investment and centrally controlled public corporations. He wanted the ZOA to collect funds for specific economic projects. At the London Conference of 1920 his views clashed with Weizmann's who wanted to found the Keren Hayesod as a general fund to improve the economy and settlement methods of Palestine, as well as to establish educational institutions. The Brandeis group refused to accept the decisions of the World Zionist Organization, represented by Weizmann. At the Cleveland convention of the ZOA in 1921, in which the issues were debated, a majority rejected Brandeis' views, and as a result he and his close associates seceded from the mainstream of Zionist activity in the U.S. and concentrated their efforts on fostering the economic development of Palestine, as, e.g., through the Palestine Economic

Corporation. Louis Lipsky, who led the opposition to Brandeis, became president, with Abraham Goldberg, Emanuel Neumann, Morris Rothenberg, and others as his collaborators. The Lipsky administration remained in office until 1930. During this period the ZOA concentrated on fund raising but was not very successful. It established the Keren Hayesod in the United States.

Article 4 of the League of Nations Mandate had made specific provision for the recognition of a "Jewish agency" to advise and cooperate with the administration of Palestine as representative of the Jewish people. U.S. Jewry, by reason of its tremendous numbers and resources, was a decisive factor in "enlarging" the Jewish Agency. Louis Marshall, the leading American "non-Zionist," convened two nonpartisan conferences to consider Palestine problems in 1924 and 1925. These meetings resulted in proposals to include non-Zionist representation in an enlarged Jewish Agency. The proposal to enlarge the Agency by the co-option of non-Zionists was also approved in principle by the Zionist Congress in 1927, and in that year, following publication of a preliminary agreement between Weizmann and Marshall, a Joint Palestine Survey Commission was appointed. It made recommendations for practical work in Palestine upon which both Zionists and non-Zionists could agree. In August 1929 the constitution of the enlarged Agency was approved and the Americans received the largest number of the 112 seats allotted to non-Zionists (44). However, due to the death of Marshall, the onset of the economic depression, the subsequent political events, and the disorganization of the American section of the Jewish Agency, the Zionists continued to control all activities and policies of the Agency.

The riots in Palestine in 1929, coupled with the U.S. economic crisis, further lowered the morale of the ZOA, whose membership declined to 8,000. There was a general clamor for Brandeis' return. At the convention in 1930, an executive committee of 18, composed mainly of Brandeis' circle, was elected with Robert Szold its chairman from 1930 to 1932. From 1932 to 1936 Morris Rothenberg functioned as president; Stephen S. Wise succeeded him from 1936 to 1938, followed by Solomon Goldman in 1938, Edmund Kaufmann in 1940 and Judge Louis E. Levinthal in 1941.

World War II. With the outbreak of World War II, the ZOA formed the American Emergency Committee for Zionist Affairs, which later became the American Zionist Emergency Council, presided over by Stephen Wise and Abba Hillel Silver. On May 9–11, 1942, at New York's Biltmore Hotel, a Zionist Con-

The 42nd annual convention of the Zionist Organization of America, New York, 1939. Courtesy Central Zionist Archives, Jerusalem. Photo Empire, New York.

vention consisting of delegates of the ZOA, Hadassah, Mizrachi, and Po'alei Zion enacted the Biltmore Program which defined the postwar Zionist aim as the establishment of Palestine as a Jewish Commonwealth. From 1945 the Zionist Emergency Council directed the energies and propaganda of the movement to influence the entire Jewish community, the U.S. government, and public opinion to support its demands in Palestine. Through these efforts American Zionists contributed decisively to the political prerequisites for the establishment of the State of Israel on May 14, 1948.

During and after the war, a dissident group, called at first Committee for a Jewish Army and later the Hebrew Committee for National Liberation, agitated in the U.S., mainly through newspaper advertisements, by expounding and supporting the ideas and acts of the Irgun Ẓeva'i Le'ummi (I.Ẓ.L.) in Palestine. The group was headed by an I.Ẓ.L. leader, Hillel Kook (who appeared in America under the name of Peter Bergson), and enlisted the support of several prominent Jews and non-Jews. The style and tactics of the "Bergson group" were the subject of sharp controversies in Zionist circles, particularly among Revisionists and their sympathizers.

In addition to their efforts in the political field, American Zionists were among the most active participants in practical aid to the *yishuv* in its struggle after 1945; they helped with "illegal" immigration, the *beriḥah,* secret shipment of arms to the Haganah, and great sums of money. The greatest number of volunteers to the *yishuv*'s fighting forces, which were called *Mitnaddevei Ḥuẓ la-Areẓ* (Maḥal), came from the United States. However, only after World War II, under the impact of the Nazi Holocaust in Europe and, later, the establishment of the State of Israel, did Zionism become accepted by the bulk of the Jewish community in America.

Opposition to Zionism. From the beginning Zionism had encountered great opposition, especially from Reform Judaism. Among the staunchest, most influential opponents were rabbis Emil G. Hirsch and Kaufmann Kohler. Other prominent Reform rabbis, however, such as Gustav Gottheil, Jacob Raisin, Bernard Felsenthal, and Maximilian Heller, supported the movement. In 1907 professors Max Margolis, Henry Malter, and Max Schloessinger, all strong sympathizers with Zionism, resigned from the Reform Hebrew Union College faculty;the Zionists charged that they were forced to resign by the College's anti-Zionist president Kohler. Among the younger generation, Stephen S. Wise, Judah L. Magnes, and Abba Hillel Silver were notable exceptions to the anti-Zionism of the Reform rabbinate. The main body of the Central Conference of American Rabbis was anti-Zionist and delivered pronouncements against Zionism until 1920. After the Balfour Declaration (1917) and the San Remo decision on Palestine (1920), the Reform movement adopted, although unofficially, a position of non-Zionism which allowed cooperation with Zionists in philanthropic enterprises. In 1935 they revised their collective negative stand on Zionism in favor of individual choice, and further conciliation occurred after the "Columbus Platform" of 1937. A small minority group, however, continued with its opposition to Zionism.

In November 1942 the American Council for Judaism was formed, composed of Reform rabbis and influential lay leaders, such as Lessing Rosenwald, with Rabbi Elmer Berger as its head. The Central Conference of American Rabbis tried to halt this split within its ranks, but to no avail. Whereas the Reform movement as a whole tended to pro-Zionism, the Council continued its anti-Zionist activities and upon the establishment of the State of Israel it stated:

> The State of Israel is not the state or homeland of the Jewish people: to Americans of Jewish faith it is a foreign state. Our single exclusive national identity is to the United States.

Jewish Orthodox circles were divided nearly from the beginning on the Zionist issue. While the Zionist Mizrachi and the Ha-Po'el ha-Mizrachi found many adherents among the East European Jews, Agudat Israel, a smaller but articulate group, was anti-Zionist out of conviction that Zionism was secularist and incompatible with Orthodox Judaism. Only during World War II did these groups abate their anti-Zionism, and in 1945, with some internal opposition, Agudat Israel declared its willingness to cooperate with the Zionists. On the fringe of Orthodoxy, extremist opposition to Zionism was continued by the Satmar Rebbe Joel Teitelbaum, who condemned the Zionists for trying to hasten the redemption by establishing a "heretical" state.

Within the lay leadership of American Jewry, Zionism at first found its strongest opponent in the American Jewish Committee, whose leadership included at various times, among others, Mayer Sulzberger, Cyrus Adler, Irving Lehmann, Louis Marshall, Jacob Schiff, Felix Warburg, Oscar Straus, Cyrus Sulzberger, and Julius Rosenwald, all wealthy, of German background, and non- or anti-Zionists. After the Balfour Declaration, however, the Committee tacitly recognized the ZOA as the representative of those Jews directly concerned with the welfare of Palestine, although within the American context the AJC, which was an unelected elite, opposed the "Congress Movement" during World War I, which was advanced by Zionists and based on mass support. During the 1920s the leaders of the AJC were approached by Weizmann in order to establish the enlarged Jewish Agency. Zionist "Diaspora nationalism," however, which the AJC saw as a threat to their position and patriotism, remained an issue of contention between them. Thus, opposition to the Zionists continued in various forms until January 1948, when Judge Proskauer, under the pressure of the pro-Zionist Jewish consensus in the U.S., declared the committee's acceptance of the Jewish state recommended by the United Nations Special Committee on Palestine (UNSCOP). However, the AJC remained apprehensive about the status of American Jews in the light of a Jewish state. It was willing to support Israel while remaining independent of direct Israel interference in its affairs. In 1950 David Ben-Gurion, as prime minister, exchanged letters on the subject with Jacob Blaustein, president of the AJC. Ben-Gurion stated that Israel represented only its own citizens and had no claim to speak in the name of the Jews in the Diaspora. The Jews of the United States, as a community and as individuals, owed political loyalty only to the United States, and the Jews in Israel had no intention of interfering in the affairs of Jewish communities abroad. The effect of these letters was the cooperation of the AJC with Israel within defined areas of agreement.

Mass Support and Fund Raising. Dedicated supporters of the Zionist movement came from the ranks of Conservative Judaism. Solomon Schechter and his faculty at the Jewish Theological Seminary supported Zionism despite the objection of the Reform-oriented board of directors of the Seminary. The meetings of the Rabbinical Assembly of America were consistently characterized by expressions of sympathy for Zionism. The Reconstructionist movement, under the leadership of Rabbi Mordecai M. Kaplan. also was always pro-Zionist. It viewed its endeavor in Palestine as a means to achieve a renaissance in Jewish life in America as well. Guided by Rabbi Kaplan's concept of "Jewish Peoplehood," Reconstructionist rabbis worked within the Zionist movement in order to achieve their twofold aim.

From the 1930s on the ZOA devoted more and more attention to fund raising, mainly in the United Palestine Appeal. There was considerable rivalry with non-Zionist overseas agencies, especially the American Jewish Joint Distribution Committee (JDC), for the allocation of funds raised in local communities. In 1939–40 the UPA and JDC combined into the United Jewish Appeal (UJA). The frequent consequence of such cooperation was a lack of emphasis on Zionist ideology in Zionist circles. The situation changed from the 1940s when fund raising and political ideology became indistinguishable. Zionist fund raising became the almost universal expression of Jewish identification and communal participation. In April 1960, following criticism from a U.S. Senate committee and other sources of the practice of returning a small proportion of funds raised for Israel for educational activities in the U.S., an agreement was reached between the Jewish Agency and the leadership of the UJA to establish an entirely American body, the Jewish Agency for Israel, Inc., to budget and allocate funds raised in the United States for immigrant needs in Israel. This body was charged with authorizing the expenditure in Israel of funds contributed in America, thus giving American Jewry a direct say and responsibility in administering its funds in Israel. Aid to Israel by Jews in the U.S. was channeled through the UJA and other overseas agencies, and through the Israel Bond Organization. From 1948 through 1968, the UJA provided over $1,100,000,000. In times of crisis for Israel, the sums collected reached unprecedented proportions, as evidenced at the time of the Six-Day War: in 1966 the sale of Israel Bonds totaled $11,000,000; in 1967, $175,000,000. In 1970–71, in the face of threats to Israel security, the goal was the largest ever, $1,000,000,000. In addition to fund raising, private investment was fostered by bodies such as the Palestine Economic Corporation (PEC). American contributors and investors were not only declared Zionists, but Jews who felt a sense of identification with the Jewish people. As a consequence, American Jewish philanthropy shifted its main priority from support of American Jewish causes to the support of Israel, and the distinction between philanthropic humanitarianism and political Zionism lost its practical significance.

Aliyah and Youth Movements. Aside from the increase in funds, there was also evidence of greater American immigration to Israel, the ultimate expression of commitment to Zionism. In the first three and a half years of the state's existence (May 1948–December 1951), out of a total of 684,201 immigrants to Israel, only

1,909 were Americans. Until 1961 immigration from the United States was less than 1.1% of the total number of immigrants. Between 1960 and 1967 immigration to Israel from the U.S. was 2,000 per year; immediately after the Six-Day War this figure rose to 5,000 per year. After 1967 a "grass roots" immigration movement started independent of the Jewish Agency, which in 1968 formed the Association of Americans and Canadians for Aliyah. The resolutions of the 27th Zionist Congress (Jerusalem, 1968) stated that all necessary help be extended to this and all other organizations seriously contemplating immigration. Immigration in 1970 and 1971 was approximately 7,000 annually. The Zionist movement in America financially assisted established educational institutions and youth movements (Iḥud Habonim, Young Judea, Benei Akiva, etc.), summer camps, and also organized tours to Israel. In the 1950s and 1960s membership in these movements declined mostly as a result of the growing Jewish affiliation to the various religious movements and their youth groups.

Organizational and Cultural Impact. After World War II, as a continuation of the framework created by the American Zionist Emergency Council, an American section of the Jewish Agency Executive was established in New York, consisting of leading members of the ZOA, Hadassah, the Labor Zionists, and Mizrachi. They participated regularly in plenary sessions of the Executive, whose main center remained in Jerusalem.

In 1957 Mizrachi and Ha-Po'el ha-Mizrachi (founded in 1925) united into the Religious Zionists of America. The women's organizations of both groups, as well as their respective youth groups, Mizrachi ha-Ẓa'ir and Benei Akiva, remained separate organizations. In 1923 Labor Zionism formed the Histadrut Campaign, which raised funds for the various institutions of the Histadrut in Israel. Pioneer Women, founded in 1926, made its main function raising funds for the women's division of the Histadrut (Mo'eẓet ha-Po'alot). The youth affiliated to Labor Zionism, Habonim, administer summer camps and year-round social and cultural programs in North America.

In the late 1960s Zionists became concerned with increasing their propaganda activities through new tactics and approaches, especially on the American campuses where the New Left and Black Nationalists developed an explicit anti-Zionist ideology which denied Israel's right to exist and supported Arab aims to destroy Israel—an ideology which even attracted a number of Jewish students. Independent radical campus groups (e.g., the

Radical Zionist Alliance) emerged throughout the U.S. to counter this ideology from a Jewish point of view.

Partly under the impact of this Zionist revival in the new generation, an important reform took place in the structure of American Zionism. Instead of the relatively weak coordinating body called the American Zionist Council, in which the main parties and organizations were represented, the Zionist Federation of America was established in 1970. Zionist affiliation of individuals became henceforth possible without the intermediary of a particular party or organization.

The voluminous literature and extensive ideological debates on the relationship between American Jewry and Israel indicated the impact made on the Diaspora by the State of Israel. American Jews showed themselves more willing and ready to be identified as Jews, to affiliate with Jewish organizations and institutions, and to send their children to Jewish schools as a result of their ties to Israel. Israel occupies an important place in synagogue activities, sermons, and various religious celebrations, and Israel's Independence Day assumes an important place in the American Jewish calendar. The Israel flag is frequently displayed in synagogues and community centers. In many synagogues prayers for the welfare of the State of Israel and world Jewry are recited on Sabbaths and holidays following that for the welfare of the United States. Both the Conservative and Reform branches attempt to establish themselves in Israel through rabbinical schools and various educational programs.

Another impact of Israel has been the use of the Hebrew language in contrast to the decline of Yiddish. Hebrew songs and Israel folk dances have become American Jewish popular culture: at weddings, bar mitzvot, and on many college campuses. Jewish art, which traditionally concentrated on East European themes, expanded to include Israel symbols; Israel crafts find a wide market among American Jews. Fiction on Israel life increases rapidly and an extensive periodical literature is directed from Israel institutions toward American Jewry.

Israel had a profound impact on the ideologies of American Jews. The anti-Zionist American Council for Judaism was the only American Jewish organization which claimed that any suggestions of an ethnic bond among Jews, especially the ideas of Zionism and the creation of the State of Israel, harmed the position of the Jews in America because it placed in question their loyalty to the United States. With the progress of the State of Israel and particularly after the Six-Day War, many of its members and supporters shifted

Demonstration in support of Israel in Lafayette Park, Washington, during the Six-Day War, June 1967. On the opposite side of the street, by the White House railings, a pro-Arab group is demonstrating. Photo U.P.I., New York.

to a more pro-Israel stance, and the Council's influence dwindled considerably. Agudat Israel, on the other hand, which before the establishment of the state held that any state not governed by *halakhah* would be illegitimate, accepted the State of Israel, as did almost all other Orthodox Jewish groups in America.

Jewish religious and welfare institutions in America, such as the National Council of Jewish Women, B'nai B'rith, and the Jewish War Veterans, as well as civic organizations such as the Anti-Defamation League and the National Communal Relations Advisory Council, all adopted an official stand of "non-Zionism." In practice, however, they support the State of Israel and demands for an American policy of friendship toward Israel. As a consequence, they reject the suggestion that Jewish ethnic traditions about Zionism and the existence of the State of Israel create conflicts of dual loyalty.

Religious and Ideological Issues. There are, however, issues of concern to some of these organizations. Orthodox Jewry in

America feels itself intimately involved in the course of religious affairs in Israel and presses the state to pursue official religious policies in accord with its own religious beliefs. Similarly, Israel rabbis command influence and respect among similar circles in the United States. The Conservative and Reform movements, on the other hand, are concerned that the legal establishment of religious Orthodoxy in Israel involved discrimination against non-Orthodox Jews there. Some demanded the separation of state and religion or the adoption of forms of religious practice closer to their own points of view. The concern of the American religious groups implies that the religious forms practiced in Israel are of direct relevance to American Jews.

After the establishment of the State of Israel, controversies also arose between Israelis and American Zionists over their relationships in the future. The Americans demanded a separation of the activities of the state from those of the Jewish Agency and the World Zionist Organization, whereas the Israelis wanted Jerusalem to be the center of all the Zionist activities. In addition, there was a great controversy about the meaning of the Diaspora and the obligation to immigrate to Israel. The Americans claimed that America was not *galut* because Jews were secure and not oppressed there (Rose Halprin) and that the Zionist Organization should not submit to the authority of Israel (Abba Hillel Silver). American Zionists wanted to be recognized as the liaison for all activities between American Jews and Israel. They demanded that, through legislation, Israel recognize their leading position in fund raising and practical work, a demand practically achieved in 1952 through the passage of the Zionist Organization and Jewish Agency Law in the Knesset and the covenant signed subsequently between the Israel government and the Jewish Agency.

American Zionists maintained that the most important issue for the Jews was their survival as a people. Since Jews will continue to live in the Diaspora, only a Zionism that recognized the essential ethnic elements of the Jewish people could keep them from cultural disintegration. For this reason a strong emphasis on cultural continuity, Hebrew, and a strong bond with Israel are the tasks of American Zionism (Ben Halpern), although since 1967 the furtherance of *aliyah* from the U.S. also became a legitimate part of Zionist activity in America. In essence this is a neo-Aḥad Ha-Am position which sees Israel as the cultural center of the Jewish people but simultaneously dependent on the moral, political, and financial assistance of the Diaspora.

In Yugoslavia. Zionism in the countries that united on Dec. 1, 1918, to form the kingdom of the Serbs, Croatians, and Slovenes sprang from three main sources: the traditional national-religious aspirations of Sephardi Jewry, which was permeated with messianic yearnings; the youth of these countries who had studied in Vienna; and the influence of the Ḥovevei Zion movement, which penetrated into these regions from Galicia, especially after the conquest of Bosnia by the Austrian army in 1878. Among the forerunners of Zionism were two rabbis in Croatia, although their activities had no reverberations in their immediate surroundings. Jekuthiel Hirschenstein, the rabbi of Varazdin, gave advice to Moshe Zaks, a Jerusalemite, who tried to engage in a kind of Zionist diplomacy in Vienna and Germany, as shown through their correspondence during the years 1835–38. Judah Hai Alkalai actively engaged in the revival of Jewish nationhood, both philosophically and in practice, and tried in vain to bring the Jews of the Serbian city of Sabac to Ereẓ Israel after the pogroms of 1865. Viennese Zionism influenced the southern Slavic countries even before the advent of Herzl. David M. Alkalai, a relative of Judah Alkalai, was a member of the Viennese Zionist student group Kadimah, founded by Nathan Birnbaum. He and his wife, Rachel, Alkalai's granddaughter, were among the few representatives from the southern Slavic countries at the First Zionist Congress (1897). The others were Marcus (Mordecai) Ehrenpreis from Djakovo and Armand Kaminka from Osijek. Immediately after the Congress, Alkalai founded an association named Zion in Belgrade and, in 1937, he became the second chairman of the Zionist Organization of Yugoslavia. At the turn of the century, Sephardi students from the southern Slavic countries, including Bulgaria, established the Zionist Esperanza Society in Vienna. A student Zionist association, Bar Giora, uniting Ashkenazi and Sephardi Jewish students from the southern Slavic countries, was organized. In 1904 the two societies held meetings together and thus laid the foundation for cooperation between the southern Slavic Zionists. Judeja, a Zionist student organization from Zagreb, joined them in 1908.

Through the initiative of the Osijek Zionists (pioneers of Herzl's political Zionism in Croatia), led by Hugo Spitzer, the Yugoslav Zionist Federation was founded in 1909 within the borders of the Hapsburg monarchy. It united the Zionist groups that had been established in the cities and towns. The first Zionist local group of this kind was founded in 1897 by Nathan Landau, a teacher in the town of Brcko in Bosnia. Other active Zionists of the early period were Gustav Seidemann, Yoḥanan Thau, Raphael Poljokan, and A. D. Levi. Under the influence of the youth who had studied in Vienna, in 1898 a group of high school students in Zagreb formed an organization that produced a generation of leaders. Led by Alexander Licht, they transformed Zagreb from a center of assimilationism into the center of Yugoslav Zionism and the seat of most of its institutions. Licht's brother Herman organized the Jewish working youth. In Belgrade, David Albala, a member of Bar Giora, founded the youth organization Gideon, which also raised a group of active Zionists. Between the Balkan War and World War I there was a discernible emigration of Jews from Bitolj (Monastir), Macedonia, some of whom reached Jerusalem. Active, organized Zionism actually began in Macedonia between the two world wars in close contact with the center in Zagreb. Leon Kamhi was the leader in Bitolj and Josef Behar in Skoplje. In Vojvodina, which belonged to Hungary, assimilationist trends prevailed until the end of World War I.

World War I brought a temporary halt to all Zionist activities in the region, due to the government's prohibition, as well as the drafting of active Zionists into the army. Before the end of the war, however, the movement came to life in Croatia, Bosnia, and also in Vojvodina, partly because of the presence of a few Russian Jewish prisoners of war and Galician Jewish soldiers in the Austrian army garrisoned there. The leader of the Zagreb Zionists then was Lav Stern. The first conference of the Yugoslav Zionist Organization assembled in Zagreb in January 1919, immediately after the establishment of the independent kingdom of Yugoslavia, with representatives from every part of the new monarchy. It served to renew the tradition of undefined unity and cooperation in the Zionist movement that had been prevalent before World War I and carried on in this role during the years between the two world wars. In 1919 a union of Jewish youth associations was established, uniting most of the students and working youth who had ties with various world Zionist youth movements. The union organized youth assemblies and summer camps. In 1920 the first *hakhsharah* and Palestine Office were founded under the chairmanship of Abraham Werber (Avishur), as a result of the influence of pioneers of the Third Aliyah who passed through Zagreb in 1919–20 and the conference of Ha-Po'el ha-Ẓa'ir in Prague (1920). *Hakhsharot* existed until the Nazi occupation, training *ḥalutzim* from Central Europe. The first pioneers from Yugoslavia went to Palestine in

1921, and their *aliyah* continued until the Holocaust, with the numbers depending upon the Mandatory entry permits ("certificates") allocated to Yugoslavia.

Under the leadership of Julius Dohany, in 1929 the Revisionists broke away from the Yugoslav Zionist Organization and set up Betar; the Zionist Organization, however, preserved its encompassing influence under the leadership of Licht, covering the General Zionists and adherents of Labor Zionism, and youth movements from the left Ha-Shomer ha-Ẓa'ir and Tekhelet-Lavan (Neẓaḥ) to General Zionists. The number of religious Zionists was small and their influence minimal.

Although there was full cooperation between the Ashkenazi and Sephardi elements of the community from the end of the 19th century onward, part of the Sephardi community tended to oppose the Zionist Organization because of complaints voiced by the World Sephardi Organization about discrimination against Sephardim in Palestine. Already with the founding of independent Yugoslavia, the frictions between the majority in the movement and the Sephardi separatists deepened because of Yugoslav political issues. The Zionist movement produced women's WIZO groups, the Maccabi movement, and Jewish choirs, orchestras, and amateur theaters. It reinvigorated the existing elementary schools, founded Hebrew kindergartens (the first in Zagreb under the direction of Mirjam Weiller), and invited teachers from Palestine. Jewish poets, writers, and researchers consciously devoted their efforts to Jewish topics and thus developed a rich Jewish literature in the Serbo-Croatian language. A monthly Zionist publication *Židovska Smotra* ("Jewish Review") appeared from 1906 to 1914. In September 1917, before the publication of the Balfour Declaration, copies of the Zionist central weekly *Židov* ("The Jew") began to appear, and it was printed up to the Nazi invasion. *Židovska Svijest* ("Jewish Consciousness") and *Jevrejski Život* ("Jewish Life"), a separatist Sephardi publication, were initiated in Sarajevo in 1918 and united with the Zionists in 1928 as *Jevrejski Glas* ("Jewish Voice"). *Gideon* and other youth publications appeared from 1919. A monthly children's publication, *Ha-Aviv,* was published from 1922 until 1941. The monthly publication *Ommanut,* under the editorship of H. Gottlieb, appeared from 1937 until March 1941. In Novi Sad, Vojvodina, various Zionist publications appeared in German, among them *Juedisches Volksblatt*. Books and pamphlets were also published by the periodicals *Židov* and *Jevrejski Narodni Kalendar*.

The Zionists of Yugoslavia worked to win control over the Jewish community councils. Almost all the Jewish communities (with the exception of the small, separate Orthodox communities) came into the hands of a stable Zionist majority until the mid-1930s. This majority was instrumental in the founding of the Federation of Jewish Communities in 1919, led by Spitzer and afterward by Fridrich Pops. The Federation of Jewish Communities was an active force behind national Jewish education, the results of which were evident even after the Holocaust: most of the survivors settled in Israel during 1944–52, and those who remained in Socialist Yugoslavia tried to retain their Judaism by keeping in close contact with the Jewish people and the State of Israel.

10 ZIONIST UTOPIAS

In the initial stages of the Zionist movement, the border line between programmatic and utopian writing was blurred. Moreover, Zionist authors and publicists often consciously made use of the utopian form in order to visualize the end product and thereby prove the feasibility of Zionism. Herzl's *Der Judenstaat* is a classic example of a book in which Zionist ideology and utopian visions are present. In a letter to Moritz Guedemann (August 22, 1895), Herzl writes of the book: "I can now say why it is no Utopia . . . There have been plenty of Utopias before and after Thomas More, but no rational person ever thought of putting them into practice. They are entertaining, but not stirring" (Complete Diaries I, 235–6). Herzl's novel *Altneuland,* which was the most famous Zionist utopia, had a great deal in common with the program presented in *Der Judenstaat. Altneuland* sought to indicate the way in which Herzl visualized the realization of Zionism—a Jewish state in which technology would be developed to the highest degree and in which the Jewish intelligentsia would find unlimited opportunities. The new culture, however, would be essentially a European culture, based on a medley of languages and devoid of distinctive Jewish character. It is thus not surprising that Aḥad Ha-Am, to whom the continuity of Jewish culture was the essence of Zionism, was outraged by the book. Herzl envisaged that the Jewish state would become a reality by 1923, 20 years after the publication of *Altneuland*.

Another Zionist utopia, *Massa le-Ereẓ Yisrael bi-Shenat Tat* ("A Journey to Ereẓ Israel in the Year 5800 (2040)," 1893), by the Hebrew writer Elhanan Leib Levinsky, which preceded *Altneuland* by ten years, reflects the Zionist dream of East European Jewry, rooted as it was in Hebrew culture. The Hebrew language and the fostering of Hebrew culture occupy a central place in the book, and Aḥad Ha-Am's vision of Ereẓ Israel becoming the spiritual center of the Jewish people reaches fulfillment. In *Ein Zukunftsblick* by Edmund Eisler (written in 1882 and published anonymously in 1885) both the political and cultural visions of the Jewish state are found. The novel describes the Jewish exodus from Europe and the creation of the state of "Judah" in Ereẓ Israel, which has Hebrew as its official language; the fledgling state is attacked by its neighbors, but vanquishes them all. Eisler even had a nightmare vision of Germany. He exchanged correspondence with Herzl on the subject of his book. In the main, the book reflected the background of European anti-Semitism and the progroms in Russia.

Edward Bellamy's book *Looking Backward, 1887–2000* had a profound influence on Zionist utopias. One example was a utopia of political Zionism by Max Austerberg-Verakoff, *Das Reich Judaea im Jahre 6000* (2241), published in 1893. The author, a non-Jew (although possibly of Jewish origin), envisaged a mass exodus of Jews from Europe, their settlement in Ereẓ Israel, and the founding there of a Jewish state with Hebrew as its official language. He discusses the attitude of the Jewish state toward the European power tha had been guilty of persecuting the Jews (Russia) and the relations between the citizens of the Jewish state and the Jews who stayed behind in the Diaspora. Austerberg-Verakoff also established contact with Herzl. Another Zionist utopia inspired by Bellamy was *Looking Ahead* (1899) by Henry Pereira Mendes. A native of England, Mendes settled in the United States and for several decades played an important role in the cultural life of American Jewry. He was one of the first American Jews to respond to Herzl's call, and his book expresses the essence of the Zionist vision: the Jewish state and Jerusalem, its capital, would be
 the center of world peace, and by the creation of the state,

the nations of the world would redress the wrongs they had perpetrated against the Jews throughout the ages. There is also a description of the mass exodus of Jews to Ereẓ Israel; those who stay behind are enjoined to be loyal citizens of their countries, without losing awareness of the temporary nature of their residence outside of Ereẓ Israel.

At the height of the Dreyfus trial (1898), a utopian extravaganza, "Anti-Goyism in Zion," was published in *Siècle*, a Parisian journal, in March 1898; it later appeared in *Die Welt* in German translation (April 1898) and was also published in Hebrew (1954). Its author was Jacques Bahar, who represented Algerian Jewry at the First Zionist Congress. His work, written under the impact of manifestations of French anti-Semitism (which also had its repercussions in Algeria), describes a "Dreyfus trial" taking place in the Jewish state, with "Anti-Goyism" playing the role of European anti-Semitism. He makes the point that in the Jewish state tolerance would prevail and a phenomenon such as the anti-Semitism that dominated the Paris scene of 1898 would be unthinkable.

Two utopias describe a Jewish state bearing the name "Israel." One, written by the Hebrew author Isaac Fernhof, describes the ascent of the poor and downtrodden Jews to Ereẓ Israel, where they create an independent state to which they give the name the State of Israel. The book is called *Shenei Dimyonot* ("Two Ideas")—one being the reality as experienced by the author, the other his vision of the Jewish state. The second utopia that refers to the Jewish state as the State of Israel was the work of the Hebrew-Yiddish writer Hillel Zeitlin. Written in 1919 under the name *In der Medinas Yisroel in Yor 2000* ("In the State of Israel in the year 2000"), it reflects the tremendous impact of the Balfour Declaration upon the Jewish masses. The author foresees the establishment of the state and its growth and development. The work appeared in serial form in *Der Moment*, the Warsaw Yiddish daily, but was never completed. The Balfour Declaration also inspired *Komemiyyut* ("Upright"), a comprehensive work written in Russia in 1920–21 by the Hebrew author Shalom Ben-Avram and published shortly thereafter in the quarterly *Ha-Tekufah*. This utopia contains an astounding accurate vision of mass *aliyah*, the founding of the Jewish state, and the Jew at last straightening his back in the young and vibrant state.

During the British Mandatory period (1918–48), a number of utopias were published in Hebrew (as *Yerushalayim ha-Benuyah* by Boris Schatz, 1924). They often reflect the contemporary situation—the struggle for Jewish labor and the opposition to the Mandatory regime. When the Jewish state is founded, the problems are foreseen as solved and all unjust decrees abolished.

11 CHRISTIAN ZIONISM

As Zionism is understood to mean a modern Jewish movement aiming at resettlement in the Land of Israel and the revival of an independent Jewish nation, "Christian Zionism," i.e., the active support of Christians for such a movement, could not have preceded the Jewish forerunners of Zionism in the second half of the 19th century. However, Christian Zionism had a long prehistory, deeply rooted in theological thought and messianic expectations. Only gradually, with the emergence of Jewish political and settlement activities in Palestine, did Christian Zionism become more and more secular, pragmatic, and political, though it often still bore the imprint of its religious tradition and motivations. Thus, even in the historic breakthrough of the Balfour Declaration, issued by the British government in 1917, when political expediency was apparently the main factor, religious motives were certainly not absent from the thoughts of men like Lloyd George and Balfour. The importance of the Christian and biblical traditions also became apparent in the attitude toward the State of Israel in the 1950s and 1960s. The Afro-Asian world (including Muslim countries), insofar as it had no biblical tradition—particularly in Central and Eastern Asia—could only gradually "discover" and evaluate the ancient roots of the Jewish renaissance in the Land of Israel, and this realization developed mostly after these states had developed formal relations with Israel on a purely utilitarian basis. The attitude of the Christian world, however, remained clearly influenced by an undercurrent of intimacy derived from the biblical tradition.

THEOLOGICAL BACKGROUND. From the time of the

Reformation, the belief that Jews should return to the Holy Land, in accordance with the biblical prophecies, became popular mainly among pietistic Protestants and certain groups of English Puritans. It was based on the millenarian concept which held, on the basis of a literal interpretation of apocalyptic prophecies, that the second coming of Jesus was at hand and that he would rule from Jerusalem for 1,000 years (the millennium). The millenarians anticipated not only the return of the Jews to their land but also their conversion to Christianity as important conditions and "signs of the time" prior to the second coming (Advent).

The Restoration movement spread from 16th-century England to other European countries and became particularly strong in the United States from the 18th century. It flooded the Protestant world with publications. Sometimes the Restorationists requested heads of state to take political measures in order to obtain rights for the Jews to settle in the Holy Land. Their activity remained without any practical results, however, until the 19th century, when essential changes took place in the character of the movement and in the motivations of Christians who supported the return of the Jews to the Land of Israel.

Some of the new sects which arose placed this belief at the center of their theology as the fulfillment of the eschatological prophecies which would bring on the end of days and the millennium. In 1830 the Plymouth Brethren were founded in England by John N. Darby (1800–82), whose doctrine of dispensationalist premillennialism asserted that all the biblical prophecies relate to the return of the Jewish people to its homeland prior to the Advent. Before the second coming, however, the Jews and all the other nations will be judged during a period of tribulation, after which Jesus and the Jewish remnant will rule over all the nations from Jerusalem. Many Protestant Fundamentalist churches adopted this outlook and continue to promote it to this day.

In 1844 the Christadelphians were established in England

by John Thomas, author of *Elpis Israel.* From the outset, this sect supported the return of Jews to the Land of Israel. Later it offered practical assistance to Jews, such as the support of the Ḥibbat Zion movement, and even the attempt to rescue Jews during the Nazi Holocaust. The Mormons, founded by Joseph Smith in the United States in 1830, held that Jews would return to their land as "a sign of the time" of the second coming. In 1841 the Mormon missionary Orson Hyde was sent to Jerusalem, where he recited a "Zionist" prayer and dedicated the land to the Jews from the top of the Mount of Olives in Jerusalem. The Adventist movement, which emerged in the United States in 1830, split into many sects. A few of these sects view the return of the Jews to the Land of Israel as a fulfillment of their eschatological beliefs, and some of them have moved their center to Israel.

In the 19th century millenarian sects, mostly American, engaged in experiments in settlement in the Holy Land in order to await the approaching Advent of Jesus. All these attempts failed, including the 1851 agricultural settlement at Monthope, near Jaffa, of the American Clorinda S. Minor and the settlement near Jaffa of Reverend G. Adams and a group of Americans from the Church of the Messiah in 1866.

EMERGENCE OF POLITICAL MOTIVES. During the 19th century, Christian politicians in various countries attempted to act on behalf of the return of the Jews to the Land of Israel, adding to their religious beliefs the political interests of their countries in the Near East. An outstanding example was Lord Anthony Ashley Cooper, Earl of Shaftesbury (1801–85), who drew up detailed projects for the settlement of Jews in Palestine under British auspices, which he presented to the government and circulated among Protestant heads of state in Europe and in the United States. The beginning of practical Jewish settlement on the land in Ereẓ Israel, and especially the establishment of the Ḥibbat Zion movement and later Theodor Herzl's political Zionism, contributed to an increase in millenarian assistance to the realization of Zionist aspirations. The Canadian theologian Henry Wentworth Monk visited Palestine and assisted in the foundation of the first Jewish settlements. The English mystic Laurence Oliphant, who eventually settled in Palestine, lent aid to the first Jewish pioneers from Russia, tried to intercede on their behalf in Constantinople, and founded an influential Christian group in London to assist the Ḥibbat Zion movement. The Zionist activities of Herzl's friend William H. Hechler also derived from a deeply religious outlook.

The most famous of the Zionist millenarians in the United States was William Blackstone (1841–1933) of Chicago, the author of *Jesus is Coming,* in which he expounded his belief in the future of the Jews in the Land of Israel according to the dispensationalist conception. He attempted a political realization of his ideas through memoranda to the president of the United States, in 1891 and in 1916, which demanded American intervention for the return of the Jews to the Land of Israel as a solution to the czarist anti-Jewish persecutions. Hundreds of eminent Americans signed these petitions, which stimulated various reactions in the general and the Jewish press. Blackstone participated in several Zionist conventions in the United States and remained a supporter of the Zionist movement until his death.

ARCHAEOLOGISTS, SCHOLARS, POLITICIANS. In the second half of the 19th century some Christians supported the return of the Jews to their homeland out of exclusively humanitarian or political motivations, distinct from theological views. In 1852 Colonel George Gawler (1796–1869) established the Association for Promoting Jewish Settlement in Palestine, which assisted the British consul in Jerusalem in the training of local Jews for agricultural work. He also published practical suggestions for Jewish settlement in Ereẓ Israel as a guarantee for establishing British influence in Syria. The Palestine Exploration Fund, established in England in 1865, was a center for energetic supporters of Jewish settlement in the Land of Israel.

Among its members were the archaeologist Charles Warren, who conducted excavations in Jerusalem and foretold Jewish rule in the country, and Claude Reignier Conder (1849–1910), a cartographer and scholar of Palestinian studies who preached and wrote on the realization of the Zionist idea. The Italian philosopher and politician Benedetto Musolino (1809–85) preached Jewish settlement in the Land of Israel as a means of bringing European culture into the Middle East in *La Gerusalemme e il Popolo Ebreo* (1851). Jean Henri Dunant (1820–1910), founder of the International Red Cross, displayed a great interest in a humane solution to the Jewish problem. From 1863 to 1876 he attempted (in vain) to rouse the Jewish organizations in Western Europe to act on behalf of Jewish settlement of Palestine, and he founded the Palestine Colonization Society in London in 1875.

In 1887 the question of Jewish settlement in Ereẓ Israel reached the British parliament. Edward Cazalet, a well-known industrialist and economist, demanded the return of the Jews to Palestine under British auspices both in his book and in his campaign speeches for parliament. He was the first Christian who regarded Ereẓ Israel as the spiritual and scientific center for Jewry, and he foresaw the idea of a Hebrew university in Jerusalem.

After Balfour Declaration. In the 20th century, mainly after the Balfour Declaration (1917), another change occurred in Christian activity on behalf of Zionism and the establishment of a Jewish state. The British Palestine Society was established and was active from 1916 to 1924 and from 1930 to 1946 in advancing common interests of British policy and Zionism. Similar Christian organizations were founded in other countries. However, the most vigorous assistance and open support of Zionist aspirations were given by several Christian groups in the United States. In 1930 the Rev. Edward Russell founded the Pro-Palestine Federation, which was joined mostly by clergy. In 1932 the American Palestine Committee was founded. Its members included prominent public figures, statesmen, and officials. The Christian Council of Palestine was founded in 1942 and had a membership of 3,000 clergymen in 1946, mostly from liberal churches. The latter two organizations merged in 1946 as the American Christian Palestine Committee, which had a very influential membership of 15,000. This organization published books and pamphlets on the justice of Zionist aspirations and later to strengthen sympathy toward the State of Israel. After the establishment of the state, gentile friends of Israel founded organizational frameworks for their activities in the form of friendship leagues.

12 ZIONIST CONGRESSES

Before Herzl, no attempt to convene general assemblies of the Jewish national movement had created an instrument similar in scope or nature to the Zionist Congresses. Herzl's aim in convening the Congress was "to close the Zionist ranks, bring about an understanding between all Zionists and to unify their endeavors . . . the Congress will show what Zionism is and wants." His other aim—to establish "the national assembly of the Jewish people"—was realized by many of the Congresses that took place both before and after his death. The problem of the location of the Congress was not confined to the First Zionist Congress alone. Several of the Congresses encountered problems in this sphere until the 23rd Congress, which met in Jerusalem (all subsequent Congresses have been held in Jerusalem). Previous venues were Basle, London, The Hague, Hamburg, Vienna, Carlsbad, Zurich, Prague, Lucerne, and Geneva. During the periods of the Ottoman regime and the British Mandate over Palestine, it proved impossible to hold the Congress in Ereẓ Israel.

The First Congress. The location of the First Zionist Congress was to have been Munich, Germany, but due to the opposition of the community and the Protestrabbiner[24], it was transferred to Basle and held on Aug. 29–31, 1897. The historical importance of the Congress lies in the formulation of the Basle Program and the foundation of the Zionist Organization, which united West and East European Zionists in both an organizational and programmatic sense. Up until that time the East European

[24]Group of German rabbis who opposed the holding of the First Zionist Congress

Ḥovevei Zion had of course engaged in practical settlement activities in Ereẓ Israel, and they now accepted political Zionism as well. The approach termed political Zionism, an essential problem debated at the Congress, was raised and defined by Herzl himself. The settlements founded to date had indeed proved the ability of the Jews to farm the land. The Jewish problem, however, could only be solved by large-scale migration and settlement of the country, which could be effected only with international assistance and recognition. By the Third Congress this was expressed in the term "charter." The means and goals of political Zionism were formulated in a key sentence, possessing four subclauses, the Basle Program.

The First Congress also devised a schedule that was followed by all subsequent Congresses: reports on the situation of Jewish communities in the Diaspora (at the first Congresses, the famous speeches of Max Nordau), lectures on Ereẓ Israel and settlement activities, and debates on cultural questions, which were extremely stormy at the first few Congresses. Herzl acted as the chairman of the Congress (as he did at all Congresses until his death) and was also elected president of the Zionist Organization.

The Congress made a tremendous impression on both Jews and non-Jews throughout the world. Herzl himself summarized the importance of the First Congress thus: "I no longer need to write the history of yesterday [the day on which the Congress opened]; it is already written by others.... Were I to sum up the Basle Congress in a word—which I shall guard against pronouncing publicly—it would be this: At Basle I founded the Jewish State" (Herzl's diary, Aug. 30, Sept. 3, 1897, *Complete Diaries,* ed. by R. Patai, 2, 580–1). Ḥayyim Naḥman Bialik even published a poem entitled *"Mikra'ei Ẓiyyon"* especially in honor of the First Congress. A full list of the participants in the First Congress with biographical and bibliographical details was compiled by H. Orlan in *Herzl Year Book,* 6 (1964–65), 133–52. There is a vast literature on the First Congress including *Warum gingen wir zum ersten*

Zionistenkongress? (1922), in which 32 participants recount the motives which prompted their participation in the first Congress, and *Sefer ha-Congress* (1923, 1950[2]), an anthology edited by Leib Yaffe. The official language of the first Congresses was German (the minutes were published in this language until the beginning of the 1930s and after that in English). The language spoken from the rostrum was, for many years, also mostly German, but since many delegates spoke a kind of Yiddishized German it was nicknamed "Kongressdeutsch."

The Second Congress. The second meeting of the Zionist Congress was held in Basle on Aug. 28–31, 1898. In his opening address, Herzl called on the Zionists to "conquer the communities," a slogan which later led to the program of "work in the present," i.e., in the Diaspora, in order to deprive various assimilationists of their self-appointed role as spokesmen of the Jewish people. At this Congress the foundations were laid for the Jewish Colonial Trust and David Wolffsohn was placed in charge of implementing the project. Leo Motzkin, who had just returned from Ereẓ Israel, presented a detailed report on the situation of both the new and the old *yishuv*. A group of Zionist Socialists demanding representation for the Jewish proletariat in the leadership of the Zionist Organization made their first appearance at this Congress. Herzl was opposed to splitting the precariously united Zionist camp. The struggle between the "political" and "practical" Zionists had been set aside at the First Congress, and the resolution to establish the Jewish Colonial Trust further narrowed the gap between the two camps.

The Third Congress. Held in Basle on Aug. 15–18, 1899, the Third Congress opened with a report by Herzl of his meetings with Kaiser William II in Constantinople (Oct. 18, 1898) and Jerusalem (Nov. 2), in addition to a casual meeting at Mikveh Israel. While these meetings produced no practical results, their demonstrative value, in the presentation of the Zionist case before the head of a great power, was immense. There was a great deal of debate

The Second Zionist Congress in Basle, 1898. Theodor Herzl is speaking. Courtesy Central Zionist Archives, Jerusalem.

about the exact meaning of the "charter," first mentioned by Herzl, and the significance of the term "public law" in the Basle Program, i.e., whether the intent was a license from all the powers or only from Turkey. Herzl was persuaded to accept the latter interpretation. It was also resolved that the Jewish Colonial Trust would confine its settlement activities to Ereẓ Israel and Syria. The "practical" Zionists failed in their attempts to gain the Congress' approval for initiating settlement activities before obtaining the "charter," and the theoretical debates on cultural matters, which occupied several Congresses from the Second on, continued. Herzl was preoccupied with political activities, and everything outside this sphere was thrust aside.

The Fourth Congress. On Aug. 13–16, 1900, the Fourth Congress was held in London. The reason for choosing London as the location of this Congress was given by Herzl in his opening speech as follows: "England, great England, free England, England looking over all the seas, will understand our aspirations. From here the Zionist idea will take its flight further and higher, of that we are sure." The Congress bore the imprint of the severe crisis in Rumanian Jewry, with many thousands forced to leave the country and those remaining behind subject to pressure and harassment. Herzl viewed the persecution of Rumanian Jewry as further proof of the urgent necessity for a Zionist solution. Since the "charter" was still a distant prospect, matters demanding immediate attention came to the fore. The position of the Jewish workers in Ereẓ Israel was also brought up at this Congress.

The Fifth Congress. Herzl presented this Congress, held in Basle on Dec. 26–30, 1901, with the greatest of his achievements—an interview with the sultan. He also presented a report on the initial activities of the Jewish Colonial Trust. These achievements, however, did not satisy many of the delegates, especially a group of young men who organized the Democratic Fraction. They advanced the concept of Zionism as an internal Jewish renaissance and demanded serious attention to the problems of Jewish culture, instead of concentrating solely on political activities, which they regarded as sterile. The main achievement of this Congress was the establishment of the Jewish National Fund (JNF) on the lines proposed by Hermann Schapira at the First Congress.

The Sixth Congress. In accordance with a resolution taken at the Fifth Congress, the Sixth took place two years after its predecessor (on Aug. 23–28, 1903, in Basle) instead of one, as had been the practice. This was the last Congress in which Herzl participated and was also the stormiest and most tragic. While the "charter" was as far as ever from Herzl's grasp, the pressure for a solution to the Jewish problem was mounting, particularly after the shock of the Kishinev pogrom in the spring of the same year. This situation gave rise to "temporary solutions," such as the El-Arish project, to which Herzl devoted much of his energies and with whose results he was bitterly disillusioned. In spite of the Kishinev pogrom, Herzl had visited Russia, where he met Minister of Interior Plehve. He also received an official offer from the British government, which was willing to allocate a territory for Jewish settlement in Uganda, East Africa. At the Congress, Herzl advanced this proposal for serious examination, while simultaneously emphasizing that "our views on Ereẓ Israel cannot and will not be subject to change. Uganda is not Zion and will never be Zion. This proposal is nothing more than a relief measure, a temporary means of allaying distress." The vote on the Uganda Scheme was as follows: 295 in favor, 178 against, and 98 abstentions. At first those opposed to the scheme left the hall, headed by Jehiel Tschlenow, but were persuaded to return by Herzl personally, who appealed to them not to destroy the Zionist Organization. The Uganda Scheme overshadowed all other matters at the Congress, such as Franz Oppenheimer's[25] lecture on cooperative settlement, a program that was

[25]German economist and sociologist who was closely associated with the Zionist movement; died in 1943

implemented some years later in the settlement Merḥavyah. Approximately one year after this Congress, Herzl died.

The Seventh Congress. The Congress, held on July 27–Aug. 2, 1905, in Basle, was opened by its new president, Nordau, who delivered a eulogy on Herzl. Immediately afterward, a stormy debate on the Uganda proposal broke out. Opposition to the scheme had grown with the return of the commission of inquiry and its negative report on conditions in Uganda, which it found unsuitable for Jewish mass settlement. Despite the opposition of the Territorialists, who were supported by Po'alei Zion, the Congress resolved to reject finally the Uganda Scheme and the notion of settlement anywhere except in Ereẓ Israel and its immediate vicinity. The Territorialists, headed by Israel Zangwill, withdrew from the Congress and the Zionist Organization and founded a separate organization, the Jewish Territorial Association. A resolution to the effect that practical settlement activities would not be delayed until public rights had been obtained, but would begin at once, was then passed. Otto Warburg, who was to become the moving spirit of practical Zionism, made his first impressive appearance at this Congress. He emphasized the political value of limited settlement and the need for introducing it in a systematic way. In place of Nordau, who refused to accept the position, Wolffsohn was elected chairman of the Executive which was equivalent to the head of the Zionist Organization. The center of the Zionist movement moved from Vienna to Cologne, where Wolffsohn lived.

The Eighth Congress. In accordance with Herzl's tradition of keeping the Zionist movement in the public eye, this Congress met at The Hague on Aug. 14–21, 1907, while the Second International Peace Conference was taking place there. The struggle between political and practical Zionists was resolved by the decision that settlement activity in Ereẓ Israel should not be delayed until after the receipt of the "charter." On the contrary, planned small-scale settlement, not exceeding the limits of the Basle Program, was to precede the charter, which would thus be obtained on the strength of these "small" achievements. Wolffsohn was the mediator between the two camps. As Herzl's close friend and loyal disciple, on the one hand, and a sober man of affairs, on the other, he was eminently suited to this function. Weizmann's famous speech on "synthetic Zionism" merged political and practical Zionism into an organic whole and laid a common foundation for both camps. He stated: "We must aspire to a charter, but our aspiration will be realized only as a result of our practical work in Ereẓ Israel." As a result of this approach, the Palestine Office was founded in Jaffa in 1908 to direct the work of agricultural settlement on behalf of the World Zionist Organization. The office was headed by Arthur Ruppin.

The Ninth Congress. Held in Hamburg on Dec. 26–30, 1909, this was the first Congress to meet in Germany. The hope that the attitude of the Turkish government toward Zionism would change after the revolution of the Young Turks, which had taken place in the previous year, was expressed by both Wolffsohn and Nordau. A very strong opposition to Wolffsohn's leadership emerged at this Congress and was led by Menahem Ussishkin, Weizmann, and Nahum Sokolow and joined by representatives of the workers in Ereẓ Israel, appearing for the first time at a Zionist Congress. They were united in their opposition to the "commercial" approach to the settlement activities, which evaluated every project by its economic efficiency. The decision to begin cooperative settlement according to the Oppenheimer plan was a great concession to the "practical" Zionists, representatives of Po'alei Zion, and the workers of Ereẓ Israel. Wolffsohn was finally reelected president of the Zionist Organization and chairman of the Executive, which also included Warburg and Jacobus Kann. Friction over Woffsohn's methods, which were also criticized by the political Zionists as not close enough to those of Herzl, did not come to an end with the closing session of this Congress.

The Tenth Congress. This Congress, held in Basle on

Aug. 9–15, 1911, earned the name of "The Peace Congress" for ending the quarrels and friction of the "Cologne period" and bringing total victory to the realistic "synthetic" trend in Zionism. In his opening address, which contained the announcement of his resignation, Wolffsohn gave his blessings to the period of Zionist history about to commence after the "Vienna period" and his own "Cologne period." Detailed discussion of practical activity in Ereẓ Israel and Hebrew culture took place. For the first time in the history of the Congresses, a whole session, led by Ussishkin, was conducted entirely in Hebrew. The relations with the Arabs was also discussed in a speech by Shelomo Kaplansky. The Zionist headquarters were transferred from Cologne to Berlin, and the new leadership consisted of the president Otto Warburg and Arthur Hantke, Shemaryahu Levin, Victor Jacobson, and Sokolow.

The Eleventh Congress. The demonstrative absence of Nordau at this Congress, held in Vienna on Sept. 2–9, 1913, was a silent protest against the abandonment of Herzl's line. Arguments about the body in charge of the Jewish Colonial Trust took place with the Executive and with Wolffsohn and his associates. Ruppin presented a detailed report on the first settlement activities on behalf of the Palestine Office. This report, together with Levin's survey of 30 years of settlement in Ereẓ Israel, were an indirect tribute to "small-scale" deeds. On the suggestion of Weizmann and Ussishkin, it was resolved to establish a Hebrew University in Jerusalem. Bialik made an impressive appearance at the closing session. Wolffsohn, who was the president of the Eleventh Congress, died a year afterward.

The Twelfth Congress. No previous Congress had met in a period so sharply distinguished from the preceding one. This was the first Congress after World War I. It was held in Carlsbad on Sept. 1–14, 1921, after the following crucial events had taken place: the Balfour Declaration, the British conquest of Palestine, the Bolshevik Revolution in Russia, mass pogroms against Ukrainian Jews, and the London Zionist Conference (1920), at which the Keren

שקל

הציונות שואפת לברוא בשביל עם ישראל בארץ ישראל מקלט בטוח עפ"י משפט גלוי של העמים.

דער ציוניזם שטרעבט צו שאפען פאר דאס יודישע-פאלק אן-עפענטליך-רעכטליך געזיכערטע היים אין ארץ ישראל

השנה החמש עשרה

№ 932 שנת תרע"ב

מר

בעיר פלך

שקל את שקל

שקל

האמצעים להשיג
את המטרה הזאת:

א. התקדמות רצויה של הישוב העברי בא"י
ע"י עובדי אדמה, אומנים ובעלי תעשיה.

ב. אגוד העם העברי והסתדרותו ע"י מוסדות מקומיות
וכלליות המתאימות לצרך זה ולחוקי הארצות.

ג. חזוק הרגש הלאומי וההכרה העצמית
של העם העברי.

ד. הכנות הנחוצות, כדי לקבל את הסכמת
הממשלות להשגת מטרת הציונות.

די מיטלען אויסצופיהרען דאס ציעל פונם ציוניזם:

א. ריכטיגע ענטוויקלונג פון דער קאלאניזאציאן
אין ארץ ישראל דורך יודישע ערדארבייטער
בעלי מלאכות און געשעפטסמענשען.

ב. ארגאניזאציאן און צוזאמענגלידערונג פון דעם
יודישען פאלק דורך ארטליכע און אלגעמיינע
אנשטאלטונגען לויט די געזעצען פון יעדען לאנד.

ג. פערשטארקען דאס יודישע פאלקס-געפיהל
און זעלבסטבעוואוסטזיין.

ד. מאכען די נויטיגע שריט, כדי צו בעקומען די הסכמה
פון די רעגירונגען אויף דאס ענדציעל פונם ציוניזם.

ציון

"*Shekel*" certificate from Warsaw, 1912. Payment of this token sum entitled the bearer to elect delegates to the World Zionist Congress. Courtesy Central Zionist Archives, Jerusalem.

Hayesod was founded. During this period the Zionist movement in America had begun to come to the fore, and the Brandeis group had clashed with Weizmann's leadership at the London Conference. The Zionist leadership had also been transformed. The "Berlin period" had come to an end with the defeat of Germany in World War I, and the group that had obtained the Balfour Declaration, led by Weizmann and Sokolow, had transferred the Zionist world center to England. At the London Conference, Weizmann was elected president of the Zionist Organization and Sokolow president of the Executive. In addition, the first years after the Balfour Declaration had been marked by anti-Jewish riots in Jerusalem (1920) and Jaffa (1921). Weizmann delivered a report on the political activities of

Presidium and executive of the World Zionist Organization at the Thirteenth Congress, Carlsbad, 1923. Seated in front row, left to right: Meir Berlin (Bar-Ilan), Chaim Weizmann, Shemaryahu Levin, Naḥum Sokolow (chairman), Leo Motzkin, Louis Lipsky, Eliezer Kaplan, Yizhak Ben-Zvi. Courtesy J.N.U.L. Photo Collection, Jerusalem.

the Zionist Organization during the war and called on the Jewish people to assist in building Ereẓ Israel. Ruppin brought the acquisition of large tracts of land in the Jezreel Valley before the Congress for approval and was opposed by the directorate of the JNF, led by Nehemiah de Lieme. Bialik, among others, came out in defense of the Jewish workers in Palestine who were the subject of attacks by the "efficiency"-minded group, opposing Weizmann's leadership. For the first time in the history of Zionism, a representative of the workers in Ereẓ Israel, Josef Sprinzak, was elected to the Executive, which thereafter was situated in London and Jerusalem.

The Thirteenth Congress. On Aug. 6–18, 1923, the 13th Congress was held in Carlsbad. Before it took place, the British Mandate over Palestine had been endorsed by the League of Nations and the Zionist Organization became officially the Jewish Agency for Palestine, mentioned in Article 4 of the Mandate and charged with taking steps "to secure the cooperation of all Jews who are willing to assist in the establishment of the Jewish National Home." At this Congress, the proposal to include non-Zionists in the Jewish Agency was debated and aroused bitter opposition from those who considered this a threat to the broad democratic basis of the Zionist Organization. Weizmann defended the proposal against its opponents until it was finally implemented six years later (1929). The possibilities of obtaining financial resources for building up Palestine were debated at length, and Chaim Arlosoroff delivered a lecture containing a proposal for a planned economic program. The Congress also resolved to open the Hebrew University in Jerusalem.

The Fourteenth Congress. This Congress, held in Vienna on Aug. 18–31, 1925, was much affected by the "prosperity" in Palestine caused by the Fourth Aliyah (mostly from Poland) and the feverish construction of houses and land speculation. It encouraged the view that private enterprise would solve the problems of building Palestine, and criticism of labor settlement methods reached its height.

David Ben-Gurion participated in the debate, delivering a speech on the workers in Palestine and their activities. Ruppin resigned as head of the Jewish Agency Settlement Department, which he had directed for approximately 18 years, and Colonel F. H. Kisch was appointed to direct the Agency's Political Department in Jerusalem.

The Fifteenth Congress. The prosperity in Palestine was followed by a severe economic crisis and unemployment, which affected nearly 8,000 workers. Hunger and poverty drove many from the country and *aliyah* dwindled. Preoccupation with "breaking the crisis" at the 15th Congress, held in Basle on Aug. 30–Sept. 11, 1927, spoiled the celebrations in honor of the 30th anniversary of the First Congress. Weizmann outlined a proposal for overcoming the crisis, and Ruppin delivered one of his brilliant Congress speeches on pioneering and its meaning for Zionism. The Executive elected did not include a labor representative and its most forceful personality was Harry Sacher. Eulogies on Aḥad Ha-Am were delivered by Martin Buber and Nahum Sokolow.

The Sixteenth Congress. Held in Zurich on July 28–Aug. 10, 1929, this Congress, like its predecessor, met in an anniversary year and was opened with a speech by Sokolow on Herzl upon the 25th anniversary of his death. Unlike its predecessor, however, this Congress met during a period of economic recovery in Palestine, improved employment conditions, and the revival of *aliyah.* Weizmann again reported on the enlargement of the Jewish Agency by non-Zionists, which was to be established after the Congress was over. Depite strong opposition to the project (mainly from the Revisionists), the debate that had lasted for seven years ended with the official establishment of the enlarged body in an impressive meeting with the participation of Weizmann, Sokolow, Herbert Samuel, Louis Marshall, Albert Einstein, Lord Melchett, Leon Blum, Sholem Asch, F. Warburg, and others. The Executive (the "Sacher regime") was severely criticized for its attitude toward Labor Zionism. The Congress ended with the election of a new Zionist Executive, joined by two Mizrachi representatives (Rabbi M. Berlin and A. Barth), two labor representatives (S. Kaplansky and Y. Sprinzak), and Ruppin.

The Seventeenth Congress. A few days after the establishment of the enlarged Jewish Agency in Zurich, bloody riots broke out in Palestine (August 1929) and were followed in quick succession by the report of the British commission of enquiry into the 1929 disturbances; the White Paper by the colonial secretary, Lord Passfield; restriction on Jewish immigration; the negative report on the possibility of Jewish settlement by Sir John Hope-Simpson; etc. The commission report and Sir John Hope-Simpson's conclusions were openly hostile to the Zionist movement, the JNF, Jewish labor and practically all other Jewish activities in Palestine. Weizmann immediately resigned as president of the Zionist Organization in protest to the new British policy. His move, in turn, resulted in the "MacDonald Letter," which retracted much of the negative elements in the new trend.

At the 17th Congress, held in Basle on June 30–July 15, 1931, a number of delegates voiced their protest to Weizmann's policy, which was based upon the fundamental need for maximum cooperation with the British government. The opposition, consisting not only of the Revisionists, but also of many other delegates, claimed that this policy was not justified. The Revisionists demanded that the creation of a Jewish majority and a Jewish state be defined officially as the final aim of Zionism, and when this demand was rejected by the majority, Vladimir Jabotinsky tore up his delegate's card with the cry: "This is no Zionist Congress," leading ultimately (in 1935) to the secession of the Revisionists from the Zionist Organization. In view of the situation, Weizmann, despite support from the labor wing, refused to withdraw his resignation, and Sokolow was chosen president of the Zionist Organization. In spite of Weizmann's official resignation, however, the Executive of the Zionist Organization, in which the strength of the labor parties had grown with the election of Chaim Arlosoroff as head of the Political Department, actually continued to act along the lines of Weizmann's policy.

The Eighteenth Congress. This Congress, held in Prague on Aug. 21–Sept. 4, 1933, bore the imprint of three events: the advent of the Nazis to power in Germany and growing persecution of German Jewry, economic inflation in Palestine, and the assassination of Arlosoroff. The conflict between the Revisionists and labor reached its height, since the labor representatives believed that the constant incitement by the Revisionists had created the setting for Arlosoroff's assassination. It was finally decided to establish a committee of inquiry into the tragedy. A special session was devoted to the celebration of Ussishkin's 70th birthday. Sokolow was reelected president of the Zionist Organization. The representation of labor on the Executive increased and included Ben-Gurion and Moshe Shertok (Sharett), who succeeded Arlosoroff as head of the Political Department.

The Nineteenth Congress. Held in Lucerne on Aug. 20–Sept. 4, 1935, this Congress was distinguished by the comprehensive and practical lectures delivered on Diaspora Jewry (Sokolow), the building of Palestine (Ben-Gurion), the JNF (Ussishkin), rescuing Jewish children from Germany—Youth Aliyah (Henrietta Szold), and the problems of Hebrew culture (Berl Katznelson). The labor faction, the largest at the Congress, worked out a program for a broad coalition and made it possible for Weizmann to resume the presidency, and Sokolow was chosen as honorary president of the Organization and the enlarged Jewish Agency. Ben-Gurion, who was reelected to the Executive, became more and more its central figure. Sokolow died within a year.

The Twentieth Congress. This Congress was held in Zurich on Aug. 3–16, 1937, and was faced with the responsibility of resolving one of the most difficult problems that had faced the Zionist movement since the controversy over the Uganda Scheme. The report of the

Royal Commission on Palestine (Peel Commission) appointed in the wake of the 1936 Arab riots proposed the establishment of a Jewish state in part of the country. There were divisions of opinion between and within the Zionist parties on the issue (with Ben-Gurion of Mapai, for example, in favor of the proposal and Katznelson against it). In the end it was decided to take note of the finding of the Royal Commission "that the field in which the Jewish National Home was to be established was understood, at the time of the Balfour Declaration, to be the whole of Palestine, including Transjordan," but at the same time, the decision of the Congress empowered the Executive to negotiate with the British government the possibility of securing a more favorable partition of western Palestine than that proposed by the Peel Commission's plan and bring the results to the Congress before a final decision was made. In addition a special session took place in Basle to mark the 40th anniversary of the First Congress. During the session, presided over by Ussishkin, delegates to the First Congress recalled the great event in their lives and in Zionist history.

The Twenty-first Congress. Held in Geneva on Aug. 16–26, 1939, the 21st Congress met on the eve of World War II. The British government had withdrawn its partition plan, conferred with representatives of Jews and Arabs (including Arab governments) at the St. James Conference in London, and published its anti-Zionist White Paper imposing tremendous restrictions on Jewish immigration and purchase of land. The delegates unanimously expressed their strong opposition to the White Paper and declared the readiness of the *yishuv* to fight against the restrictions. Katznelson extolled the "illegal" immigration program and called for all the energies of the Zionist movement to be channeled into extending its scope, in view of the threatening political situation in Europe. In the atmosphere of impending war the Executive was reelected for another term. Weizmann closed the Congress with the emotion-filled statement: "I have no prayer but this: that we will all meet again alive." Ussishkin, the president of the Congress, expressed his grave concern for the fate of Polish Jewry.

The Twenty-second Congress. The Congress met in Basle on Dec. 9–24, 1946, after World War II and the Nazi Holocaust, which had exterminated most of European Jewry. The *yishuv* had participated in the British war effort and had waged an armed struggle against White Paper restrictions. The Revisionists had returned to the Zionist Organization and were represented at the Congress. The Biltmore Program (1942) on the establishment of Palestine as a Jewish commonwealth had been approved as the program of the Zionist movement at the first international Zionist conference after the war (New York, 1945). The Anglo-American commission of inquiry (1946) had recommended, inter alia, the abolition of a number of existing restrictions and the settlement of 100,000 Jews in Palestine. The British government had refused to accept these recommendations, and the armed resistance of the *yishuv* had increased. Leaders of the *yishuv* and the Jewish Agency had been arrested (1946). The Morrison-Grady plan for the cantonization of Palestine and its division into four districts (Jewish, Arab, Jerusalem, and Negev) had been announced. The British had proposed a Jewish-Arab conference in London to reach an agreed solution, and the release of the imprisoned Jewish leaders as a preliminary to this conference. The Congress was therefore faced with the necessity of taking a stand on both the Morrison-Grady proposal and the London Conference. Weizmann stressed the importance of the decision on the establishment of a Jewish state in Palestine and the sympathy with which Zionism and the aspirations of the *yishuv* were regarded by President Truman and American opinion. The Congress approved the political program of the Zionist Organization "to establish a Jewish commonwealth integrated into the world democratic structure," turned down the plan for the cantonization of Palestine, and also resolved that "in existing circumstances, the Zionist movement is unable to participate in the London Conference." Weizmann, who was opposed to this last resolution and favored participation in the London Conference resigned from the presidency, and for the first time in the history of the Zionist Organization the Congress failed to elect a new president.

The Twenty-third Congress. The Congress met in Jerusalem on Aug. 14–30, 1951. Weizmann, now president of the State of Israel, was unable to attend, but in a message to the delegates defined the new situation: "There is a deep symbolism in the fact that the Zionist Congress has not met in our ancient land until it has become ours again . . . It is only now, since we have attained independence and statehood, that we can fully appraise the paramount place held by Zionist Congresses in the evolution of our movement." The opening ceremony of the Congress took place, symbolically, by Herzl's grave in Jerusalem. The chairman of the Executive, Berl Locker, summed up the history of the Zionist movement and described the road it had taken from Basle to Jerusalem. The central issue debated at the Congress was the status of the Zionist movement after the establishment of a Jewish state. The Basle Program, no longer meeting the requirements of the new reality following 1948, was replaced by the "Jerusalem Program", whose essential clause was: "The task of Zionism is the consolidation of the State of Israel, the ingathering of the exiles in Ereẓ Israel and the fostering of the unity of the Jewish people." The coalition formed after the Congress included all the factions except for the Zionist Revisionists— Ḥerut. Two chairmen were elected to the Executive: Naḥum Goldmann in New York and Berl Locker in Jerusalem. One of the resolutions, demanding official recognition of the status of the Zionist Organization by the state, was implemented after the Congress in the World Zionist Organization-Jewish Agency for Palestine Status Law passed by the Knesset on Nov. 24, 1952.

The Twenty-fourth Congress. The Congress, held on April 24–May 7, 1956, was overshadowed by the security situation of the State of Israel, which was threatened by the arms streaming especially into Egypt from the Soviet bloc.

Internal affairs in the spheres of *aliyah,* settlement, and organization of fund raising were also discussed. It was decided to concentrate all funds in the hands of the Keren Hayesod and United Israel Appeal. Naḥum Goldmann was elected president of the Zionist Organization, an office which had been unfilled since 1946.

The Twenty-fifth Congress. The central issues debated at this Congress, held on Dec. 27, 1960–Jan. 11, 1961, were: the relationship of the government of Israel to the Zionist Organization and its official status, in light of the sharp criticism leveled against the Organization by Ben-Gurion; *aliyah;* absorption; Jewish culture and education in the Diaspora. Goldmann was reelected president and chairman of the Executive. After the Congress, Moshe Sharett was elected chairman of the Jerusalem Executive in place of B. Locker, who resigned.

The Twenty-sixth Congress. The slogan "Facing the Diaspora," coined in Goldmann's opening address, was the center of debate at this Congress, held on Dec. 30, 1964–Jan. 10, 1965. After the establishment of the state, Goldmann felt it was necessary to regard the aims of Zionism as the survival of the Jewish nation in the Diaspora and the assistance of the state to the Jewish people. The debate, as usual at Congresses held after the establishment of the state, spread to the sphere of relations between the state and the Zionist Organization, *aliyah* obligations, etc. The Congress resolved on the following as the first of the tasks and functions of the Zionist movement: "The deepening of Zionist awareness and its dissemination as a way of life, based on the recognition of the uniqueness of the Jewish people and the continuity of its history, the unity of the nation despite its dispersion, the mutual commitment of all its parts and their common responsibility for its historic fate, and the recognition of the decisive mission of the State of Israel in assuring its future." Goldmann was reelected president of the Zionist Organization. Sharett, chairman of the Jerusalem Executive, sent his greetings in writing due to illness. He died a few months later.

Binyanei ha-Ummah in Jerusalem, site of the Zionist Congresses from 1956, lit up for the 27th Congress, 1968. Courtesy Government Press Office, Tel Aviv.

The Twenty-seventh Congress. The Congress was held on June 9–19, 1968, the first in reunited Jerusalem after the Six-Day War. An innovation at this Congress was the participation of youth delegations, students, and members of the *aliyah* movement. The question of *aliyah* was the focal point of the debates, and the decision of the Israel government to establish a Ministry of Immigrant Absorption was approved. Additional paragraphs on the goals of Zionism were added to the Jerusalem Program: "The unity of the Jewish people and the centrality of Israel in its life; the ingathering of the Jewish people in its historic homeland Ereẓ Israel through *aliyah* from all lands; the strengthening of the State of Israel founded on the prophetic ideals of justice and peace; the preservation of the identity of the Jewish people through the fostering of Jewish education, Hebrew, and of Jewish spiritual and cultural values; the protection of Jewish rights everywhere." Goldmann resigned as president of the Zionist Organization and no one was chosen to take his place. Louis Pincus, who had been elected chairman of the Executive after the death of Sharett, was reelected to this post.

The Twenty-eighth Congress. Held in Jerusalem on January 18–28, 1972. For the first time in many years, instead of the interparty agreements to determine the appointment of delegates to previous congresses, elections were held in most countries. The membership drive which preceded the elections revealed a membership of the World Zionist Organization approaching 900,000. Most of the delegates from Israel were nominated by the political parties, in proportion to their Knesset strengths. The Sephardi and Oriental communities were represented by about 90 delegates and observers. The large representation of youth, through the World Union of Jewish Students and the Zionist youth movements, was another notable feature. Louis Pincus was re-elected chairman of the Zionist Executive. The Congress concentrated on the specific tasks of the Zionist Movement in the Diaspora, such as Jewish education, youth work, and the promotion of *aliyah* from the free countries. Considerable attention was devoted to such social problems as the cultural and economic gaps between sections of the population in Israel and the acute housing shortage. A prominent theme at the Congress was the struggle of Soviet Jewry for the right to *aliyah*. A resolution to the effect that Zionist leaders who failed to settle in Israel after two terms of office should forfeit their right to re-election, was declared unconstitutional.

Congress Minutes. Minutes of the 1st to the 27th Congresses were published in special volumes from 1898 until 1969. The minutes of the 1st to the 19th Congresses came out in German. Minutes of the First Congress came out in a second edition (Prague, 1911), with introductions by Nordau and Wolffsohn, and were also translated into Hebrew with supplements by H. Orlan (1947) and with the addition of forewords by surviving participants in the First Congress. From the 16th Congress (1929) minutes also include discussions of the Jewish Agency Council, which took place immediately after the closing session of the Congress. Hebrew became the language of Congress minutes with the 19th Congress, whose minutes are also in German; from the 20th Congress, the official records are only in Hebrew. Hugo Schachtel published the following reference works for the minutes of the first Congresses: an index of the first six Congresses (1905), an index of the Seventh Congress (1906), and the resolutions of the first seven Congresses (all in German, 1906). An index of the minutes of the first four Congresses was compiled at Tel Aviv University (1966–69).

A vast and multilingual literature on the Congresses is to be found in newspapers, journals, and special books, especially during the periods in which Congresses were held. Various catalogues of journals and newspapers are extremely rich in this material, especially the index of *Ḥamishim Shenot Ha-Po'el ha-Ẓa'ir,* and *Zionism and Palestine* (11 vols., 1946–56).

13 ZIONIST BIBLIOGRAPHY

Zionist literature developed in many languages: German (*Rome and Jerusalem* by Moses Hess), Hebrew (*Derishat Ẓiyyon* by Ẓevi Hirsch Kalischer and the articles of D. Gordon), and gradually in many other languages, not only in countries with large Jewish populations. It also appeared in many forms, from thick volumes to leaflets and periodicals issued at various intervals (dailies, weeklies, monthlies, yearbooks, collections commemorating special occasions, etc.). The variety of form is reflected in the variety of genre: feature writing, essays, chronicles, belles lettres in all its forms (fiction, plays, poetry, etc.), historical research and documentation, and so forth. Zionist literature covers the period from the 1860s to the present and, including all the books, leaflets, articles, and so on, encompasses millions of items.

A difficulty in cataloging this wealth of material is that in the early days of Ḥibbat Zion, the border between "Zionist" material and works on Ereẓ Israel in general was very vague, and this lack of a clear distinction between the two categories was not overcome in later years. Even after the establishment of the State of Israel it was difficult to draw a distinct line between literature on the state and writings on the Zionist movement. Throughout the existence of Zionist literature, therefore, the terms, "Ḥibbat Zion," "Zionist movement," "Ereẓ Israel," and the "State of Israel," have been viewed as loosely synonymous, although the special scope of each concept was clear. Thus it is difficult to differentiate bibliographically between the history of the *yishuv* from the beginning of the 1880s and the history of the movement and political Zionism.

This overlapping in concepts is inevitably reflected in the majority of the works cited below. Characteristic is the subtitle of a recent platform for research, which is entitled *Ha-Ẓiyyonut: Me'assef le-Toledot ha-Tenu'ah ha-Ẓiyyonit ve-ha-Yishuv ha-Yehudi be-Ereẓ Yisrael* ("Zionism: Journal of the History of the Zionist Movement and the *Yishuv* in Ereẓ Israel," vol. 1, 1970). The same problem of exact definition exists in the bibliography *Esrim Shenot Medinat Yisrael* ("Twenty Years of the State of Israel," 1970) by A. Neuberg, in which much Zionist material is found, and the index volumes titled *Palestine and Zionism* (all these items are discussed below).

BIBLIOGRAPHIES. As a rule, the bibliographies dealing with Zionism are listed in Shunami's *Bibliography of Jewish Bibliographies* (1965[2]), but not all the material on this subject is found under the headings "Zionism" or "Zionist" in the index (p. 990), and a considerable amount of relevant material is found in other divisions. Bibliographical attention was first paid to the subject of Zionism at the end of the 19th century, even before the advent of Theodor Herzl. Practical efforts intensified with the advent of political Zionism, especially when newspapers throughout the world began to display an interest in Zionism. At a meeting of Russian members of the "Actions Committee" in Minsk, following the Minsk Conference (1902), it was decided to charge G. Belkowsky with the task of publishing a comprehensive bibliography on Zionism. The book came out in Russia under the title *Ukazatel literatury o sionizme* (St. Petersburg, 1903). It did not cite the names of the editors of the bibliography, which Belkowsky revealed after many years in a detailed article on this project (*Haolam*, Sept. 10, 1942, p. 425). The work listed over 4,000 entries in a variety of languages, in three categories: (1) Jewish nationalism; (2) Zionism: Theory and Practice; and (3) Ereẓ Israel. The second of the three parts, which was to appear later and include literature in Hebrew and Yiddish, was not published because of the conditions in czarist Russia at the time. Hebrew works on Zionism were recorded afterward by William Zeitlin in his bibliography *Bibliotheca Sionistica* (Frankfort, 1909; reprint from ZHB, vols. 12–13, 1908–09; includes works from 1852 to 1905).

At the same time a bibliographical project of vast dimensions on Palestine, entitled *Die Palaestina Literatur,* began to be carried out under the editorship of Peter Thomsen. Up to 1971, six volumes had been published, covering the literature from 1895 to 1939 (although the title page of the sixth volume states that it goes down to 1944). This series was published in Germany from 1908 to 1956 (the beginning of the sixth volume includes a biography of Thomsen). Material on Zionism is found only in the first four volumes and in the section on contemporary Palestine; a vast amount of material is listed in several languages (inter alia, bibliographies other than those recorded by S. Shunami).

Since 1944 many bibliographies have appeared, some of a general nature and some devoted to various bodies and institutions of the Zionist movement and Zionist Organization. Among the latest general and detailed bibliographies that include Zionist literature in various languages is *Bibliografiah Ẓiyyonit* (1943), by Abraham Levinson (with the cooperation of N. M. Gelber), which lists 2,400 entries in 17 languages. Bibliographical notations have been added to each section of Yiẓḥak Gruenbaum's work *Ha-Tenu'ah ha-Ẓiyyonit* (vols. 1–4, 1942–54) by G. Kressel (1–2) and Israel Klausner (3–4). With the establishment of the State of Israel, Sophie A. Udin published an important bibliographical listing in English entitled "A List of References Leading to the Establishment of the State of Israel" (in *The Journal of Educational Sociology,* 22:3 (Nov. 1948), 239–47). Finally, *The State of Israel* (1948–68), by Assia Neuberg, contains much material on Zionism in a variety of languages (1970).

Any bibliography, no matter how complete, is by its nature unable to be entirely up-to-date in recording the continuous publication of works each year. Therefore annual bibliographical listings are included in various yearbooks: the *American Jewish Yearbook*, the *Palestine*

Yearbook, the *Zionist Yearbook*, the *Jewish Book Annual*, etc. The most complete and correct ongoing bibliographical listing, however, is that published in each edition of the bibliographical quarterly of the Jewish National and University Library in Jerusalem, *Kirjath Sepher*, in the section on "Zionism, Ereẓ Israel, the State of Israel," which covers material published in Israel and abroad. The Zionist Archives in Jerusalem have published a bibliographical bulletin in various forms and at irregular intervals since 1936 (mimeographed). A vast amount of material on Zionism can also be found in the many bibliographies on personalities active in the field; these are listed in the section "Personal Bibliographies" in Shunami. The same is true of bibliographies on institutions and organizations within the Zionist movement, e.g., *Madrikh Bibliografi le-Sifrut Ẓiyyonit-Datit* ("A Bibliographical Guide to Literature on Religious Zionism," 1960[2]), by Yiẓḥak Raphael, which goes beyond the field defined in its title and also includes articles in periodicals and the press, and *Ha-Po'el ha-Mizrachi be-Ereẓ Yisrael* (1968), by Yosef Salmon, which also includes articles.

PRESS AND PERIODICALS. The press and periodicals, Jewish and non-Jewish, in all languages, contain much important material on the history of the Ḥibbat Zion movement, political Zionism, and everything pertaining to Ereẓ Israel over the past generations, from first-hand documentation (statements, press releases) to news items, commentary, reaction, essays, and research. Periodicals of all sorts, issued at varying intervals, whether published by official institutions of the Zionist Organization or its sympathizers or by those opposed or openly hostile to Zionism, reach into the thousands; and recent research has led to the conclusion that periodical literature attacking Zionism—whether published by Jews or non-Jews—is no less important for the study of Zionism than the publications of official Zionist organs or Zionist sympathizers.

In the beginning the scope of the Zionist press was limited, in direct relation to the size of the movement itself.

In the 1860s and 1870s, the Jewish press, in all languages, was generally hostile, or at least apathetic, to the Jewish nationalist movement, with the exception of the *Jewish Chronicle* in England, *Der Israelit* and *Die Juedische Presse* in Germany, *The Occident* in the United States, and the Hebrew *Ha-Maggid* (Prussia). A pioneer of Zionist journalism in Germany was *Selbstemanzipation,* edited by N. Birnbaum, and its successor *Zion,* edited by H. Loewe and Willy Bambus (until Bambus came into conflict with Herzl before the First Zionist Congress). Then Herzl began to publish the weekly *Die Welt* (in German), which later became the first official organ of the Zionist Organization. Afterward organs of the Zionist organizations in various countries began to appear in a number of languages. Over the years Zionist newspapers have been established wherever a Zionist organization functioned, and some non-Zionist newspapers became pro-Zionist or tempered their opposition. At the same time, however (and until World War I), the Jewish press that was not particularly sympathetic toward Zionism—from the Orthodox and Reform movements to the leftist parties in Eastern Europe—was also a substantial force. The change in their attitude came about gradually, as the achievements of the Zionist movement and the *yishuv* became more noticeable and, by the outbreak of World War II, the future of the Jews in Europe grew darker and darker. Finally, a radical change in attitude came about during and after the Holocaust, which practically reversed the situation that had existed during the 1860s and 1870s: a very small minority of the press remained opposed to the Zionist movement and the State of Israel and the majority were devoted to them to one degree or another. Because of this change in attitude, it was practically unnecessary for the Zionist movement to maintain its own organs, although such a press does continue to exist in many countries.

The Hebrew press holds a unique position. Even when it was employed to preach the doctrines of the Haskalah and indifference toward Jewish nationalism and Zionism, the

Hebrew language was, by its very nature, a kind of living bridge to Ereẓ Israel. After the illusions of the Haskalah in Eastern Europe had been destroyed, therefore, the Hebrew press was the most loyal instrument of the Ḥibbat Zion movement and afterward of political Zionism, each paper expressing a difference in orientation. Sharp opposition to Jewish nationalism and Zionism in the Hebrew press was inconsequential compared to the overwhelming majority of pro-Zionist publications. The opposition began with *Ha-Emet,* a socialist-oriented paper edited by A. S. Liebermann, and after a number of years it was also expressed in extreme Orthodox circles, thus appearing at opposite poles of the spectrum. Over the years this opposition has taken various forms (today as the pro-Arab Israel Communists, Rakaḥ, and the Neturei Karta, respectively). An impressive symbol of the developments discussed above was the development of the Zionist leadership and its expression in the press and Hebrew literature through such personalities as Lilienblum, Aḥad-Ha-Am, Sokolow, and many others.

LIST OF NEWSPAPERS AND INDEXES TO THEIR CONTENTS. These two instruments of aid never kept up with the developments in the field of Jewish and Zionist journalism. For decades lists of Jewish newspapers have appeared, both in various lexicons and separately. Comprehensive listings are the *Tentative List of Jewish Periodicals in Axis-Occupied Countries* (1947), covering the period between the two world wars, and Joseph Fraenkel's *The Jewish Press of the World* (1967[6]), which reflects the situation after World War II. In this period, the distinction between Zionist and non-Zionist publications has become blurred, and any comprehensive list of Jewish publications reflects principally Zionist or pro-Zionist publications (for lists of publications, including those prepared by Fraenkel, see Shunami, Bibliography, second edition, index).

More problematic is the task of getting to the vast amount of material in the press. Indexes of the press, long accepted as standard in the world at large, are still rather innovations in the realm of the Jewish and Hebrew press. Only lately have really useful indexes come into being, but this venture is still in its infancy. One thing must be stressed in regard to material on Zionism: it is not to be found under subject headings such as "Zionism" and the like. Over the last generation Zionism encompassed the entire Jewish world and is thus to be found under thousands of other subject headings. Among the indexes included by Shunami and others that have been issued recently, the following deserve special attention: (1) S. A. Udin and S. Landress (eds.), *Palestine and Zionism* (vols. 1–11, 1949–58) is organized according to a dictionary catalog (as are the two following works), so that "Zionism" is scattered among an abundance of sources; at the end of each volume of this important index to periodicals is a separate index to books and pamphlets, and it also covers material published in languages other than English from 1946 to 1956. (2) *Index to Jewish Periodicals,* edited by Miriam Leikind, has been published in Cleveland, Ohio, since 1964 (seven volumes through 1970) and covers material from 1963 onward. (3) Index to *Ha-Po'el ha-Ẓa'ir,* edited by Isa and G. Kressel (1968). The index to this weekly during the 50 years of its existence is essentially an index to all the events in the Zionist movement, the *yishuv,* and the labor movement during this period and is the largest index of this kind (in its dimensions and number of entries—more than 100,000) that has yet been published in Hebrew. It is also worth noting that an event located in the index to one newspaper can easily be found, according to the dates, in the rest of the press. (4) The quarterly of the Jewish National and University Library, *Kirjath Sepher,* lists (beginning with no. 21) with exactness the contents of periodicals on Jewish studies and important articles in the daily press. Anyone wishing to keep up with what is going on in all fields of Jewish studies or any one or set of fields therein must go over each and every issue; for the sake of expediency, however, Issachar Yoel has compiled the *Index of Articles on Jewish Studies* (for 1966ff.), which reviews the yearly output according to special categories, including Ereẓ Israel, Zionism, and State of Israel. It includes an index to the largest number of newspapers and periodicals in this ramified field.

ENCYCLOPEDIAS AND LEXICONS OF ZIONISM. Every Jewish lexicon obviously contains much material on Zionism, whether on personalities or Zionist affairs. Nonetheless, throughout the decades the need was felt for a special lexicon of Zionism, which would cover all aspects of this subject. The first attempt at this task, which still holds a position of major importance, was the lexicon published by the Zionist Federation in Germany in 1909, *Zionistisches A-B-C Buch*. The entries therein on personalities and Zionist affairs are written with exactitude and provide a comprehensive picture of the Zionist Organization, through the end of the first decade of its existence. The participants in putting the volume together were the heads of the Zionist movement in Germany and Austria. The second venture into this field was the *Leksikon Ẓiyyoni* (1924) of the Hebrew writer S. L. Zitron; however, it is restricted to personalities only. A Zionist lexicon (in Yiddish) of greater dimensions, whose intention was to cover personalities, Zionist affairs, the names of settlements in Ereẓ Israel, etc., began to come out in Warsaw under the title *Tsiyionistisher Leksikon*, under the editorship of B. Zweibaum; however, only one volume was published (1935; up to the middle of the letter "*bet*"). Another Yiddish lexicon published in Warsaw, *Yidisher Gezelshaftlekher Leksikon*, edited by Reuven Ben-Shem (Feldschuh), met a similar fate. Its first volume, which also included personalities, institutions, affairs, etc., came out close to the outbreak of World War II and is preserved in only a few copies throughout the world. It goes up to the middle of the letter "*vav*" and covers primarily Polish Jewry, but it is considered a Zionist lexicon because of the wealth of Zionist material covered therein.

In Palestine, Moshe Kleinman aspired to publish the *Enẓiklopedyah le-Ẓiyyonut* (1947), but was prevented from
 issuing more than one volume (which goes up to the end of

the letter "*gimmel*") by the conditions in the country and finally by his death. Since 1957 *Enẓiklopedyah shel ha-Ẓiyyonut ha-Datit,* edited by Y. Raphael (assistant editor G. Bat-Yehudah), has been published in Jerusalem; it covers personalities only. A large encyclopedic venture covering personalities is David Tidhar's *Enẓiklopedyah le-Ḥalutzei ha-Yishuv u-Vonav,* published from 1947 (19 volumes),which lists biographies of Ereẓ Israel personalities alphabetically, but the indexes to each volume and to the work as a whole facilitate locating an entry. This work contains a wealth of Zionist material, especially in the latter volumes, which contain biographies of personalities in Ereẓ Israel mostly from Eastern Europe, the United States, England, etc. The *Leksikon la-Sifrut ha-Ivrit ba-Dorot ha-Aḥaronim,* by G. Kressel, also contains entries on many Zionist personalities. A two-volume work in English, *Encyclopedia of Zionism,* covering both personalities and Zionist events and affairs, was published in New York under the editorship of Raphael Patai (1971). Note should also be made of the various Jewish *Who's Who* volumes in English, Hebrew, and other languages that have come out in Israel and abroad.

JOURNALS, RESEARCH INSTITUTES, ARCHIVES. Material on research into the history of Zionism is found in abundance in Jewish periodicals throughout the world. Especially rich in material are the official organs of the Zionist movement (*Selbstemanzipation, Die Welt, Juedische Rundschau, Haolam,* etc.). Since the beginning of the Zionist movement, however, the need for a special forum for Zionist research has made itself felt. In 1905 a forum of this type appeared for the first time in Germany, known as *Die Stimme der Wahrheit* and subtitled *Jahrbuch fuer wissenschlaftlichen Zionismus* (edited by L. Schoen). The notation "the volume of the first year" expressed the intention to perpetuate this publication, which was not realized. Since then collections honoring the memory of Herzl, for example, have turned into platforms for Zionist research: *Theodor Herzl, A Memorial,* edited by Meyer

Weisgal (New York, 1929), and the *Herzl-Jahrbuch*, an annual for research on Herzl and Zionism, only one issue of which (by T. Nussenblatt) was published (1933). In Israel three collections were put out (one of which was in two volumes; 1950–56) under the title *Shivat Ẓiyyon;* they were intended to become an annual (edited by a staff of editors), but publication ceased. In the United States, Raphael Patai published the *Herzl Year Book* (6 vols. 1958–65). In 1970 the first collection on the history of the Zionist movement and the *yishuv* in Ereẓ Israel, *Ha-Ẓiyyonut*, was published under the editorship of Daniel Carpi. All these collections contain mostly research papers and documentary material.

Research institutes have been established at Tel Aviv University (named in honor of Chaim Weizmann) and the Hebrew University, Jerusalem (named in honor of Israel Goldstein). The former has already put out a number of books that investigate various aspects of the history of the *yishuv* and Zionism. The largest and most important archive for the history of Zionism throughout the world is the Central Zionist Archive in Jerusalem, but other archives are found in New York, in Bet ha-Tefuẓot of the University of Tel Aviv, etc.

GLOSSARY

Actions Committee, early name of the Zionist General Council, the supreme institution of the World Zionist Organization in the interim between Congresses. The Zionist Executive's name was then the "Small Actions Committee."

Agudat Israel, world organization of Orthodox Jews, founded in Kattowitz in 1912.

Aḥdut ha-Avodah, Zionist Socialist Labor Party in Palestine founded in 1919. In 1930 this movement merged with *Ha-Poel ha-Ẓair* and formed *Mapai.*

Aliyah, (1) immigration to Ereẓ Israel; (2) one of the waves of immigration to Ereẓ Israel from the early 1880s.

Alliance Israélite Universelle, French organization founded in 1860 to defend Jewish civil and religious liberties and to provide education for backward Jewish communities.

Asefat ha-Nivḥarim, representative assembly elected by Jews in Palestine during the period of the British Mandate (1920–48).

Ashkenazi (pl. **Ashkenazim**), German or West-, Central-, or East-European Jew(s), as contrasted with Sephardi(m).

Balfour Declaration, official statement (Nov. 2, 1917) issued by British foreign secretary Arthur James Balfour, declaring that the British government favored the establishment of a national home for the Jewish people in Palestine.

Bar mitzvah, ceremony marking the initiation of a boy at the age of 13 into the Jewish religious community.

Bene Akiva, religious Zionist pioneering youth movement affiliated with *Ha-Poel ha-Mizrachi* founded in 1929.

Benei Moshe, secret order of *Ḥovevei Zion* founded in Odessa in 1889 whose aims were the spiritual renaissance of the Jewish people and the return to Ereẓ Israel.

Beriḥah Movement, ("flight"), organized underground operation moving Jews out of Central and Eastern Europe between 1944 and 1948 as a step toward their "illegal" immigration to Palestine: also name of the spontaneous mass movement of Jewish survivors from Europe toward Ereẓ Israel.

Betar, youth organization of the Zionist *Revisionist* party whose members played prominent roles in the *Irgun Ẓevai Le'ummi* and *Loḥamei Ḥerut Israel.*

Bilu, first modern movement for pioneering and agricultural settlement in Ereẓ Israel, founded in 1882 in Kharkov, Russia.

Bund, Jewish socialist party founded in Vilna in 1897, supporting Jewish national rights, Yiddishist, and anti-Zionist.

Congresses (Zionist), regular conferences of representatives of the Zionist movement instituted by Theodor Herzl in 1897.

Conservative Judaism, trend in Judaism developed in the United States in the 20th century which, while opposing extreme changes in traditional observances, permits certain modifications of *halakhah* in response to the changing needs of the Jewish people.

Democratic Fraction, radical opposition faction in the Zionist movement between 1901 and 1904 that demanded greater cultural activity and immediate settlement in Ereẓ Israel.

Diaspora, Jews living in the "dispersion" outside Ereẓ Israel; area of Jewish settlement outside Ereẓ Israel.

Dorshei Zion, Zionist society established in Bulgaria in the late 19th century.

D. P. (Displaced Person), term used to describe people who had been driven out of their homes by the Nazis during World War II, primarily survivors of concentration or forced labor camps.

Dunam, unit of land area (1,000 sq. m., c. 1/4 acre), used in Israel.

Ereẓ Israel, Land of Israel; Palestine.

Ezrat Aḥim, Zionist society established in Bulgaria in the late 19th century.

Ezra Society, organization that supported Jewish agricultural settlers in Ereẓ Israel and Syria formed in Berlin in 1886.

Galut, "exile"; the condition of the Jewish people in dispersion.

General Zionists, Zionist party whose members were those who did not join the first Zionist political parties and especially advocated private enterprise.

Habonim, world organization of Zionist youth movements founded in Great Britain in 1929.

Hadassah, The Women's Zionist Organization of America, largest Zionist organization in the world and one of the largest women's organizations in the U.S.

Haganah, clandestine Jewish organization for armed self-defense in Ereẓ Israel under the British Mandate, which eventually evolved into a people's militia and became the basis for the Israel army.

Haham, title of chief rabbi of the Spanish and Portuguese congregations in London, England.

Hakhsharah ("preparation"), organized training in the Diaspora of pioneers for agricultural settlement in Ereẓ Israel.

Halakhah (pl. **halakhot**), an accepted decision in rabbinic law. Also refers to those parts of the Talmud concerned with legal matters.

Ḥalutz (pl. **ḥalutzim**), pioneer, especially in agriculture, in Ereẓ Israel.

Ḥalutziyyut, pioneering.

Ha-Noar ha-Ẓiyyoni, pioneering Zionist youth movement originating in E. Europe.

Ha-Po'el ha-Mizrachi, religious pioneering and labor movement in Ereẓ Israel founded in 1922.

Ha-Shomer ha-Ẓa'ir, Zionist youth organization and former Palestinian political party formed in Galicia in 1913, it participated in 1948 in the formation of *Mapam.*

Ḥasid, adherent of Ḥasidism.

Ḥasidism, (1) religious revivalist movement of popular mysticism among Jews of Germany in the Middle Ages; (2) religious movement founded by Israel ben Eliezer Ba'al Shem Tov in the first half of the 18th century.

Haskalah, "Enlightenment"; movement for spreading modern European culture among Jews c. 1750–1880. An adherent was termed *maskil.*

Ḥeder, (lit. "room"), school for teaching children Jewish religious observance.

Ḥeder metukkan, a new type of Jewish school established in Russia at the end of the 19th century that derived its inspiration from Jewish nationalism and developed into an educational movement.

He-Ḥalutz (Heb. "the pioneer"), association of Jewish youth whose aim was to train its members to settle on the land in Israel.

Herut, political movement and party in Ereẓ Israel established in 1948 as a successor-group to *Irgun Ẓevai Le'ummi.*

Ḥibbat Zion, see Ḥovevei Zion.

Hilfsverein der Deutschen Juden, central charitable society of German Jewry founded in Berlin in 1901 to assist Jews in E. Europe and oriental countries.

Histadrut (abbr. for Heb. **Ha-Histadrut ha-Kelalit shel ha-Ovedim ha-Ivriyyim be-Ereẓ Israel**), Ereẓ Israel Jewish Labor Federation, founded in 1920; subsequently renamed Histadrut ha-Ovedim be-Ereẓ Israel.

Holocaust, the organized mass persecution and annihilation of European Jewry by the Nazis (1933–1945).

Horah, folk dance of pioneer Ereẓ Israel derived chiefly from the Rumanian *hora.*

Ḥovevei Zion, federation of Ḥibbat Zion, early (pre-Herzl) Zionist movement in Russia.

I.Ẓ.L. (initials of Heb. **Irgun Ẓevai Le'ummi;** "National Military Organization"), underground Jewish organization in Ereẓ Israel founded in 1931, which engaged from 1937 in retaliatory acts against Arab attacks and later against the British mandatory authorities.

Jewish Agency, international nongovernment body, representative and executive of the World Zionist Organization, whose aims are to assist and encourage development and settlement in Ereẓ Israel.

Jewish Colonial Trust, first bank of the Zionist Organization, established in 1899. Originally registered in Britain, it became an Israel Company in 1955.

Jewish Legion, Jewish units in British army during World War I.

Jewish National Fund, institution of the World Zionist Organization for the acquisition, development and afforestation of land in Palestine, founded at the 5th Zionist Congress (1901).

Kabbalah, the Jewish mystical tradition.

Kabbalist, student of Kabbalah.

Kadimah, first Jewish students' nationalist society, founded in Vienna in 1882.

Keneset Yisrael, comprehensive communal organization of the Jews in Palestine during the British Mandate.

Keren Hayesod, chief financial instrument of the Zionist Organization.

Kibbutz (pl. **kibbutzim**), large-size commune constituting a settlement in Ereẓ Israel based mainly on agriculture but engaging also in industry.

Knesset, parliament of the State of Israel.

Kristallnacht (Ger. "crystal night," meaning "night of broken glass"), organized destruction of synagogues, Jewish houses, and shops, accompanied by mass arrests of Jews, which took place in Germany and Austria under the Nazis on the night of Nov. 9–10, 1938.

 Leḥi (abbr. for Heb. **Loḥamei Ḥerut Israel,** "Fighters for the

Freedom of Israel" also L.H.Y.), radically anti-British armed underground organization in Palestine, founded in 1940 by dissidents from I.Ẓ.L.

LḤY, see Leḥi.

Maccabi, world union of Jewish athletic organizations, its first branches were founded in Berlin in 1895.

Maḥal, volunteers from abroad, mainly Jews, in the Israel Defense Forces who participated in the War of Independence in 1948–49.

Mandate, Palestine, responsibility for the administration of Palestine conferred on Britain by the League of Nations in 1922; mandatory government: the British administration of Palestine.

Mapam, left-wing labor-Zionist Israel party formed in 1948 by the fusion of *Ha-Shomer ha-Za'ir* and *Aḥdut ha-Avodah-Po'alei Zion.*

Maskil (pl. **maskilim**), adherent of Haskalah ("Enlightenment") movement.

Mishnah, earliest codification of Jewish Oral Law.

Mizrachi, religious Zionist movement, founded in 1902 as a religious faction of the World Zionist Organization.

Moshav, smallholders' cooperative agricultural settlement in Israel.

Negev, the southern, mostly arid, area of Israel.

Neology, trend of Reform Judaism in Hungary forming separate congregations after 1868.

New Zionist Organization, organization established by the Revisionists party in 1935 after its break with the World Zionist Organization.

Numerus Clausus, amount fixed as maximal number in the admission of persons to institutions of higher learning frequently applied to Jews in Central and Eastern Europe.

Orthodoxy (Orthodox Judaism), modern term for the strictly traditional sector of Jewry.

Palmaḥ (abbr. for Hebr. *peluggot mahaẓ;* "shock companies"), striking arm of the Haganah.

Partition plan(s), proposals for dividing Ereẓ Israel into autonomous areas.

Peel Commission, British Royal Commission appointed by the British government in 1936 to inquire into the Palestine problem and make recommendations for its solution.

Pioneer Women, worldwide labor Zionist women's organization founded in New York City in 1925.

Po'alei Ẓion, political party whose ideology consisted of a combination of Zionism and Socialism founded in Russia toward the end of the 19th century.

Reconstructionism, trend in Jewish thought originating in the United States.

Reform Judaism, trend in Judaism advocating modification of Orthodoxy in conformity with the exigencies of contemporary life and thought.

Revisionists, movement of maximalist political Zionists founded in 1925 and led by Vladimir Jabotinsky.

Sephardi (pl. **Sephardim**), Jew(s) of Spain and Portugal and their descendants, wherever resident, as contrasted with Ashkenazi(m).

Shali'aḥ (pl. **sheliḥim**), in Jewish law, messenger, agent; in modern times, an emissary from Ereẓ Israel to Jewish communities or organizations abroad for the purpose of fund-raising, organizing pioneer immigrants, education, etc.

Shekel, a silver unit of weight, later a permanent accepted coin among the Jews.

Simḥat Torah, holiday marking the completion in the synagogue of the annual cycle of reading the Pentateuch.

Six-Day War, brief war in June 1967 when Israel reacted to Arab threats and blockade by defeating the Egyptian, Jordanian, and Syrian armies.

Talmud, "teaching"; compendium of discussions on the Mishnah by generations of scholars and jurists in many academies over a period of several centuries. The Jerusalem (or Palestinian) Talmud mainly contained the discussions of the Palestinian sages. The Babylonian Talmud incorporates the parallel discussion in the Babylonian academies.

Territorialism, 20th century trend in Jewish public life supporting the creation of an autonomous territory for Jewish mass-settlement outside Ereẓ Israel.

Torah, Pentateuch or the Pentateuchal scroll for reading in synagogue; entire body of traditional Jewish teaching and literature.

Uganda Scheme, plan suggested by the British government in 1903 to establish an autonomous Jewish settlement area in East Africa.

Ulpan, center for study by adults, particularly applied to intensive Hebrew courses for new immigrants in Israel.

Va'ad Le'ummi, national council of the Jewish community in Ereẓ Israel during the period of the British Mandate.

War of Independence, war of 1947–49 when the Jews of Israel fought off Arab invading armies and ensured the establishment of the new State.

White Paper(s), report(s) issued by British government, frequently statements of policy, as issued in connection with Palestine during the Mandate period.

WIZO, women's Zionist organization founded in London in 1920.

Yishuv, settlement; more specifically, the Jewish community of Ereẓ Israel in the pre-State period. The pre-Zionist community is generally designated the "old yishuv" and the community evolving from 1880, the "new yishuv."

Young Judea, U.S. Zionist youth organization founded in 1909 by Jewish students.

Youth Aliyah, organization for transferring young persons to Israel and educating them there.

Ze'irei Zion, Zionist and moderate socialist labor movement, active mainly in Russia in the first two decades of the 20th century.

Zionist Commission (1918), commission appointed in 1918 by the British government to advise the British military authorities in Palestine on the implementation of the Balfour Declaration.

Ẓiyyonei Zion, the organized opposition to Herzl in connection with the Uganda Scheme.

BIBLIOGRAPHY

GENERAL:

N. Sokolow, *History of Zionism*, 2 vols. (1919).

A. Boehm, *Die zionistische Bewegung*, 2 vols. (1935–37).

I. Cohen, *The Zionist Movement* (1946).

B. Halpern, *The Idea of the Jewish State* (1961).

A. Hertzberg (ed.), *The Zionist Idea* (1960).

R. Learsi, *Fulfillment: Epic Story of Zionism* (1951).

Learsi, *Fulfillment: Epic Story of Zionism* (1951).

W. Z. Laqueur, *History of Zionism* (1972).

Ch. Weizmann, *Trial and Error* (1948).

Y. Gruenbaum, *Ha-Tenu'ah ha-Ẓiyyonit*, 4 vols. (1942–54), partial translation into Eng. *History of Zionism*, 2 vols. (1943–46).

J. Heller, *The Zionist Idea* (1947).

L. Stein, *The Balfour Declaration* (1961).

C. Sykes, *Crossroads to Israel* (1965).

A. Bein, in: *Herzl Year Book* (1959), 1–27, includes bibliography.

ḤIBBAT ZION:

N. Sokolow, *Hibbath Zion* (1935).

idem, *History of Zionism*, 1 (1919).

Y. Gruenbaum, *History of Zionism*, 1 (1943).

A. Boehm, *Die zionistische Bewegung*, 1 (1935), 96–150.

A. Levinson, *Bibliografiah Ẓiyyonut* (1943), 51–69.

A. Druyanow, *Ketavim le-Toledot Ḥibbat Ẓiyyon*, 3 vols. (1919, 1925, 1932).

idem, *Pinsker u-Zemanno* (1953).

Ḥ. Ḥissin, *Mi-Yoman Aḥad ha-Bilu'im* (1928).

B. Dinaburg, *Tekufat Ḥibbat Ẓiyyon* (1932, 1934).

S. Jawnieli, *Sefer ha-Ẓiyyonut: Tekufat Ḥibbat Ẓiyyon* 2 vols. (1942, 1961[2]).

S. Breiman, in : *Shivat Ẓiyyon*, 1 (1950), 138–68; 2–3 (1953), 83–227.

I. Klausner, *Ḥibbat Ẓiyyon be-Rumanyah* (1958).

idem, *Be-Hitorer Am* (1962).

idem, *Mi-Katoviẓ ad Basel* (1965).

N. M. Gelber, *Toledot ha-Tenu'ah ha-Ẓiyyonit be-Galiẓyah,* 1 (1958), passim.
M. L. Lilienblum, *Derekh La'avor Ge'ullim* (1899).
T. Lavi et al. (eds.), *Pinkas ha-Kehillot, Romanyah,* 1 (1970), 47–60, 213–4 (bibl.).
ZIONIST SOCIALISM:
J. Frankel, *Socialism and Jewish Nationalism in Russia* (dissertation, Cambridge University, 1961).
B. Borochov, *Ketavim,* ed. by L. Levite et al., 3 vols (1955–66).
M. Mishkinsky, in: YIVOA, 14 (1969).
idem, *Yesodot Le'ummiyyim be-Hithavvutah shel Tenu'at ha-Po'alim ha-Yehudit be-Rusyah* (dissertation, Hebrew University, 1965).
idem, in: *Zion,* 31 nos. 1–2 (1966).
I. Kolatt, *Ideologyah u-Meẓi'ut bi-Tenu'at ha-Avodah be-Ereẓ Yisrael* (dissertation, Hebrew University, 1964).
Y. Ritov, *Perakim be-Toledot Ẓe'irei Ẓiyyon—Ẓ. S.* (1964).
M. Minc, *Ber Borochov* (Heb.; dissertation, Hebrew University, 1968).
idem, in: *Ba-Derekh,* 5 (1970).
ZIONIST POLICY:
C. Sykes, *Crossroads to Israel* (1965).
H. M. Sachar, *The Emergence of the Middle East 1914–1924* (1969).
Ch. Weizmann, *Trial and Error* (1948).
O. K. Rabinowicz, in : *Herzl Year Book,* 1 (1958), 1–106.
M. Medzini, *Ha-Mediniyyut ha-Ẓiyyonit me-Reshitah ve-ad Moto shel Herzl* (1934).
R. G. Weisbord, *African Zion . . .* (1966).
N. Friedman, J. De Haas, H. M. Kallen et al., *A Memorandum on the Relations between the Ottoman Government and the Zionist Administration* (1913).
I. Friedman, in: *Jewish Social Studies,* 27 (1965), 147–67, 236–49.
idem, in: *Journal of Contemporary History,* 5 no. 2 (1970).
P. A. Alsberg, in: *Shivat Ẓiyyon,* 4 (1956), 161–209.
Y. Rabi, in: *Middle Eastern Studies,* 4 (Apr. 1968), 198–242.
L. Stein, *The Balfour Declaration* (1961).
M. Vereté, in: *Zion,* 32 (1967), 76–114.
idem, in: *Middle Eastern Studies,* 6 no 1 (Jan. 1970).
J. Kimche, *The Unromantics—the Great Powers and the Balfour Declaration* (1968).
M. Medzini, *Eser Shanim shel Mediniyyut Arẓiyisre'elit* (1928).
F. E. Manuel, *The Realities of American-Palestine Relations* (1949).

idem, in: *Shivat Ẓiyyon*, 4 (1956), 210–39.
Zionist Organization, *Political Report* (1921).
H. L. Samuel, *Memoirs* (1955).
F. H. Kisch, *Palestine Diary* (1938).
Ch. Arlosoroff, *Yoman Yerushalayim* (1950).
M. Sharett, *Yoman Medini*, 2 vols. (1968–70).
R. Meinertzhagen, *Middle East Diary 1917–1956* (1959).
ESCO Foundation for Palestine: *Palestine, A Study of Jewish, Arab, and British Policies*, 2 vols. (1947).
V. Jabotinsky, *The Story of the Jewish Legion* (1945).
H. Parzen, in: *Herzl Year Book*, 4 (1962), 345–94.
S. L. Hattis, *The Bi-National Idea in Palestine during Mandatory Times* (1970).
Y. Bauer, *From Diplomacy to Resistance* (1970).
Ḍ. Joseph, *British Rule in Palestine* (1948).
B. Dinur (ed.), *Sefer Toledot ha-Haganah* (1954ff.).
D. Ben-Gurion, *Medinat Yisrael ha-Meḥuddeshet*, 1 (1969).
ZIONIST ORGANIZATION:
Zionist Organization, *Protocols of the Zionist Congresses*, in particular of the 1st (1897) and 23rd (1951).
idem, *The New Constitution of the World Zionist Organization* (1960).
Jewish Agency, *Constitution of the Jewish Agency for Palestine* (1950).
Zionist Organization, *Reports of the Executive of the ZO submitted to the Congresses*, in particular to the 22nd (1946).
idem, *The Jubilee of the 1st Zionist Congress* (1947).
ZIONISM IN AUSTRIA:
J. Fraenkel, *The Jews of Austria* (1967), passim.
H. Gold (ed.), *Geschichte der Juden in Wien* (1966).
IN AUSTRALIA AND NEW ZEALAND:
M. Freilich, *Zion in Our Time—Memoirs of an Australian Zionist* (1967).
A. Wynn, *Fortunes of Samuel Wynn* (1968).
IN BULGARIA:
A. Romano, J. Ben, and N. Levy (eds.), *Yahadut Bulgaryah* (1967), 87–606.
Ch. Keshales, *Korot Yehudei Bulgaryah* (1969).
N. M. Gelber, in: JSOS, 8 (1946), 103–26.
IN CZECHOSLOVAKIA:
F. Weltsch (ed.), *Prag vi-Yrushalayim* (1953).
 Ch. Yahil, *Devarim al ha-Ẓiyyonut ha-Tchekhoslovakit* (1967).

idem, in: *Gesher*, no 59–60 (1969).
The Jews of Czechoslovakia, 2 vols. (1967–71).
IN FRANCE:
André Spire, *Le Mouvement sioniste 1894–1918* (1919).
idem, *Poèmes Juifs* (1919, 1959).
A. Bein, *Introduction au sionisme* (1939[2]).
A. Blumel, *Léon Blum, juif et sioniste* (1951).
IN GERMANY:
M. Bodenheimer, *Prelude to Israel* (1963).
R. Lichtheim, *Die Geschichte des deutschen Zionismus* (1954).
idem, *Rueckkehr* (1970).
K. Blumenfeld, *Erlebte Judenfrage* (1962, Heb. 1963).
E. Auerbach, *Pionier der Verwirklichung* (1970).
IN GREAT BRITAIN:
P. Goodman, *Zionism in England, 1899–1949* (1949).
J. Fraenkel, in: *Zionist Year Book* (1959–60), 283–312.
idem, in: *YIVO Bleter*, 43 (1966), 72–147.
Ch. Weizmann, *Trial and Error* (1949), passim.
Zionist Federation of the United Kingdom, *Annual Report* (1968).
IN HOLLAND:
Jaarverslagen van het Bondsbestuur van de Nederlandse Zionistenbond; Bishviley Jachid (1950).
IN HUNGARY:
Z. Zehavi, *Toledot ha-Ẓiyyonut be-Hungaryah*, 1 (1966).
IN ITALY:
D. Lattes, in: D. Carpi et al. (eds.), *Scritti in Memoria di Leone Carpi* (1967), 208–18.
A. J. M. Pacifici, *ibid.*, 219–29.
S. Minervi, *Angelo Levi-Bianchini e la sua opera nel Levante 1918–20* (1967).
E. Castelbolognese (ed.), H. E. Sereni, *Ha-Aviv ha-Kadosh* (1947), an anthology of diaries, letters, and essays.
IN LATIN AMERICA:
P. Schwartzman, *Judiós en América . . .* (1963), index.
I. Austri-Dann (ed.), *Yorbukh fun Meksikaner Yidentum* (1950–52), 331–51.
M. Senderey, *Di Geshikhte fun dem Yidishn Yishuv in Chile* (1956), 231–56.
J. Shatzky, *Communidades Judías en Latino América* (1952).
Communidades Judías de Latino América (1968).
Primero Congreso Sionista Latino Americano (1946).
Primera Convención Juvenil Judía Latino Americana (1962).

IN NORTH AFRICA AND ASIA:
H. J. Cohen, *Ha-Pe'ilut ha-Ẓiyyonit be-Iraq* (1969), incl. bibl..
J. M. Landau, *Ha-Yehudim be-Miẓrayim ba-Me'ah ha-Tesha-Esreh* (1967), 126–35.
IN POLAND:
N. M. Gelber, *Toledot ha-Tenu'ah ha-Ẓiyyonit be-Galiẓyah*, 2 vols. (1958).
Y. Gruenbaum (ed.), *Warsaw*, 1 (1953), 357–466; 2 (1959).
I. Schwarzbart, *Tsvishn Beyde Velt-Milkhomes* (1958).
L. Spizman (ed.), *Antologye fun der Khalutsisher Bavegung*, 3 vols. (1959–62).
H. M. Rabinowicz, *The Legacy of Polish Jewry: 1919–1939* (1965).
A. Tartakower, in: *Algemeyne Entsiklopedye Yidn*, 6 (1963), 147–63.
IN RUMANIA:
T. Lavi et al. (eds), *Pinkas ha-Kehillot, Romanyah*, 1 (1970), 47–61, 101–6, 177–89, 209–24 (incl. comprehensive bibl.).
M. Landau, in: *Gesher*, 3 no. 1 (1957), 77–94; 3 no. 2 (1957), 78–91; 3 no. 3 (1957), 101–13.
IN RUSSIA:
L. Greenberg, *The Jews in Russia*, 2 (1951), 160–202.
J. B. Schechtman, *Zionism and the Zionists in the Soviet Union* (1966).
idem, in: L. Kochan (ed.), *The Jews in Soviet Russia* (1970), 99–124.
G. G. Goldman, *Zionism under Soviet Rule 1917–1928* (1960).
G. Aronson, in: J. Frumkin, G. Aronson and A. Gildenweiser (eds.), *Russian Jewry 1860–1917* (1966), 144–71.
I. Ben-Zvi, *ibid.*, 209–18.
S. Baron, *Russian Jews under Tsars and Soviets* (1964), index.
A. Rafaeli (Zenziper), *Pa'amei ha-Ge'ullah* (1951).
idem, *Ha-Ma'avak la-Ge'ullah* (1956).
M. Nurock, *Ve'idat Ẓiyyonei Rusyah* (1963).
Y. Gruenbaum, *Ha-Tenu'ah ha-Ẓiyyonit be-Hitpatteḥutah*, 3, 4 (1949, 1954).
I. Klausner, *Oppoziẓyah le-Herzl* (1960).
A. Levinsohn, *Be-Reshit ha-Tenu'ah* (1947).
Y. Erez (ed.) *Sefer Z. S.* (1963).
B. West, *Struggle of a Generation: The Jews Under Soviet Rule* (1959).
Y. Eliash, *Zikhronot Ẓiyyoni me-Rusyah* (1955).
B. Z. Dinur, *Be-Olam she-Shaka 1884–1914* (1958).
idem, *Bi-Ymei Milḥamah u-Mahpekhah 1914–1921* (1960).

J. Rabinovich, *Mi-Moskva ad Yerushalayim* (1957).

He-Avar le-Divrei Yemei ha-Yehudim ve-ha-Yahadut be-Rusyah (1952).
IN SOUTH AFRICA:
M. Gitlin, *The Vision Amazing* (1950).
IN THE UNITED STATES:
I. S. Meyer (ed.), *Early History of Zionism in America* (1958), includes a series of articles and comprehensive bibliographies.
M. Feinstein, *American Zionism 1884–1908* (1965).
A. Friesel, *Ha-Tenu'ah ha-Ẓiyyonit be-Arẓot ha-Berit ba-Shanim 1897–1914* (1970), includes a comprehensive bibliography.
idem, in: D. Carpi (ed.), *Ha-Ẓiyyonut*, 1 (1970), 121–49.
N. W. Cohen, in: *American Jewish Historical Society—Publications*, 40 (1950/51), 361–94.
S. Udin (ed.), *Fifty Years of American Zionism 1897–1947; A Documentary Record* (1947).
R. J. H. Gottheil, *The Aims of Zionism* (1899).
idem, *Zionism* (1914).
M. Rischin, in: *American Jewish Historical Society—Publications*, 49 (1959/60), 188–201.
Y. Shapiro, *Leadership of the American Zionist Organization 1897–1930* (Ph. D. thesis, Columbia, 1964).
S. S. Wise, *Challenging Years* (1949).
S. Halperin, *The Political World of American Zionism* (1961).
C. Reznikoff (ed.), *Louis Marshall, Champion of Liberty*, 2 vols. (1957), index and passim.
B. Halpern, *The American Jew, Zionist Analysis* (1956).
R. Patai (ed.), *Herzl Year Book*, 5 (1963), contains a series of studies in the history of Zionism in America 1894–1919.
H. Parzen, *ibid.*, 4 (1962), 345; 6 (1965), 311–68.
idem, in: *Jewish Social Studies*, 23 (1961), 235–64.
ZIONIST UTOPIAS:
G. Kressel (ed.), *Ḥezyonei Medinah* (1954).
idem, in: I. Cohn and D. Sadan (eds.), *Me'assef le-Divrei Sifrut, Bikkoret ve-Hagut*, 8–9 (1968), 456–69.
CHRISTIAN ZIONISM:
M. Vereté, in: *Zion*, 33 (1968), 145–79.
N. M. Gelber, *Vorgeschichte des Zionismus 1695–1845* (1927).
F. Kobler, *The Vision Was There* (1956).
A. M. Hyamson, in: *American Jewish Historical Society—Publications*, 26 (1918) 127–64.
N. Sokolow, *History of Zionism*, 2 vols. (1919–68), passim, index.

Y. Malachy, in: *Herzl Year Book*, 5 (1963), 175–208. 6 (1964/65), 265–302.
B. Tuchman, *Bible and Sword* (1956).
CONGRESSES:
N. M. Gelber, *Ha-Kongressim ha-Ẓiyyoniyyim* (1956).

INDEX